is Marriage for White People?

is Marriage for White People?

HOW THE AFRICAN AMERICAN MARRIAGE DECLINE AFFECTS EVERYONE

Ralph Richard Banks

DUTTON

DUTTON
Published by Penguin Group (USA) Inc.
375 Hudson Street, New York, New York 10014, U.S.A.
Penguin Group (Canada), 90 Eglinton Avenue East, Suite 700, Toronto, Ontario M4P 2Y3, Canada (a division of Pearson Penguin Canada Inc.); Penguin Books Ltd, 80 Strand, London WC2R 0RL, England; Penguin Ireland, 25 St Stephen's Green, Dublin 2, Ireland (a division of Penguin Books Ltd); Penguin Group (Australia), 250 Camberwell Road, Camberwell, Victoria 3124, Australia (a division of Pearson Australia Group Pty Ltd); Penguin Books India Pvt Ltd, 11 Community Centre, Panchsheel Park, New Delhi–110 017, India; Penguin Group (NZ), 67 Apollo Drive, Rosedale, Auckland 0632, New Zealand (a division of Pearson New Zealand Ltd); Penguin Books (South Africa) (Pty) Ltd, 24 Sturdee Avenue, Rosebank, Johannesburg 2196, South Africa

Penguin Books Ltd, Registered Offices: 80 Strand, London WC2R 0RL, England

Published by Dutton, a member of Penguin Group (USA) Inc.

First printing, September 2011
1 3 5 7 9 10 8 6 4 2

LIBRARY OF CONGRESS CATALOGING-IN-PUBLICATION DATA

Banks, Ralph Richard.
Is marriage for white people? : how the African American marriage decline affects everyone / Ralph Richard Banks.
p. cm.
Includes bibliographical references and index.
ISBN 978-0-525-95201-5
1. Marriage—United States. 2. African Americans—Marriage. 3. African American families. 4. Interracial marriage—United States. I. Title.
HQ536.B3225 2011
306.81089'96073—dc22
2010047353

Printed in the United States of America
Set in Warnock Pro
Designed by Alissa Amell

All names and identifying characteristics have been changed to protect the privacy of the individuals involved.

For my brilliant and beautiful wife, Jennifer Lynn Eberhardt

CONTENTS

is Marriage for White People?

Reexamine everything. Go back to where you started, or as far back as you can, examine all of it, travel your road again and tell the truth about it. Sing or shout or testify or keep it to yourself: but know whence you came.

—James Baldwin, *The Price of the Ticket*

INTRODUCTION

On a bitter cold day in January 2009, throngs formed on the National Mall in the predawn darkness, and as the skies lightened, the crowd swelled to a million strong. Children atop fathers' shoulders; old ladies in wheelchairs thankful to have lived to see this day; college students barely old enough to vote; white-collar professionals with rooms at four-star hotels; and blue-collar workers who had journeyed three days by bus—they came from all parts of the nation and all walks of life to join in the making of history.

My family had made the journey as well. Like most people, we had never attended a presidential inauguration. And I was hesitant to go to this one—concerned about the cost, the crowds, our children missing school—but my wife, a woman who by her own admission never cared much for politics, insisted. So from California to D.C., with three young boys in tow, we went.

After the swearing in, we joined thousands of others lining the route for the inaugural parade. No sooner had the presidential limousine appeared, it seemed, than it stopped and its door opened. Into the frigid air emerged our new president and first lady. They held hands and smiled as they walked, waving to the crowd, whispering into each other's ears, sharing a laugh. They seemed to be having fun. Together.

For all the African Americans who have occupied the spotlight—from Oprah Winfrey to Bill Cosby, Michael Jordan to Tiger Woods, Condoleezza Rice to Colin Powell—virtually none have done so as a couple, much less been as prominent as the president and first lady. Their residency at 1600 Pennsylvania Avenue not only places them at the center of our political life, it embeds them in our cultural imagination. They're the iconic family with whom we are all called to feel kinship: two accomplished parents, adorable children, a doting grandmother, and—since moving into the most fabled home in the land—a dog. They're like the Huxtables—only real, and better.

But the captivating image of Barack and Michelle also accentuates a sobering reality. As African Americans, they are extraordinary in the most ordinary way: They are a married couple raising their children together.

Over the past half century, African Americans have become the most unmarried people in our nation. By far. We are the least likely to marry and the most likely to divorce; we maintain fewer committed and enduring relationships than any other group. Not since slavery have black men and women been as unpartnered as we are now.

Although the African American marriage decline is especially pronounced among the poor, it is apparent as well among the affluent: doctors, lawyers, corporate professionals. Black women of all socioeconomic classes remain single in part because the ranks of black men have been decimated by incarceration, educational failure, and economic disadvantage. In recent years, two black women have graduated college for every one black man. Two to one. Every year. As a result, college-educated black women are more likely than college-educated women of other races to remain unmarried or to wed a less-educated man who earns less than they do. More than half of married black women who have graduated from college have a less-educated husband who did not. Yet despite the shortage of black male peers, black women do not marry men of other races. Black women marry across class lines, but not race lines. They marry down but not out. Thus, they lead the most racially segregated intimate lives of any Americans.

Why? Why are black women the least likely to marry out? What are the consequences of the unprecedented rates at which they marry down or remain unmarried? These are the questions at the heart of my inquiry. I find the answers in two very different types of evidence. For more than a year, I traveled the country interviewing scores of professional black women at length about their relationships with men. Their stories, told with courage and candor, are certain to resonate deeply with some readers and to surprise or even shock others. Before I conducted my first interview, I devoted several years to the study of the black marriage decline. I began, as law professors typically do, with judicial decisions and legislative enactments but soon found myself immersed in history, social science, and government data about the United States population.

Throughout this book I repeatedly invoke the idea of the relationship market. Although love cannot be bought or sold, the market metaphor highlights two developments that account for the marriage decline. One is that the rules of the market have changed, so that people marry for different reasons and with different expectations than in earlier eras. The other development is equally unprecedented: that women have moved ahead economically and educationally as men have begun to fall behind.

Researching this book has been illuminating—indeed, liberating. But writing it has been a struggle. Although the intersection of race and family has been one of my intellectual preoccupations since my undergraduate days more than twenty years ago, and a professional focus since I joined the Stanford Law School faculty more than a decade ago, finding my voice in these pages has not been easy. This book confronts some uncomfortable truths about relationships between black men and women.

This book begins with African Americans, but it does not end with them. The story I tell of African Americans and marriage may seem exceptional—and in some ways it is—but it is also representative, distinct more in degree than in kind. Americans of all races are substantially less likely to be married now than their predecessors were a few generations ago. And throughout society, many men are struggling economically, victims of technological change and an increasingly global market for labor. As a majority of our nation's college graduates, women are becoming better positioned than men to take advantage of the economic opportunities of the coming decades. And today's high-achieving women are already more likely than ever to marry men who are either lower earning or less educated than they are.

As particular as the black experience may seem, it implicates readers of all races. The terrain of marriage and intimacy is shifting, for everyone, as never before. Black people are at the center of a social transformation whose reverberations encompass us all.

CHAPTER I

The Marriage Decline

Audrey Jones is thirty-nine years old. A native of southeast Washington, D.C., she is the child of parents who have been married for nearly half a century. After graduating from high school, she attended Spelman College in Atlanta, then business school in New York. During her studies, she traveled the world and became multilingual. When she returned to D.C., she took a job with a multinational consulting company, where she found business solutions for one client after another. The company has rewarded her with increased responsibilities and compensation, and she now earns more than her father and mother ever did, combined. More important, though, she enjoys her work; it is challenging and fulfilling. She cherishes the life that she has made for herself: her family, her friends, her church community.

There is only one thing missing in this woman's rich and full life. At its mention, Audrey's voice softens, her eyes glance downward, and she takes a breath before explaining, "At this point in my life, I thought I'd be married with children." Sitting across from her in a Dupont Circle restaurant, I can hardly believe she isn't. This woman is the proverbial "good catch": smart, funny, well educated, attractive. She has a big job but not a big ego.

Audrey still hopes to marry. But as she stares at forty, she confronts a possibility that her younger self could not have imagined: "I'm trying to get to a point where I accept that marriage may never happen for me," she says. "That may be my reality. This may not be the life that I had hoped for, but this is the life I have to live."

As a black woman, Audrey Jones belongs to the most unmarried group of people in our nation.[1] Nearly seven out of every ten black women are unmarried, and as many as three out of ten may never marry.[2] For black women, being unmarried has become the new normal, single the new black.

It wasn't always so. Through the middle of the twentieth century, approximately nine out of ten black women married. Now, black women are about half as likely to be married as their 1950s counterparts.[3] Marriage has also declined among black men,[4] fewer than half of whom are husbands.[5]

Children are the most impressionable witnesses to the fracturing of black intimacy. As a fifteen-year-old African American girl in Massachusetts explains, "I don't know anyone who's married, or anybody who [has] stayed married."[6] A poignant image of the African American marriage decline comes from a journalist's account of her visit to a class of black sixth-grade students in Washington, D.C. When one of the boys says he wants to be a good father, she offers to invite some married couples to speak to the class about child rearing. The boy objects: "Oh, no. We're not interested in the part about marriage. Only about how to be good fathers." The author writes: "And that's when the other boy chimed in, speaking as if the words left a nasty taste in his mouth: 'Marriage is for white people.' "

Or is it?

White adults, men and women alike, are more than twice as likely to be single now as in 1970.[7] More American women in their early thirties are single today than ever in our nation's history.

African Americans lead the marriage decline; other groups follow. White women are as unmarried now as black women were in the 1970s.[8] And in 1965, when Daniel Patrick Moynihan famously declared single-parent African American families a "tangle of pathology,"[9] slightly less than 25 percent of black children in the United States were born to unmarried parents.[10] Now that figure substantially exceeds 25 percent—for *white* children. With respect to marriage and childbearing, white follows black, a pattern that exemplifies the universality of the African American family experience.

Still, marriage has diminished more among African Americans than among any other Americans, including whites, with whom I typically contrast African Americans for ease of exposition. Black women are only half as likely as white women to be married,[11] and more than three times as likely as white women never to marry.[12] As others marry, black women often remain alone.[13] Marriage is not all that's lacking in their lives. Black women are three times as likely as white women never even to live with an intimate partner. Some women find solace in humor, as in the case of one never-married fifty-something-year-old black woman from Los Angeles who reports that she and her friend refer to themselves as "virtual virgins." These women are sexually experienced, but they have been without an intimate relationship for so long that they feel as though they have forgotten what sex is like. Other black women can relate: Research by sociologist Averil Clarke suggests that college-educated black women are more likely than any other group of women in our nation to be celibate.

One might suppose that because African Americans marry less frequently and, on average, are older (and presumably more mature) when they do,[14] black spouses might be particularly compatible, and thus more likely to stay together. Yet black spouses are, by some estimates, nearly twice as likely as their white counterparts to divorce.[15] A November 2010 study by the Pew Research Center found that half of black couples divorce within the first ten years of marriage, while less than a third of white couples do so. Eventually, more than two out of every three black marriages will dissolve.

One might also expect marriage to be more stable and widespread among African Americans because they are highly religious.[16] African Americans are more likely than other Americans to describe religion as "very important" in their lives,[17] and to pray daily and to attend church weekly,[18] all characteristics that tend to bolster marriage. Yet the centrality of religion in the lives of African Americans seems not to have buffered the black marriage decline.

From the Poor to the Middle Class

Discussions of the African American marriage decline often fixate on the black poor, the so-called underclass—those economically disadvantaged, uneducated residents of blighted urban areas. It is the near disappearance of marriage among that group that has attracted the attention of scholars, who attempt to explain it, and of policymakers, who attempt to remedy it. Books have been written, conferences convened, legislators briefed, all in the hope of addressing the precipitous drop in marriage among the black poor. Scholarly examinations of the black middle class, in contrast, either devote scant attention to marriage or assume that successful African Americans are exempt from the influences that have decimated marriage among the poor. Some commentators have attributed the waning of marriage among the black poor to the loss of the middle-class role models as they left the inner city for the suburbs.

But, in fact, the African American marriage decline is not limited to the poor. It now encompasses the middle and upper-middle class, too, a grouping that I refer to simply, for the sake of convenience, as the middle class.[19] Indeed, by some measures the racial gap in marriage is actually wider among the prosperous than among the impoverished. While college-educated black women are more likely to marry than poor black women, they are still substantially less likely to marry than their white counterparts. College-educated black women are twice as likely as their white counterparts to be unmarried. Although within each racial group marriage rates and marital stability have declined the most among poor people, college-educated black women are no more likely to marry, or stay married, than white women who have only completed high school.

The marriage gap is also apparent among middle-class black men. Among men, higher earnings are associated with a greater likelihood of marriage. Yet black men who are employed and economically stable are less likely to have ever married than white men with comparable incomes. Moreover, the marriage gap between black men and white men actually widens at the top of the income distribution. For white men, as income increases so does the likelihood of marriage. But a black man who earns more than a hundred thousand dollars per year is *less* likely to have ever married than a black man who earns seventy-five thousand dollars per year. The highest-earning black men are more than twice as likely as their white counterparts never to have married.

The decline of marriage among the black middle class is important in part because the black middle class is large.[20] Its fortunes figure prominently in the future of the race. Notwithstanding the persistence of stereotypes equating race and poverty, more African Americans are middle-class than poor.[21] And despite the unprecedented number of black men who are incarcerated, there are still more African American men and women in their twenties and thirties who have been to college than to jail.[22] In fact, African Americans in their late teens or early twenties are more than twice as likely to be in college as in jail.[23]

Although the black middle class is large, it is fragile. Middle-class black adults are more likely than their white counterparts to be among the first generation of their family to have graduated from college. Black middle-class families are, to put it simply, poorer than their white counterparts; they rarely benefit from the cushion of intergenerational wealth possessed by some white families.[24] Having only come into affluence recently, even apparently well-off blacks are often only a few missed paychecks away from financial ruin.

The marriage decline restricts the growth and security of the black middle class. Consider, for example, that although college-educated black women earn salaries comparable to college-educated white women,[25] white women have much higher household incomes, in large part because they are more likely to be married.[26] This is one significant way in which the marriage gap limits the growth of the black middle class.

The middle-class marriage decline undermines the next generation as well. Many professionally successful, college-educated black women remain childless because they don't want to have a child without being married.[27] Moreover, when middle-class African Americans do have children, they less successfully transmit their class status to those children. Research has shown that children from middle-class black families are more likely than their white counterparts to fare worse than their parents.[28] One likely contributing factor is that these children more frequently lack the economic and parenting benefits of a functional two-parent household, and as a result are less equipped than other children to thrive as adults.

(Partial) Explanations

The most common explanations for the racial gap in marriage are, at best, partial. One common intuition attributes the marriage gap to slavery. Harvard sociologist Orlando Patterson, for example, argues that slavery scarred African American gender relations in a way that has yet to be undone.[29] Patterson is the latest in a long line of sociologists who have emphasized the destructive effect of slavery on African American families. More than a century ago, the pioneering scholar W. E. B. Du Bois wrote what slavery meant: "No legal marriage. No legal family. No legal control over children."[30] Du Bois concluded that "no amount of kindliness in individual owners could save the system from its deadly work of disintegrating the ancient Negro home."[31]

Another common explanation attributes the marriage gap to African culture. The idea here is that the African societies from which the slaves were taken featured extended family structures in which marriage was less pivotal. Children were reared not solely by a mother and father but by an extended web of relatives. The African culture explanation became popular during the 1970s in part in response to the negative connotations of the slavery account. Whereas the slavery explanation depicts contemporary black family patterns as an unhealed wound from a painful past, the African culture theory situates the black family as an expression of cultural diversity: different, but not deficient.

Neither slavery nor African culture fully explains the black marriage decline. Both founder on the issue of timing. However severe slavery's effect on the black family,[32] it is unlikely that slavery wholly accounts for a racial gap in marriage that developed a century after slavery's abolition. So, too, is it fanciful to attribute that marriage decline to the African cultures from which African Americans' ancestors were taken centuries earlier.

Other explanations identify influences contemporaneous with the decline itself. The dominant explanation is the so-called marriageable man theory developed by the sociologist William Julius Wilson three decades ago.[33] Wilson asserts that deindustrialization undermined employment opportunities for less-educated men in urban areas, leaving many men unable to support a family and therefore less attractive as spouses.[34]

An alternative explanation attributes the marriage decline to government welfare programs that lessen a woman's incentive to marry, either by reducing benefits upon marriage or simply by making it economically possible for a woman to live without the financial support of a husband. Conservative commentator Charles Murray became the best-known proponent of this argument after the publication of his 1984 book *Losing Ground: American Social Policy, 1950–1980.* To the question "Does welfare undermine the family?" he replies, "It does, and the effect is large."[35] This view has been embraced more recently by a younger generation of conservative policy analysts.[36]

These explanations may help to explain the waning of marriage among the black poor, but not among African Americans who are college-educated and economically stable. It is the deterioration of marriage among this group that animates my inquiry: Why are middle-class black men and women so much less likely than other middle-class Americans to marry or stay married? 

Living Free

Some imagine that middle-class black women don't marry simply because they don't want to. And of course there are black women who are perfectly content to remain unmarried and childless. Tina Ingram is one of them. Her career has led her from a corporate law firm to politics, and finally to New York City, where she manages the legal and business affairs of a major music industry personality. Now in her forties, she earns enough to support a lifestyle she could only have dreamed of as the child of working-class parents. Her freedom to pursue personal interests and professional opportunities without needing anyone else's approval or agreement makes her the envy of friends whose options are—there's no other way to put it—limited by their husbands and children. Tina is by no means a loner. She babysits her nieces and takes her mom to the doctor; she is there for her married mom friends, who often have less energy for her than she does for them. Her life in many ways is charmed. That it doesn't include a husband or children matters little to her. She is not opposed to marriage, but she doesn't feel compelled to wed either. "As a child," she says, "I never really saw myself getting married. I've never had the vision of the marriage or the wedding or any of that stuff." Nor has she felt any urge to have children. She enjoys children and takes her role as an aunt seriously, but birthday parties, holiday gatherings, and weekend trips to the zoo are more than enough to satisfy her need to nurture a young person.

Although she sometimes wonders whether when she's old and gray she'll regret not marrying, for now she sees little reason to do so. She loves her life as it is. She'd give up a lot if she married or had children—her freedom, her independence—and she's not sure what she'd gain. "I don't feel like I'm missing anything," she explains. "I'm content. My life right now is so full that it's hard to view the absence of a marriage as a bad thing. There's no flaw in my life that I'm trying to fix; there's no hole that I'm trying to fill."

Unfulfilled Hopes

But most unmarried black women are not like Tina. As the writer Debra Dickerson observes, black women may accept solitude, but most of them don't choose it.[37] Successful black women—like women of all races—may not want to marry young, and they certainly don't want to settle for anyone. But most do want a husband and children. For these women, being single is not a freedom they embrace so much as a condition they manage. Their unfulfilled dreams are yet another cost of the marriage decline.

Some of these women live with the creeping sense that they may never marry. Rachel Lewis, a beautiful, accomplished forty-three-year-old investment manager in Chicago, recalls collapsing into a heap of self-pity after chancing upon an old business school friend on the train one day. The friend was rushing to get home in time for a dinner party that she and her husband were hosting. As the friend talked of her husband and two sons—showing pictures on her cell phone that her children had taken of themselves—Rachel, usually a model of composure, felt her insides churning.

"It hit me," she says. "I didn't expect it to, but it did. Just seeing her on the train and hearing her talk about her husband and little boys . . ." Her voice trails off. "I just thought, 'That's the life I should have.' How is it that she gets to go home to her husband and I come home alone, go to the gym, and make dinner for myself?

"It's not like I'm saying, 'Why don't I have a Nobel Peace Prize?' " she pleads. "I'm just saying, 'Why don't I have *that*?' "

Why indeed? Many single black women, who have succeeded in every other aspect of life, grapple with this question. One middle-age, never-married black woman from Cleveland describes how she and her friends cope: "We focus on our careers, our friends, go back to school, whatever," she says. "We fill our lives with other things."

As I sat in that Dupont Circle restaurant that day talking with Audrey, the D.C. corporate professional, I could see that in many ways her life was blessed. Her relationship with her parents, her church family, her friends, her well-maintained home, and her career—these were all sources of meaning and fulfillment. Yet it still wasn't quite enough.

As our time together neared its end, Audrey shared with me a story about a recent encounter with her neighbors, a gay couple living on the other side of her backyard fence. Hand-in-hand, with big smiles across their faces, they announced to Audrey, "We got married!" They were among the first same-sex couples in D.C. to do so. Audrey did her best to muster the smile that their news warranted. "Great!" she said. "Congratulations!" She tried to make her kind words sound heartfelt, not hollow. It wasn't that she begrudged them their happiness. She wanted them to have the life they wanted. It's just that it was the life she wanted too. And when the newlyweds left, she couldn't help but say to herself, in a voice barely above a whisper: "Even they can get married."

As I listen to Audrey recount this exchange, I wonder if she knows how sad she sounds, or just how long and deep the sigh accompanying her lament had been. "Even they can get married." Her words echoed in my mind long after we left the restaurant.

We each sought an answer to the same question: *Why hadn't she?*

CHAPTER 2

What Has Become of Marriage?

To understand why black women like Audrey are not married, we need to understand the changing status of marriage in the relationship market.[38] During the past several decades, the restrictions governing marriage and other intimate relationships have been relaxed. Compared to earlier eras, it is easier to exit a marriage, and there is less incentive to enter one. People are freer than ever not to marry, yet they also expect more emotional compatibility and fulfillment when they do.

Divorce

The changing rules of divorce exemplify the relaxation of restrictions that had long governed marriage. In 1956, a Pennsylvania court declared: "The fact that married people do not get along well together does not justify a divorce." Mr. and Mrs. Rankin wanted to divorce and introduced evidence that Mr. Rankin had threatened his wife with a gun and that she had spit in his face, thrown hot water on him, and nearly slashed him with a butcher knife. Yet the court denied the petition for divorce, reasoning that "Testimony which proves merely an unhappy union, the parties being high strung temperamentally and unsuited to each other and neither being wholly innocent of the causes which resulted in the failure of their marriage, is insufficient to sustain a decree [of divorce]. If both are equally at fault, neither can clearly be said to be the innocent and injured spouse, and the law will leave them where they put themselves."[39] Which is to say, married.

In Pennsylvania, as throughout the nation, a spouse seeking a divorce had to show both that he or she was innocent of any wrongdoing and that the other spouse was at fault. If both spouses were at fault, as were the Rankins, then neither was entitled to a divorce. However effective such stringent rules were in actually keeping couples together, they vividly reflect the ethos of marriage that prevailed throughout much of American history.

It wasn't until the 1970s that courts and legislatures began to allow couples to divorce without a showing of wrongdoing and blamelessness. Now, a court will grant a divorce even if only one of the spouses no longer wants to be married, and despite the fact that the other spouse may have done all he or she could to make the marriage work.

Sex and Children

Just as changes in the law have made it easier to exit a marriage, legal changes have decreased the need to enter one. For most of American history, the law designated marriage as the sole legitimate setting for sexual relationships and for the rearing of children. Recent controversies about the legal regulation of sexual intimacy have focused on same-sex relationships, but for most of American history, states were free to designate any sexual relationship between unmarried people as a crime. Put simply, nonmarital sex—even between two adults of the opposite sex who were not married to anyone else—could be a criminal offense. Unmarried couples with children endured the legal disabilities associated with "illegitimacy." The children were often unable to inherit from their father, and the father was neither required to support his children nor accorded parental rights. These rules helped to channel people into marriage.

Since the 1970s, courts have relaxed these restrictions by vindicating individuals' rights to structure their intimate lives as they choose. In most states, the rights and obligations of parenthood depend virtually not at all on whether the parents are married to each other. The Supreme Court has struck down most state laws that disadvantaged the children of unmarried parents or categorically denied parental rights to unwed fathers.[40] A father is now obligated to support his child even if he never marries the child's mother. Not only is sex between unmarried people no longer illegal, many states now accord unmarried couples who live together some of the same rights as married couples.[41]

The loosening of the legal link between sex and marriage was spurred by the availability of birth control and abortion. After the Pill was introduced in 1960 and the Supreme Court invalidated bans on the sale and use of contraceptives,[42] more than half of all adult women began to use the oral contraceptive.[43] In 1972, *Roe v. Wade* further expanded sexual freedom by according constitutional protection to abortion.[44] As a result of these developments, pregnancy could be avoided or, when necessary, ended. The ability to reliably disconnect sex from procreation undermined the case for limiting sex to marriage, either as a matter of personal decision or public policy. Marriage thus became untethered from one of the purposes that once defined it.

The Emancipation of Marriage

For much of human history, people married for other reasons as well. Marriage was a means of organizing economic activity. During agrarian times, for example, men and women married in part to gain a business partner. Families expected their children's marriages to serve the family's needs; parents directed their children into marriages that would establish ties with other families, thus converting strangers into kin who could provide support in times of need. Over time, as societies changed, marriage, for the most part, shed these roles.

Through the mid-twentieth century in the United States, men married to gain a homemaker and women married to gain economic support. Spouses were bound together by the interdependence that resulted from their role specialization. Now, of course, fewer marriages conform to that model. With the entry of women into the workforce, both spouses typically work for pay, and the roles of husband and wife are less distinct than they once were.

The cumulative effect of all these changes is that it has become more possible to lead one's life outside the bounds of marriage. Making a living, having sex, rearing children, setting up a household with a partner—none of these requires marriage. Although claims about the legal significance of marriage abound, the reality is that marriage entails fewer legal rights now than ever in American history. Some state and federal laws still turn on whether one is married,[45] but much less so than in the past. And in any event those laws often burden married couples more than benefit them.[46]

One might then wonder not why marriage has declined, but instead how it has survived. Why would anyone marry when, as a matter of law or economic necessity, there seems to be so little reason to do so?

The Persistence of the Ideal

Marriage survives because its symbolic significance persists. Marriage confers a sort of social prestige, what the sociologist Andrew Cherlin describes as the "ultimate merit badge." Marriage has become a marker of status and achievement.

The federal government has long accorded marriage great importance. In passing the Personal Responsibility and Work Opportunity Reconciliation Act of 1996, Congress described marriage as "the foundation of a successful society."[47] The law aimed "to end dependence by promoting marriage" and to foster the "formation and maintenance of two-parent families."[48] President George W. Bush continued governmental endorsement of marriage when he promised in 2001 to "give unprecedented support to strengthening marriages"[49] and then undertook a $1.5 billion "Healthy Marriage Initiative."[50] This initiative supported a wide array of programs, including communications skills workshops, websites, and public-service announcements such as "He may not always be charming, but he'll always be your prince"; "The wedding is just the icing on the cake"; and "It's the one family member you get to choose."[51]

Some states began their own marriage promotion efforts—rallies led by "marriage ambassadors," campaigns to convince churches to require premarital counseling, studies publicizing the devastating economic effect of rising divorce rates. When I visited Georgia to learn about its marriage promotion efforts, I didn't have to look far. Adjacent to my downtown Atlanta hotel stood a billboard featuring a sleeping newborn beside the words: "For Children's Sake." Below, in bold black letters—hardly subtle—the sign ordered: "Get Married, Stay Married."[52]

Justifications for marriage promotion programs typically invoke social science rather than morality. Proponents often cite the economic benefits of marriage. The governor of Oklahoma, for example, has said that he became a proponent of marriage promotion after economists at the state's university attributed the state's lackluster economic performance to its high divorce rate. Marriage is also lauded in terms of its benefits for the couple's children. One need not doubt the legitimacy of these benefits in order to suspect that many people continue to embrace marriage because they believe it is morally right, or even religiously mandated. Indeed, I suspect that the diminishing practical significance of marriage has accentuated its cultural cachet.

Although marriage is not as universal and as stable a social institution as in earlier eras, it remains, for many Americans at least, an aspiration. According to a recent assessment by Andrew Cherlin, annual surveys of high school seniors completed since the 1970s have consistently shown that four out of five young women, and seven out of ten young men, report that they expect to marry, and that "having a good marriage and family life" is extremely important.[53] These numbers have not declined during the past few decades.

The cultural primacy of marriage is also reflected in the controversy about same-sex marriage. Both sides premise their arguments on the unrivaled importance of marriage.[54] One side argues that the institution is too meaningful to keep same-sex couples out, and the other that it is too sacred to allow them in. Although marriage has traditionally been defined by state law, the United States Congress entered the debate by passing the Defense of Marriage Act in 1996, which defines marriage, for purposes of all federal programs, as a relationship between a man and a woman. And, of course, the very fact that gay and lesbian activists so ardently pursue the right to marry suggests that marriage occupies a special place in the American cultural firmament. If one were only concerned about legal rights, then domestic partnership legislation—which is certainly more politically attainable than the right to marry—would be a sensible goal. Indeed, in my home state of California, the same-sex marriage debate has been especially fierce, even while state legislation provides for domestic partnerships that confer nearly identical legal rights as same-sex marriage under state law.

The European Contrast

The cultural salience of marriage in the United States contrasts sharply with the situation in most European countries. In those European nations where marriage has declined the most as a social institution—that is, where marriage rates are lowest—it has faded as a cultural ideal as well. Consider Sweden, for example, where marriage rates have declined substantially during the past several decades. A majority of Swedish adults are unmarried,[55] and as many as one out of three Swedish women will never marry, a rate comparable to that of African Americans in the United States. As many as 60 percent of Swedish children are born to unmarried parents. Although marriage rates in Sweden are lower than those in the United States, the Swedish government has undertaken no efforts to promote marriage, and its decline is not perceived as a crisis.

The Swedes are untroubled by the marriage decline in part because, unlike in the United States, couples maintain long-term stable relationships without being married. In Sweden, cohabitation is becoming practically indistinguishable from marriage,[56] so much so that nonmarital cohabitating relationships in Sweden may be more stable than marriages in the United States![57] Thus, a child born to unmarried Swedish parents who cohabit—as the overwhelming majority of unmarried parents in Sweden do[58]—may face less risk of family disruption than a child born to the average married couple here in the United States.[59]

The situation is similar in France, where many heterosexual couples do not marry even though they are in long-term and committed relationships. A French friend who lives in the United States reports: "My relatives in France don't get married anymore." In fact, he continues, "When I got married, they thought it was odd." His family didn't condemn his choice or oppose his marriage, but they were perplexed. "Why marry?" they wondered. Why embrace a legal institution to which people seem to feel less and less attraction? When civil unions became available in France, many heterosexual couples chose that option.[60] The cultural divergence between the United States on one hand and countries like France and Sweden on the other is reflected in the results of a recent survey that asked people whether they agreed with the statement "Marriage is an outdated institution."[61] Only 10 percent of Americans, but 20 percent of Swedes and 36 percent of French respondents, answered "yes."

Although cohabitation rates are high in the United States, living together without being married is still regarded as different from being married. In the United States marriage remains a way for couples to signal, to themselves and others, the seriousness of their relationship. Couples who live together without being married typically intend to do so temporarily, either as a matter of convenience or as a potential prelude to marriage. More than half of all couples who decide to marry will also decide to live together before saying "I do."[62] Most cohabiting couples in the United States either separate or marry within a few years.[63] Couples who have lived together for a decade or more without marrying remain rare.

The New Meaning of Marriage

The paradox of marriage in the United States, then, is that its cultural prominence persists even as it has shed many of the social functions that traditionally prompted people to marry. Marriage is more a relationship and less an institution these days. As the meaning of marriage has shifted, so, too, have people's expectations of it. Perhaps more than ever, marriage is understood now as a means of personal fulfillment and individual growth. The primary purpose of marriage, in the view of most Americans, is the establishment of a mutually fulfilling relationship, one in which understanding and emotional intimacy prevail.[64] Marriage now is less a means of building a life and more a means of enjoying one's life. More finish line than starting gate, marriage often comes after other milestones of adulthood have been met: living together, buying a car and house, having children.[65] People take pride in marriage as an achievement. To enjoy that achievement requires a certain degree of financial stability. According to one nationally representative study conducted in 2001, more than four out of five Americans agreed that "it is extremely important to be economically set before you get married."[66]

The new view of marriage is reflected in the findings of a 2007 survey by the Pew Research Center. Throughout history and across different societies children have been pivotal to the prevailing conception of marriage. Yet when respondents to the Pew survey were provided with a list of items and asked to identify which were "very important" to a successful marriage, they ranked children near the bottom of the list.[67] Practically every other consideration—shared religious beliefs, shared interests, a happy sexual relationship—ranked as more important than children. The survey respondents were even more likely to judge "sharing household chores" as more important to a successful marriage than children. The Americans surveyed said by a margin of nearly three to one that "the main purpose of marriage is . . . the 'mutual happiness and fulfillment'" of the couple, rather than the "'bearing and raising of children.'"[68]

What better way to find happiness and fulfillment than by marrying one's soul mate? In a national survey conducted in 2001, nearly nineteen out of twenty never-married adults agreed that "when you marry, you want your spouse to be your soul mate, first and foremost."[69] Fulfilling the roles long associated with marriage—reliable business partner, a responsible parent, a faithful sexual intimate—is no longer sufficient. People are expecting their spouses to meet ever more of their emotional needs.

These heightened expectations lead people to want to marry a peer. Contemporary marriages tend to be between socioeconomic equals, a development made possible by the advanced education of women and their increased entry into high-status professions. Doctors used to expect to marry nurses; now they look to marry other doctors.

Such marriages are probably happier and more emotionally satisfying than the marriages of earlier eras. Spouses are more emotionally compatible and more likely to enjoy each other's company. Yet the expectations that many people bring to marriage are now so high that it is quite difficult to meet them. As historian Stephanie Coontz observes, marriages are more satisfying but also more fragile. Spouses are more attuned to each other, but they are also less tolerant of lagging attraction or diminished passion; they are more inclined to divorce for reasons that would have seemed petty or trivial a few generations ago.

High expectations have also contributed to a divergence in the marital experiences of the poor and the affluent.[70] Affluent, well-educated people continue to marry, and their marriages are much more stable than media references to a 50 percent divorce rate suggest.[71] Poor people, in contrast, are less likely to marry and less likely to stay married when they do. If marriage is less a necessity and more, as the sociologist Frank Furstenberg notes, a luxury, then it takes money. It is something that people do after they've established a measure of stability and reached other milestones. A job, a house, a car—these all typically come before marriage now. And if those goals are not accomplished, then often neither is marriage.

Middle-class black women don't lack the resources to marry, and they don't lack the desire to wed either. But they find it difficult to establish the intimate relationships that they want, the type of relationship that women of all races want. Monica Wilson, a church administrator from Washington, D.C., is forty-eight years old and has never been married. "I would like to be married," she says. "But I don't regret any of my decisions"—a reference to the men she might have married but didn't. She wasn't willing to settle for just anyone. Now, at her stage of life, she wonders, "Maybe marriage is not meant for me. I know some older women who have never been married. I hope I'm not one of them, but maybe I am."

Expectations of marriage have shifted throughout society in ways that make its promise more difficult to attain. But to understand why black women, even the most successful among them, remain unmarried, we need to consider the specific barriers they encounter in the relationship market.

CHAPTER 3

The Man Shortage

The heightened expectations that Americans bring to the marriage market are not the only things that have spurred the African American marriage decline. The relative number and characteristics of buyers and sellers also matter. Just as the meaning of marriage has changed in the past half century, so, too, has the supply of potential partners shifted. Black women confront a tighter relationship market than any other group of women because there are too few black men for them to marry.

There are three major contributors to the man shortage. First, black men's incarceration constricts the market for poor and working-class black women. Second, interracial marriage depletes the pool of men for middle-class, college-educated black women. Third, the economic prospects for many men have worsened while those for women have improved. This economic repositioning is most apparent among African Americans, but it extends throughout our society.

Incarceration

The most talked-about aspect of the numbers problem is the unprecedented rate at which black men are incarcerated. For black women, the boom in the prison population has both decimated the ranks of potential spouses and taken men from their families—brothers, cousins, nephews. Black women know all too well the magnitude of the incarceration problem among black men. As a public school teacher I interviewed in Chicago said, "I had jury duty once and my girlfriend said, 'Go down there and meet a lawyer.' Another friend said, 'Nah, you got to be careful who you meet. Just because he's in a suit doesn't mean he's a lawyer. He might be the one who needs the lawyer.'" They laughed, but they all knew it was true. Too true.

Since the mid-1980s, the United States has become the world leader in incarceration, imprisoning more people (both in absolute numbers and as a percentage of the population) than any other country and than at any other time in U.S. history.[72] Over the past several decades, the U.S. inmate population has increased fivefold, from less than 150 to more than 700 inmates for every 100,000 residents. Only South Africa during apartheid and the former Soviet Union have incarcerated comparable percentages of their population; our incarceration rate dwarfs those of every Western democracy. According to sociologist Bruce Western, the United States' incarceration rate is seven times the average among European nations.[73] The rise of mass incarceration stems primarily from the enactment of draconian sentencing schemes and the establishment of the war on drugs in the 1980s.[74] Punitive policies gained support from both Republicans such as Ronald Reagan and Democrats such as Bill Clinton, whose 1994 crime bill spurred prison construction and enacted harsh sentencing policies.

Black men have borne the brunt of the rise in mass incarceration. More black men are in prison now than at any time in our nation's history.[75] More than two million people in the United States are in jail or prison,[76] and 40 percent of them, more than 840,000, are African Americans.[77] At any given time, one in ten black men in their early thirties is incarcerated,[78] and for men in their early twenties, the incarceration rate is closer to one in eight.[79] Some researchers have estimated that more than a quarter of all black men will spend some time in prison.[80] Black men are eight times as likely as white men to be incarcerated.[81]

The risk of imprisonment for African Americans depends very much on their socioeconomic status. The young black men who end up in jail are not, by and large, people who otherwise would have been working as a loan officer at a bank or managing the local Ford dealership. The occupants of our nation's jails and prisons are drawn overwhelmingly from poor urban areas. Among this group, the likelihood that a black man will spend time in prison is extraordinarily high. Bruce Western has calculated that among "black male dropouts born since the mid-1960s, 60 to 70 percent go to prison."[82] Our nation's prisons have become the destination for so many of the black boys who drop out of high school that researchers and activists have coined the term "school-to-prison pipeline." In some urban areas, three out of four black boys drop out of high school. While more than half of black dropouts end up in jail, fewer than one in ten college-educated black men will spend time in prison.[83] For whites, incarceration is also concentrated among the most disadvantaged, though the rates at each educational level are much lower than for blacks.

Not surprisingly, incarceration strains existing relationships. When men are imprisoned, marriages tend to dissolve and nonmarital relationships tend to unravel. Resentments simmer. Women left on the outside develop other relationships. But the gravest cost of incarceration may fall on the children of prisoners. Incarcerated men are often fathers but rarely husbands. They are less likely than nonincarcerated men to be married,[84] but no less likely to have children.

The marriage prospects for these men, even after they're released from prison, are bleak. Ex-felons are not appealing as potential spouses. For men, income is one of the strongest predictors of marriage. A man's appeal as a spouse, and perhaps his readiness to assume the role of husband, typically increases as his earnings rise. Yet formerly incarcerated men do not fare well economically. While the same personal characteristics that landed them in jail depress their wages once they get out, some portion of their economic disadvantage also stems from the fact that they've been incarcerated. At a time when competition for jobs is especially intense, the mark of a prison record relegates an ex-con to the end of the hiring line. In fact, some employers in urban areas with large numbers of formerly incarcerated black men may discriminate against any black man who applies for a low-skill, entry-level position.[85] Compounding the problem, young men who have spent a number of years in the penitentiary have been socialized within that environment, and as a result are unlikely to have developed the sort of social skills that many jobs now demand—and that help romantic relationships thrive.

Apart from all this, there's another reason that incarceration diminishes men's marriage rates: stigma. Although incarceration is widespread in poor urban areas, a woman who marries a formerly incarcerated man still assumes the burden of his prison past. Ethnographic research suggests that poor women may be especially unwilling to share this stigma,[86] since they also tend to view marriage as a means of gaining a certain middle-class respectability.[87]

Statistical analyses further support the hypothesis that increased incarceration rates among men have undermined marriage rates for women. In one recent study, University of Chicago professor Kerwin Kofi Charles and National Taiwan University professor Ming Ching Luoh gathered data about the incarceration rates in different metropolitan areas across time. They found that the higher the incarceration rates of black men, the lower the marriage rates of black women.[88] According to these researchers, more incarceration for men means less marriage for women. As one might expect, the marriage decline was most apparent among less-educated women.

The Interracial Marriage Gap

While incarceration decimates the ranks of potential partners for poor and working-class black women, interracial marriage severely diminishes the pool of black men available to college-educated black women.

Black men are between two and three times as likely as black women to marry someone of a different race.[89] Estimates are that more than one out of five black men marry interracially, whereas fewer than one out of ten black women do.[90] Consider the implications of this sex asymmetry for the African American relationship market. Imagine, for example, a population with one hundred black men and one hundred black women. If the men marry outside of their racial group ("outmarry") at three times the rate of the women, then if ten women outmarry, thirty men will do so, leaving ninety women but only seventy men. Suppose that forty African American couples then marry one another. Now only thirty men and fifty women remain—an appealing ratio for the men, but not for the women.

For decades, the gap in the interracial marriage rates of black men and black women has been a source of tension. Some black women take it personally. "Black men dating White women," according to a 1993 article in *Ebony,* can "cause most single Black women to see red."[91] A 1998 *Essence* readers poll revealed that almost two-thirds of black women felt upset when black men married or dated white women.[92] They felt unappreciated, inadequate, unwanted. As one twenty-nine-year-old black woman in Los Angeles says in another *Ebony* article, "[E]very time I turn around and I see a fine Brother dating outside his race, I just feel disgusted. I feel like, what's wrong with us? Why do you choose her over me?"[93] Another *Ebony* reader responded: "Black men I encounter are either dating or married to white women; they aren't interested in the sisters."[94]

The imbalance hits professional black women especially hard, because the black men they might regard as the most desirable—college graduates with good jobs—are also the most likely to marry interracially.[95] Consequently, the African American gender gap in interracial marriage is widest among the black middle class. Moreover, some black women think that successful black men often wed white women who don't have much going for them. Sociologists explain such relationships as a "status exchange" in which the man benefits from the woman's whiteness, and the woman gains from the man's educational and professional accomplishments.[96] The suspicion is that well-educated, high-earning black men are so enamored of the idea of having a white spouse that they often marry white women who are less educated and of lower status in every way except for race. Empirical support for the "status exchange" theory remains mixed,[97] but the idea that successful black men will accept low-status white women remains an article of faith for many black women.

That belief is reflected in a joke recounted by the late writer Bebe Moore Campbell in the early 1990s: "Two wealthy black businessmen are strolling down the street and one says to the other, 'Man, let's try to get a date with the next white woman we see.' His friend agrees and soon they notice two white women approaching them. One is young and pretty; the other is over seventy, not very attractive, and has difficulty walking. One of the men says quickly, 'I want the old one.' His amazed companion asks, 'Why in the world do you prefer her?' His friend responds, 'Because she's been white longer.'"[98]

Campbell says that "for many African-American women, the thought of black men, particularly those who are successful, dating or marrying white women is like being passed over for the prom by the boy of their dreams, causing them pain, rage, and an overwhelming sense of betrayal and personal rejection."[99]

This same sentiment has been reflected in the movie version of Terry McMillan's best-selling *Waiting to Exhale,* in which a black woman seizes on the race of her husband's girlfriend. "I give you eleven fuckin' years of my life, and you're leaving me for a white woman?"

He responds defiantly, "Would it be better if she were black?"

Without missing a beat, she says, "No, it'd be better if you were."

Similarly, in Spike Lee's *Jungle Fever,* when Wesley Snipes's character, Flipper, falls for the white office assistant, his wife seems as upset about his paramour's race as about her husband's infidelity. "White?" she exclaims. "Are you on crack or something?"

The movie suggests that he might as well be. Flipper's transgression simultaneously betrays his wife, leaves his daughter without a father, and embodies the failure of black men to play their rightful role in the black family. His family's brightly lit home—with Spelman and Morehouse memorabilia on display—was a haven from the rough, litter-strewn Harlem streets through which Flipper walked his daughter to school. His family was an oasis of black middle-class stability until he strayed, causing all they had built to crumble. Lee accentuates this theme of destruction by coupling Flipper's sexual transgression with another, more obvious sort. Flipper's brother Gator is a crackhead, who is beyond redemption. He begs people for money, smokes it up, then returns for more. When Gator's mother refuses a request, Gator dances for her—a series of slick moves that only highlight his own pitifulness—and eventually gets what he wants. His father, a stern and religious man, is less forgiving and when Gator's desperation borders on violence, his father shoots him dead.

What's striking here is the parallel that Lee constructs between addiction to crack cocaine and an ill-advised interracial affair. In this framing, the black family is destroyed not only by the scourge of drugs, but also by the willingness of black men to have sex with white women. Flipper and Gator have failed the family equally if in different ways—one lured by cocaine, the other by a white woman—weakening a community they instead should have helped to strengthen.

Jungle Fever may have captured the tenor of the times in the late 1980s and early 1990s, but opposition to interracial marriage among black women seems to have become more muted over the years. The anger of the early 1990s has softened into the disappointment of the second decade of the twenty-first century.

In 2010, the black singer and actress Jill Scott—known both for her tender love songs and her wild natural hair—expressed her dismay in *Essence* magazine upon discovering that her "handsome, African-American, intelligent and seemingly wealthy" new friend was "happily married to a White woman." The realization made her "spirit wince" as her body felt an "inner pinch, like a mosquito under a summer dress."

Similarly, some of the women interviewed for this book were troubled by black men who partnered with nonblack women. As one woman explains: "If I see a black man with a white woman, there's a part of me that feels sadness and a part of me that feels anger. I may not want that black man, but I probably know some black woman who does." Another woman had for years adamantly opposed interracial marriage but more recently has tried to become more accepting, especially as friends enter interracial relationships. "I don't roll my eyes when I see an interracial couple now," she says, sounding proud of herself. " 'Maybe they do love each other,' I think. I try not to judge."

It is tempting to fixate on the increasing rate of interracial marriage among black men—more than ten times as many African American men were intermarried in 2000 as in 1960. But the increased rate of interracial marriage for black men is only part of the story. What's important is the gap between the rates of interracial marriage for black men and for black women. Not only do black women outmarry less frequently than black men, they outmarry less than any other minority group. Moreover, the rate of interracial marriage among black women has increased more slowly than that of any other minority group. Asian Americans and Latinos, men and women alike, are three or more times as likely as black women to marry outside their group.[100] What is striking, then, is that as black men join other groups in a racially integrated relationship market, black women remain romantically segregated. Later in the book I unravel the multifaceted causes of that puzzling phenomenon.

The Success Gap

The third reason that black women confront a shortage of men is that black men lag behind them both educationally and professionally. Black girls outperform their male counterparts as early as elementary school.[101] By high school the boys' failures become glaring. Consider these simple facts: Nationwide, fewer than half of all black boys graduate from high school,[102] a figure that sinks to 25 percent in the state of New York, one of the most populous in the nation.[103]

The result is that black women vastly outnumber black men in college, where there are more than 1,400,000 black women, but fewer than 900,000 black men.[104] Not only do more black women enter college, they outperform the men once they get there. Nationwide, black women have surpassed their male counterparts even in typically male-dominated and often lucrative fields such as computer science. Each year, black women earn twice as many bachelor's degrees as black men.[105] At historically black colleges—renowned for their success with African Americans—fewer than a third of black male students graduate within six years.[106]

In postgraduate education black women outnumber black men more than two to one.[107] In 2008, there were 125,000 African American women enrolled in graduate school, but only 58,000 African American men. The African American gender gap is also substantial in traditionally prestigious professions such as law and medicine. According to data compiled by the National Center for Education Statistics, black women received 751 medical degrees and 1,893 law degrees in 2008, while black men received only 396 medical degrees and 1,109 law degrees.[108]

This gender gap has developed over the past forty years. In 1970, roughly equal percentages of black men and women had graduated from college.[109] By 1990, black women had moved ahead.[110] Now, the gender gap in college completion among African Americans is wider than ever.[111] Multiple explanations for this development have been offered, with none gaining a consensus. What is clear, though, is that the educational attainment of young black men continues to lag behind that of black women.

The Value of a Degree

Black women are receiving the overwhelming majority of college degrees among African Americans at the same time that those degrees have become more valuable.[112] The earnings gap between the educational haves and have-nots has grown wider over the last few decades due to an evolving labor market. As jobs have been automated or outsourced overseas, opportunities for the least-educated workers have diminished dramatically. And among less-educated workers, men have suffered more than women. David Autor, an economist at the Massachusetts Institute of Technology, has documented this phenomenon in eye-opening detail.[113]

According to Autor, the decline in jobs for less-educated workers has been uneven across industries. Jobs in the industrial sector, including manufacturing steel and building cars, have declined precipitously,[114] and the remaining jobs pay far less than they did before deindustrialization. Well-paying and secure factory jobs are now less plentiful because this work moved overseas to cheaper labor markets, leaving fewer jobs for men with less education. The job opportunities remaining for less-educated workers tend to be female-dominated service positions that cannot easily be outsourced,[115] such as home health care aides, child care providers, and food service workers.

These changes are reflected in the statistical data concerning earnings and employment. According to Autor's analysis, black male high school dropouts are nearly 25 percent less likely to have a job now than they were in 1979.[116] Even those who are employed earn substantially less than their counterparts did three decades ago. Although the labor market has become less favorable for less-educated workers generally, black women have fared better than other groups, in part because their earnings thirty or forty years ago were so low. Black women workers without a high school diploma actually earn slightly more now (in inflation-adjusted dollars) than their counterparts did three decades ago.

The divergent earnings trajectories of black men and women is pronounced among high school graduates. According to Autor's analysis, black men with only a high school diploma are 14 percent less likely to be employed today than their counterparts were thirty years ago, and those who are employed earn about 12 percent less, on average, than their counterparts did three decades ago. In contrast, over that same period, the earnings of black female high school graduates have risen.

These changes in the labor market are not temporary. The recent recession may have exacerbated the effects of deindustrialization, but it did not cause this shift. Most of those industrial jobs that have disappeared are not coming back. Their demise reflects the restructuring of our economy in response to advancing technology and the global labor market that technology has made possible.

While social scientists have thoroughly documented the transformation of the labor market through statistical analyses of earnings and employment rates, I see the shift reflected in the lives of my own family. My sister and her husband each graduated from high school in the late 1970s. Both have been in the labor market consistently since then, my sister as a hotel housekeeper, her husband as an industrial worker. Her work is neither glamorous nor high-paying, but it's consistent. Someone has to clean those rooms. Her husband's work, however, is a different story. He's been laid off more than once and has bounced down the economic ladder with each new job, rung by rung. In fact, as I write these words, he's unemployed. When he is working, he makes more than his wife. But the trajectory of their employment opportunities is clear: Hers are, if not improving, at least steady; his are slowly but surely declining.

The shifting labor market has affected my other family members as well. A favorite cousin joined Republic Steel within days of his high school graduation in the early 1970s. The work was arduous. He labored in front of a blast furnace and came home every day grimy, sweaty, and exhausted. But the job paid well. With overtime he earned more than friends who had gone to college. My cousin thought he'd one day retire from Republic Steel, just as his father had done after more than forty years on the assembly line at Ford. But over time my cousin began to want out. The problem wasn't his back pain and stiff neck—that he could manage—but the increasing precariousness of the steel industry. Wave after wave of layoffs swept the plant. My cousin, a progressive man, made the sort of decision that few men do: Rather than lose his job along with his buddies from the plant, he left a dying industry for a growing one. Now, my 6′4″, 220-pound cousin is a nurse, and his economic future is secure.

As the job market for less-educated workers has weakened, the market for highly educated workers has grown stronger. While high school dropouts earn about 16 percent less than their counterparts thirty years ago did, college graduates over that same period have experienced earnings gains of between 10 percent and 37 percent.[117] Wages have fallen at the bottom of the job ladder, and they have risen at the top,[118] widening the wage gap between less- and more-educated workers. College graduates have long earned more than high school graduates, but the earnings gap has been growing for the past thirty years. Now, according to Autor's estimates, college graduates earn nearly double the wages of high school graduates.[119] The gap between high school dropouts and college graduates is greater still.

While black women overall still earn less than black men, the female-male earnings gap is narrower among African Americans than any other racial group. Black women earn almost 95 percent of what black men earn, up from 75 percent thirty years ago.[120] As impressive as that progress may seem, that 95 percent figure undoubtedly understates the earning power of black women relative to black men. Such statistics don't take into account the large number of black men who, for one reason or another, have dropped out of the labor market. Moreover, black women already occupy a majority of the professional and managerial jobs among African Americans.[121] Fifty years ago, women occupied less than a quarter of the professional and management jobs held by blacks. Today they fill roughly 60 percent of such jobs.[122] Furthermore, during the past three decades, the earnings of black female college graduates have increased *more than four times as much* as the earnings of their black male counterparts.[123]

These developments led sociologist Orlando Patterson to conclude in the late 1990s that African American women are now "poised to assume leadership in almost all areas of the Afro-American community and to outperform Afro-American men at middle- and upper-class levels of the wider society and economy."[124] His assessment reflects a social fact now too well established to be denied: Where black men fail, black women succeed. Advanced education brings higher wages, and black women are twice as likely as black men to receive that education. As today's young adults move into their peak earning years, black women will outearn black men.

The educational and economic gulf between black men and women signifies the fracturing of black America. The fortunes of African Americans are polarizing. Some have taken advantage of the opportunities opened by the advances of the civil rights era, while others have fallen victim to deindustrialization and mass incarceration. Black America has bifurcated into two communities: one moving ahead, one lagging behind. The divide between these two groups is not only economic; it is cultural and social as well. The depth of that divide is apparent in the views of African Americans themselves. A national poll conducted in 2007 found that more than six in ten African Americans believed the values of the poor and the middle class had diverged during the previous decade.[125] Nearly four in ten African Americans thought that they should no longer be viewed as members of a single race.

If black America is splintering into two Americas, one prosperous and one poor, then it is also the case that one is disproportionately female, the other disproportionately male. Two dynamics are operating at once: the widening of the class divide and the development of a gender divide. This recognition allows us to reconcile the fact of unprecedented incarceration rates for young black men with the fact that more than twice as many African American young adults are in school as in prison.

The success gap between black men and women provides some context for understanding the growth of incarceration, as discussed earlier in the chapter. A big part of the reason that so many black men are incarcerated is that black men are disproportionately likely to be poorly educated and, in turn, to lack viable employment opportunities in the mainstream economy. The growth of incarceration is parasitic upon black men's educational and economic failures.

The success gap also helps us to make sense of the irritation that some black women feel about interracial marriage by black men. There are many fewer high-achieving black men than women. Recall that two black women graduate college for every one man. Yet a large percentage of that small group of high-achieving men marry outside the race. Many black women thus experience interracial marriage by black men as a loss they can ill afford.

White Follows Black

The success gap between men and women is not confined to African Americans: The same trend is reshaping gender relations throughout society.[126] In the 1970s, women were a third or less of college graduates.[127] Now, more women than men graduate from college,[128] and more women than men enroll in graduate school.[129] Adults between the ages of thirty and forty-four are the first group in U.S. history comprised of more female than male college graduates.[130]

The same labor market shifts that have diminished the economic prospects of black men and boosted those of black women also affect other groups. While men still earn more than women,[131] the degree by which the gap has narrowed over the past few decades is striking. According to a study by the Pew Research Center, women's earnings grew 44 percent between 1970 and 2007, compared to a meager 6 percent for men.[132] Among workers with postgraduate degrees, wage growth has also been greater for women.[133] The shrinking economic gap between genders is also apparent in employment rates. Over the past few decades, at every level of education, the likelihood of employment for men has remained flat or even declined, while it has risen for women.[134]

The erosion of the earnings advantage that men enjoyed for so long has been exacerbated by the recent recession. It struck men particularly hard. According to one estimate, men accounted for nearly 75 percent of the jobs lost during that period.[135] So while men generally still earn substantially more than women, the gap is narrowing.[136] And although the recession is temporary, it accentuates a long-term trend.

Marriage and the Success Gap

The economic decline of men diminishes their appeal in the eyes of women. It has long been the case that a man's value in the marriage market depends on his income potential. Although the view that a husband's role is to support the family is less universal now than decades ago, it is still widely held. A 2010 poll by the Pew Research Center finds that more than two-thirds of Americans think that a man who is about to marry should be able to support his family, while only a third think the same about a woman.

Fifty years ago, the fact that a man earned a meager income influenced who he married; today it influences whether he marries. As I discussed in Chapter 2, people are no longer compelled to marry, and when they do marry they expect a lot from the relationship. Poor people, no less than middle-class people, seek emotional intimacy and understanding in marriage. They want a nurturing partner with whom they can grow as a person. These goals require a degree of economic stability that many poor couples never attain. Even poor couples who live together and have a child often postpone marriage in the hope that they'll get the stable job and nice apartment that they think should precede it.[137] They don't think that marriage allows a person to become stable; they think a person needs to be stable in order to have a good marriage. While middle-class people postpone marriage, the poor more often end up forgoing it altogether.

The marriage market plight of low-income men is likely exacerbated by the growth in income inequality. The success of those men with advanced degrees and high incomes casts a shadow, as it were, over the marriage prospects of the economically marginal men, diminishing even further their likelihood of marital bliss. Women will compare the less successful men to their more successful counterparts, and are more likely to find lower achievers wanting than they might have a generation or more ago.[138]

Low-income black men confront another difficulty: that black women in particular value economic security in a husband. Research from the 1990s found that black women gave more weight to a husband's economic status than did white women. Research polling data from

2010 seems to confirm that in evaluating potential mates, economic stability still matters more for African Americans than for other groups.[139] This helps to explain why at every income level, black men are substantially less likely than their white counterparts to have married. Black women may want their husbands to be economically stable because if a black couple encounters economic difficulties, their in-laws are much less likely than those of white couples to be able to offer assistance. (Black men are concerned about economic stability too; they are more likely than other groups of men to think that the ability to earn a living is an important consideration in evaluating a prospective wife.) So as men become more economically marginal, their chances for a successful marriage diminish.

Just as labor market difficulties undermine a man's appeal as a potential spouse, professional success enhances that of women. It may have been the case decades ago—when the husband earned the income and the wife cared for the home and the children—that women with professional aspirations were disadvantaged in the marriage market. But now that is clearly not the case. The breadwinner/homemaker model of marriage has been supplanted by a new norm. In most families, both spouses work for pay, so a woman's advanced education now stands to benefit both her and her husband. Moreover, men whose own income has declined may view prosperous women as especially desirable. Thus, marriage rates remain high for college-educated women, even as they decline for the poor.

However, for black women the situation is different. They confront a shortage of successful black men. Some professional black women marry black male peers. But most professional black women either remain unmarried or marry a less-educated man. That so many college-educated black women marry working-class men depletes the pool of men for less-educated women.

If the fortunes of white men and women diverge as they have among blacks, then in the years to come, professional white women may confront the same challenges that professional black women do today. The lives of each group of women will embody the same irony: The potential realization of their hopes for marriage is bolstered by their successes yet undermined by men's failures.

CHAPTER 4

The Market

Here's an e-mail I received from a friend:

FIVE RULES FOR MEN TO FOLLOW FOR A HAPPY LIFE:

1. It's important to have a woman who helps at home, cooks from time to time, cleans up, and has a job.

2. It's important to have a woman who makes you laugh.

3. It's important to have a woman you can trust and who doesn't lie to you.

4. It's important to have a woman who is good in bed and who likes to be with you.

5. And it is very, very important that these four women do not know each other.

Once I stopped laughing, I replied to my friend's missive. "Thanks," I wrote, not only for the humor but for underscoring the widespread and deeply rooted expectation of monogamy. Only with the final rule do we learn that the man is a scoundrel, the women duped. For how else could a woman come to share a man?

However dominant the cultural ideal of monogamy, people's actual relationships are varied. National data suggest that, in any given year, more than one in ten men is involved in concurrent relationships.[140] Some concurrent relationships are brief, as when one begins not long before another ends. But some endure for years.

Man Sharing

Although people of all races engage in concurrent sexual relationships, the evidence suggests that such relationships are more common among African Americans than other groups. Concurrent relationships were certainly familiar to a number of the professional black women I interviewed. Linda Carlson, a consultant in Atlanta, has been seeing the same man since her divorce some years earlier. "A great guy," she tells me. "Never been married." For her birthday, he surprised her with a weekend trip to New York City, where they stayed in a luxury hotel, ate at fine restaurants, and enjoyed a Broadway play. I surmised that her bachelor beau might be ready for marriage after all.

But, in fact, the birthday revelry was one-sided. In the few years they had been dating, he had never missed her birthday, but she had never spent one of his with him.

"What's that about?" I ask. She shrugs, then mentions that he likes to visit his family on his birthday. I could tell without having to ask that she suspects more.

Linda jokes that "Don't Ask, Don't Tell" is their rule, and that it works fine for them. Linda's friend never promised that she'd be the only one, much less mentioned marriage. But he never outright lied to her, at least as far as she knew. He keeps his cards close to his vest, and she does not ask too many questions. They rely instead on tacit understandings.

The prevalence of nonmonogamous relationships has been a topic of discussion in the black community for decades. More than twenty years ago, psychologist and relationship counselor Audrey Chapman wrote the controversial book *Man Sharing: Dilemma or Choice,*[141] in which she described the predicament faced by a growing number of women. Chapman contended that many women, willingly or not, would at some point in their lives share a man with other women. And she suggested that there are healthy ways to navigate these touchy relationships. More recently, man sharing has received attention in print and broadcast media. *Essence* magazine offered the story of a woman who heard from her lover only every three weeks. "It was like flying standby," she said. "He had openings, and you were happy he could accommodate you."[142]

When *Nightline* went to Atlanta in 2010 to interview successful black women there about why they were unmarried, the women reported that the problem wasn't meeting men; it was exclusivity. Some of the women said that they hadn't had an exclusive relationship with a black man in more than a decade. Intrigued by the *Nightline* episode, I tracked down some of these women in Atlanta and interviewed them myself. I wanted to understand how such beautiful, accomplished, and intelligent women could have trouble finding husbands. “The numbers are in their favor,” one said, referring to the dearth of successful black men. “They take advantage,” added another.

Interviews with other women unearthed similar stories. One female physician suspects that, at some level, many women know their man has other partners. “In my clinical experience dealing with a largely African American female population,” she says, “women are not surprised by the fact that their men are cheating on them.” She describes a common response after telling a black woman that she has a sexually transmitted disease. “She knows she hasn’t slept around, yet she doesn’t look surprised.” This happened not once or twice but, according to the physician, many times with different women. “They aren’t shocked and they aren’t mad,” the doctor explains. “I have yet to see one black woman say, ‘Oh, no, let me go get my gun, I’m going to kill him.’ It hasn’t happened. It’s just quiet acceptance.”

The evidence that many African Americans maintain long-standing, nonexclusive relationships is more than anecdotal. Research confirms what personal stories suggest—that man sharing is a reality for many black women. In the late 1980s, a team led by Professor Edward Laumann at the University of Chicago initiated one of the most rigorous and thorough studies ever of sexual behaviors and relationship patterns. Their research project spanned many years and produced numerous publications.[143] Laumann and colleagues examined, among other things, the types of intimate sexual relationships in which people engage. The researchers found that most sexually intimate relationships are monogamous, and typically last for at least several months.[144] In Laumann’s study, African Americans were the least likely of all groups to have a monogamous relationship.[145] And while relationships that were concurrent tended to overlap briefly, in one predominantly African American Chicago neighborhood, the researchers found that almost two out of every five men had simultaneous relationships with more than one sex partner.[146] Most of those concurrent relationships endured for six months or more.[147] The researchers found that a majority of men from that neighborhood—60 percent—had had another partner during the course of their current relationship. For some men, no doubt, concurrent relationships had become the new normal.

Laumann and colleagues found that black men were substantially more likely to be in long-term concurrent relationships than white men, for whom monogamy or short-term relationship overlaps were more common.[148] Among men who did not live with their intimate partner, black men were less than half as likely as white men to have only one partner, and more than twice as likely to maintain long-term concurrent relationships. Even among men who lived with a woman, the racial difference in concurrent relationships was substantial. Black men with a live-in partner were more than five times as likely as their white counterparts to also be involved in a long-term relationship with another woman. In fact, more than a third of black male cohabitants had a long-term relationship with an additional partner. Other data are consistent with these findings.[149]

There is evidence that man sharing extends to marital relationships as well; black married men are substantially more likely than any other group of men (or women) to engage in an extramarital relationship.[150] Some research has found, astoundingly, that even taking into account individual characteristics associated with fidelity (e.g., views about sex, marriage, or religiosity), black married men are twice as likely as white married men to have a relationship with another woman.[151]

Some researchers have misleadingly described nonmonogamous relationships as a form of polygamy.[152] Some African Americans in particular link concurrent relationships to the African past, as though current-day man-sharing arrangements are the polygamous legacy of the African homeland. But this explanation for contemporary man sharing is no more sensible than attributing the black marriage decline to the extended family of African tribal cultures. Polygamy is a marriage-like relationship in which the parties live together and assume the rights and obligations of spouses. In societies that permit polygamy (and there have been many of them), men with multiple wives are required to support those wives. Man sharing is less like polygamy and more like "friends with benefits," nonexclusive sexual relationships unencumbered by the obligations of committed partnerships.[153]

Distrust and Discord

Man-sharing relationships contribute to the African American marriage decline in a number of ways. First, these nonexclusive relationships are not on the serious commitment track. As one man told me, "If you have four quality women you're dating and they're in a rotation, who's going to rush into a marriage?" The more common long-term concurrent relationships become, the more acceptable they will seem to many black men in particular.[154] These changing norms haven't escaped black women. As a single female friend noted on her Facebook page: "I've seen five of my white male friends propose or get married, yet almost all the black males I know in their same age category are happily single, trying to keep a few candidates in rotation until they get bored with partying and PlayStation and decide to 'give up the ghost' on their single days—usually when their moms start verbally harassing them about grandkids and stop cooking Sunday and holiday dinners [for them] because they feel they should have daughters-in-law to do it."

The prevalence of man-sharing relationships also makes it more difficult for men and women alike to sustain a committed intimate relationship with anyone. For black men, the surfeit of black women makes it enticing to remain single, and likely causes black men's standards for a wife to rise. Even if a man decides he wants to marry, the variety of women he has enjoyed may nurture an unrealistic standard. I know men who expect in a wife some combination of the best of all the women they have dated. Although a natural consequence of the relationship market, such a sense of entitlement makes a relationship with any woman difficult. There is a popular discourse about whether black women are too picky, but from all that I have seen, it is black men, particularly sought-after and successful black men, who are the pickiest of all.

These men can maintain absurdly high standards because they are under no pressure to commit—the options are endless. Why cash in when you can continue to play? In my conversations with men, they typically didn't put it so bluntly. Instead, they made oblique references to how much fun it is to be single. They talked about not being in any rush to marry, about cherishing their freedom. They talked about their hesitancy to commit to marriage when they've seen so many go wrong. They talked about how difficult it is to find the right woman, a quest ironically rendered more challenging by the knowledge that there are so many of them out there.

While man sharing may heighten men's expectations of women, it may diminish women's expectations of men. When a committed partnership is not on the horizon, and the prospect of a long-term payoff is bleak, the sensible thing to do is focus on the short term, take one's benefits from the relationship *now,* not wait for them in the future. "You've gotta put up with so much mess from these men," says Linda, the Atlanta consultant, "you might as well get paid. He'd better take you to the nicest places, buy you things, because you know you're going to have to put up with the usual mess." This isn't her approach, she tells me, but it is one that, given the circumstances, she understands. "You make him pay either for the benefit he gets from being with you or you make him pay for his transgressions."

A single friend describes a trip to New York to visit a woman he'd just begun to date. His first night there he stopped at a grocery store, picked up salmon, salad, and vegetables, and cooked dinner for her. "It was a great dinner," he boasts. But for her, a home-cooked meal wasn't enough. The next day she wanted to go to brunch at a five-star hotel. "The parking alone will be fifty bucks," he complained to her. He suggested a quaint place in Brooklyn. Good food, reasonable prices, he said. He was trying to be practical. She heard "cheap." He was paying, but she wanted to call the shots. They disagreed; he packed his bag and left.

"I just couldn't see dropping two hundred, three hundred dollars on brunch," he tells me. And, he had felt certain that at the restaurant her eyes would settle on the most expensive item on the menu. And that she'd want champagne. "What's brunch without a mimosa?" he mimics. He had confronted this situation before—a woman with dollar signs in her eyes—and he wanted no part of it. If she was determined to squeeze what she could out of him, it was only because she knew that he, like other men, wanted the benefits of a relationship but none of the obligations.

This cycle breeds suspicion on both sides. It leaves some black men cynical, wary of relationships with black women, and always ready to assume the worst. Some men become hypervigilant about any effort to take advantage of them, to use them for what they have, rather than appreciate who they are. And the woman who suspects she is one of many paramours is left to wonder which of her rivals is getting that two-hundred-dollar brunch. Bitterness, resentment, distrust—these are the consequences of man sharing.

What Men Want

So why do black men choose nonexclusive relationships rather than marriage? Deviant values are not to blame. Black men maintain nonexclusive relationships for the same reason as other men: because they can. There is probably some truth to the notion that women are more inclined toward marriage than are men. That difference could reflect millennia of evolution. Or it could reflect socialization and the influence of culture. Or it could simply be that women hear a biological clock ticking when men do not. Whatever the reason, men in their twenties and thirties seem less inclined to marry than women.

Man sharing results from a relationship market in which women vastly outnumber men. Faced with so many options, some men reason—as one black man bluntly told researchers in a study of unmarried parents—"Why have one woman when you can have ten?"[155]

Many men are content to wait to marry. As one of the women interviewed by *Nightline* noted, "You meet these great guys, have a good relationship, good rapport, and then it's like 'I'll keep you around and hopefully when I'm ready to settle down you'll be there.'" Another woman added that "every now and then they'll check in to make sure you're still single." The other women understood, concluding almost in unison: "That's the back pocket girl." Men with so many options can imagine a much worse scenario than being single and young—or even single and not so young.

Maurice Dawson, a fifty-three-year-old businessman who lives in a leafy suburb of Philadelphia, has an impressive record—a career as a competitive athlete, a business degree, and currently an executive position with a Fortune 500 company. Although now happily married since his midforties, he admits to looking back fondly, a bit too fondly some might say, on his single days. "You have more fun on a day-to-day basis if you're single," he tells me. When I ask why, he raises an eyebrow and looks at me, as if to say, "You can't be seriously asking me that question." When I press him, he explains, "Man, your thirties, even into your forties, you go out, you're making money, you got a job, you got your health—your life can be great." And part of this "greatness" involves relationships with beautiful black women. From the way Maurice talks about his single days, I can see that he was in no rush to leave them behind. But as he approached fifty—and began to look back over his life and assess its significance—he accepted that it was time to move on.

Studies conducted by sociologist Scott South suggest that black men in particular are, like Maurice, in no rush to marry. During the 1990s, South analyzed data from the nationally representative and government-funded National Survey of Families and Households in order to assess the extent to which racial differences in the desire to marry account for the lower likelihood of an African American marrying.[156] He found that black men are more reluctant to marry than black women, white men, or white women. One of the reasons that black men are more content to remain single, South concluded, is that compared to white men, they are less likely to believe that their sex life will improve if they marry. South reasoned that the supposed sexual benefits of marriage may appeal less to black men because the sex ratio tilts so heavily in their favor. So, while black women don't marry because they have too few options, some black men don't marry because they have too many.

Why Women Accept It

But why do women who want to marry stay with a man who doesn't? Here, as elsewhere, the market holds the key. As men become scarcer they become better able to dictate the terms of relationships.

And black women are not the only ones confronting a market in which men are in short supply. Consider the women students at the University of North Carolina, Chapel Hill. A 2009 *New York Times* investigation of the changing culture of intimate relationships at the school begins, "Another ladies night, not by choice."[157] At UNC, as at many schools, men are becoming scarce; the numbers imbalance makes it hard for women to find a man, and shapes what happens once they do. "Girls feel pressured to do more than they're comfortable with to lock it down," one woman notes. And as the relationship progresses, women feel pressured to overlook indiscretions to keep a man. As for a man's cheating, "That's a thing that girls let slide, because you have to," one female student explains. "If you don't let it slide, you don't have a boyfriend."

Some social science research suggests that the shortage of men on some college campuses is one of the many factors that contribute to the widespread practice of "hooking up," a reference to a sexual encounter without any commitment or even any relationship beyond a physical one.[158] As Kathleen Bogle notes in her book *Hooking Up: Sex, Dating, and Relationships on Campus,* "Men are now a scarce resource on campus [and gain] power in *lack* of numbers." The fewer men there are, the greater their power to dictate the terms of relationships, leaving women little choice but to "adapt to a script that is particularly beneficial to some college men."[159] Sociologists Jeremy Uecker and Mark Regnerus reach a similar conclusion through a systematic analysis of a nationally representative sample of college women. They compare colleges with varying gender balances and conclude that when men are scarce, the balance of power in a relationship favors men. Women on such campuses are more likely to think that the men there don't treat women well and are unwilling to commit to an exclusive romantic relationship.

In college and elsewhere, appealing black men are in short supply, and desirable black women are abundant. That's the central fact shaping interactions in the relationship market. Their negotiation of the terms of their relationship—including the question of exclusivity—is influenced by the power that each can bring to bear. And each party's relative power derives in part from the demographics of the relationship market. Generally, whichever party belongs to the group in shorter supply gains an advantage. In China, for example, as a result of the country's one-child policy, there are many fewer women than men, which puts men in the position of having to compete. Women, by virtue of their scarcity, have more relationship options than the men do. Researchers find that this scarcity of women has prompted families with young boys to save money at higher than normal rates so that their son can eventually attract a wife in a competitive marketplace.[160]

With African Americans, in contrast, the numbers imbalance favors men. What this means is that for a black man and black woman negotiating a relationship, the man will have more options and more opportunities outside the relationship than the woman. If for whatever reason their relationship negotiation breaks down—if they can't agree about what sort of relationship to have—the man will encounter a surfeit of beautiful, accomplished, single black women. The woman, in contrast, will have to contend with a much shallower pool of desirable men.

More favorable options outside the relationship give the man more power within it. The easier it is for him to find the type of relationship he wants elsewhere, the less willing he is to compromise in this one. The woman, conversely, is more willing to compromise in a relationship if the alternatives don't appear any better. For the man and woman alike, their available options establish, in this relationship negotiation, the least disagreeable "deal" for which they'd be willing to settle.

It is in this way that options outside the relationship influence behavior within it. The quality and extent of those options exert their force simply by the fact of their existence. Neither party needs to invoke the options for them to have their effect. All that's required is for the man and woman to both have a sense of the abundance or paucity of opportunities awaiting them if they don't reach an agreement.

So, in Linda's case, even if her friend offers relationship terms that she finds less than ideal, his terms might represent the best deal she can expect to encounter on the "open market." This option may also seem more appealing than a return to single life. Saddled with the knowledge that other women with less demanding standards might quickly swoop up her partner on the market, she feels the pressure to accept a deal that does not conform to her expectations. In this way, the numbers imbalance gives black men the power to dictate the terms of their intimate relationships. The market metaphor leads us to this conclusion: Black men tend to use their disproportionate power to establish relationships that are intimate but not committed, that entail sex but not marriage, and that offer benefits without responsibilities.

The small group of successful black men have the greatest market power of all. They have the numbers on their side in two ways. First, as a result of incarceration and other factors, there are fewer black men than women in the population. Second, successful black men are scarce, especially relative to the large numbers of high-achieving black women. The failure of so many black men increases the value of successful black men—and that power seems to be intoxicating: a currency often used to avoid commitment rather than to attract a wife.

Black women are keenly aware of the paucity of successful black men, and that shortage shapes their intimate relationships as well as their perceptions of prospective partners. As one woman explained, "The black men that are on my level are like, 'I know I'm in demand, I have the pick of whoever I want. So why would I limit it?' The sad thing is that they *do* have their pick," she conceded. She could see that a man with so many options was not the man for her.

Linda, like many other women, is making the best of a bad situation. She wants the companionship of a man who is "on her level." She wants a man who is accomplished, with whom she'll have something to talk about. As intelligent, interesting, and delightful as Linda is, in terms of the market, women like her are plentiful; men like her friend are not. If she doesn't offer him a nonexclusive relationship, someone else will. And she'll confront the same dilemma with the next man. So Linda accepts the relationship he offers; it is better, she reasons, than being alone.

The dynamics in Linda's relationship are mirrored in the sexual behaviors study conducted by Laumann and colleagues in Chicago. The researchers not only found that multiple-partner relationships were more common among African Americans, they also discovered that for blacks—but not for whites—multiple-partner relationships were the most common among better-educated men.[161] Black men who had completed college or higher were the least likely to have a single long-term partner and the most likely to be in a relationship with multiple sexual partners.[162] Among the white men, the researchers found no relation between the men's education level and their likelihood of having long-term concurrent relationships.[163] For whites, whether high school dropouts or college graduates, the rate of long-term concurrent relationships was uniformly low.

One explanation for this pattern of results is that highly educated black men wield more power in the relationship market than either less-educated black men or white men of any education level. Highly educated black men are, in the eyes of many women, more desirable than less-educated black men. And well-educated black men are scarcer than well-educated white men. Some of the most desirable men, emboldened by their scarcity and the resulting plethora of options, negotiate the relationship deals that they think work to their advantage: sex and female companionship without commitment.

Disease

Man sharing not only shapes the emotional terrain between black men and women. It also undermines their physical health, particularly that of black women.[164] Black women are more likely than any other group of people to be infected with herpes, according to a 2010 study from the Centers for Disease Control and Prevention.[165] The study concluded that the incidence of the virus was more than three times higher among blacks than among whites. Most alarmingly, almost half of all black women have herpes.[166] As with other sexually transmitted diseases, women are more susceptible than men, and black women were more than three times as likely as white women or Mexican American women to be infected.

The increased incidence of herpes among black women is not a result of promiscuity among women or unsafe sexual practices—neither of these is the primary culprit. The available evidence indicates that African Americans are no less likely than other groups to use condoms.[167] Nor can the high rate of herpes infection among black women be attributed to an exposure to a greater number of sexual partners. Even among black women with fewer than four lifetime partners, infection rates are more than three times higher among African Americans than whites (34 percent versus 9 percent).[168] Black women with between two and four partners are more likely to be infected with herpes than white women who have more than ten partners.

Concurrent relationships contribute to the high rate of herpes infection among black women.[169] Black women are more likely to be involved in multipartner relationships than white women, and these multipartner relationships dramatically increase the risk of contracting a sexually transmitted disease. In these relationships, black men are the promiscuous ones, but black women bear more of the costs. Start with one man with herpes who is having sex with four different women, then multiply that many times over, and you can imagine the infection explosion. Women, by virtue of biology, acquire the infection more readily upon exposure than men, and the consequences of infection are often more severe.

Recent statistics from the Centers for Disease Control and Prevention further confirm the high number of sexual partners among black men.[170] A 2005 report showed that nearly 22 percent of African American men reported having three or more sexual partners in the past twelve months.[171] Black men are also significantly more likely to have a high number of lifetime sexual partners than men of other races.[172]

Black women are disproportionately represented among HIV cases as well. Although black men account for a larger share of total HIV cases than black women, within gender groups, the racial disproportion is greater for black women. Black men constitute approximately 40 percent of HIV+ men, while black women are 60 percent or more of HIV+ women. According to incidence rates provided by the Centers for Disease Control and Prevention, black women are nearly fifteen times as likely as white women to be newly infected with HIV.[173] And they are more likely than white women to have contracted the disease through heterosexual contact.[174] Estimates are that more than three out of every four HIV+ black women have been infected through sex with a man.[175] And because women may pass the virus on to their newborns, African American children comprise nearly two-thirds of all HIV+ young children in the United States.[176]

As with herpes, concurrent relationships contribute to the disparity. For women who are already infected with herpes, the risk of contracting HIV is compounded. Researchers have shown that the likelihood of HIV infection depends in part on the presence of other sexually transmitted diseases. Put simply, a woman is more likely to acquire the virus if she already has another sexually transmitted disease—like herpes—that provides an entryway for HIV. That makes man sharing a source, for some, of lifelong physical jeopardy.

Their struggles with men leave some black women hardened. A businesswoman in Atlanta recalls a man telling her, straight out, "You look like one of those sisters who don't cut a brother slack." Her response? "I proceeded to curse him out." The man's observation upset her, she says, because "I've heard that from other men." When I suggest that maybe she *doesn't* cut a brother slack, she says without equivocation, "I don't." And then in her own defense, "Why should I? They're not cutting me any slack."

Other women remove themselves from the fray. Audrey, the never-married corporate professional from D.C., has decided that "right now, I feel I should just be still. I'm trying to get to the point where I accept that marriage may never happen for me," she says. "I don't want to think negatively, but as more time passes, the less hopeful I am."

She sometimes thinks of the Obamas in assessing her own failed romantic history. "What's so different about Michelle compared to a lot of these other women who are not married, including myself?" she wonders aloud. "Did she just happen to be at the right law firm at the right time? Is it just the luck of the draw?"

Her own hopes for marriage have dimmed, she says, as men have come and gone with no wedding ring, just a long list of excuses. "Is it men?" she wonders. "Or is there something wrong with me?" Her experiences have nurtured a wariness that leaves her wondering, with every new man she meets, "OK, how long before you act the fool?" She sometimes feels that she is "just waiting for the costume to come off."

CHAPTER 5

What About the Children?

Annelise Hemphill is pregnant. It is 1999. She is twenty-eight years old and faced with the prospect of unwed motherhood. She is college-educated and works full-time as the executive assistant to the CEO of a Fortune 500 company. She has been in an exclusive relationship with her baby's father for the past year. When she tells him she's pregnant, his response betrays neither happiness nor regret. They hadn't planned to have a child. Annelise's pregnancy is testament to what even teenagers ought to know: No birth control method works all the time.

Unwed Childbearing

The situation Annelise confronted arises more frequently with black women than with anyone else. Black women have more unintended pregnancies, and are more likely to become unmarried mothers, than any other group of women. The statistics would shock if they weren't so familiar: Seven out of ten black children are born to unmarried parents.[177] Five out of every six black children will spend some portion of their childhood living with a single parent.[178] Almost four out of ten black single mothers are poor.[179]

The high rate of unwed childbearing among blacks has long been the focus of scholarly and popular attention.[180] But unwed motherhood is not unique to African Americans. I mentioned in Chapter 1 that more than 25 percent of white children are born to unmarried parents. That statistic actually understates the extent to which marriage and child-bearing have been decoupled for some white women. A better measure is the percentage of mothers who are unmarried when they have their first child. For white women, that figure is 35 percent. For younger women, the rate is higher still: According to the University of Texas sociologist Mark Regnerus, the percentage of first births to unmarried white women between the ages of twenty and twenty-four—ages that used to be the prime years for marriage and childbearing—rises to 60 percent.

Misconceptions about unwed mothers abound. While the image persists of the unwed teenage mother, scared to reveal her pregnancy to her parents because they didn't know she was having sex, the reality is that most unwed mothers are not teenagers—they are women like Annelise, in their twenties, or even thirties.[181] Teenagers figure less prominently than ever among the group of unmarried black mothers. (Teenage pregnancy rates, although still high compared to those of some other nations, are near record lows in the United States.[182])

Nor are black women getting pregnant more frequently now than they were thirty or forty years ago. In fact, just like white women, today's black women are less likely to get pregnant, and on the whole have fewer children, than their predecessors. The percentage of black children born to unwed parents exceeds 70 percent not because single, black women are getting pregnant more often, but because black women are so much more likely to be single. Unwed childbearing is yet another consequence of the marriage decline.

There is a substantial and growing body of research concerning unwed childbearing that aims to answer the question: Why don't more black women wait until they are married to have children? But what the public hears most often is the commentary of politicians and of celebrities such as Bill Cosby, a talented comedian and generous philanthropist but an uninformed social critic. According to Cosby, the explanation for unwed childbearing is simple: deficient values. "[T]he lower economic and lower-middle economic people are not holding their end in this deal,"[183] he declared in 2004, during a commemoration of the Supreme Court's historic *Brown v. Board of Education* school desegregation decision. "No longer is a person embarrassed because they're pregnant without a husband," he said. That interpretation became a staple of his subsequent speaking tour and book with Harvard professor Alvin Poussaint: Poor blacks have embraced deviant values that account for their continued disadvantage.[184]

But Cosby is wrong. The best available research makes clear that poor black women don't marry for the same reason that many other women don't: They set a high bar for marriage. They want to marry; they hope to marry. But not until they and their partner are stable, with a job, a car, a home. They do not remain unmarried because they reject the institution, so much as because they expect the same from it as do other Americans. They differ from their affluent white counterparts less in their values than in their circumstances.

Recent studies of single mothers, for example, have found that many don't marry their child's father because they doubt his ability to contribute economically and his commitment to the relationship.[185] And with good reason. The fathers are often not financially stable, and are dogged by the kinds of problems—drug abuse, unemployment, violence, infidelity—that tend to shadow low-income, undereducated black men. Statistics suggest these women are correct to suspect that their chances for marital success are slim. The majority of marriages among poor African Americans do end in divorce,[186] and those that survive are often troubled. The life circumstances of poor black women thus create a cruel dilemma. If they were to have children only after their hopes for marriage were fulfilled, many would remain childless. It is partly because their hope for a stable marriage seems destined to remain unfulfilled that they have children without a husband.

Middle-class black women confront this dilemma as well. The racial gap in unwed childbearing spans the socioeconomic spectrum, just as the racial disparity in marriage does. Middle-class black women are more likely to become unwed mothers than their white counterparts.[187]

The Middle-Class Predicament

Yet being an unwed mother is a distinction that middle-class black women wear uneasily. "The worst thing in life to me was to be single, black, and pregnant," Annelise, the executive assistant, explains. "I just thought it was a loaded portfolio that I didn't want any part of."

Her aversion to becoming a single mother, though, had little to do with the burden of raising children alone. "I had an ultrasound in Beverly Hills," she recalls. "I remember sitting in the waiting room at the doctor's office and being the only black person there. I could feel these white women looking at me and noting that I didn't have a ring." What

Annelise feared was not the life of the single mother so much as the image of the single mother, the stigma of having a child but no husband. She didn't want strangers—white people, especially—to view her as a stereotype: unwed black mother; immoral, promiscuous, irresponsible; inclined to birth one child after another, often by different men, with nary a thought to how she might support them. She didn't want others to see her through that lens, and she didn't want to think of herself that way.

For all of their achievements, many successful, college-educated black women struggle against the image of the unmarried welfare mother. They have worked hard to better themselves, but they still worry about being measured against a stereotype. That's not what their parents raised them to be, not what they envisioned for themselves as they spent late nights at the library, amassed internships and honors, then carefully proofread the résumé that would land them the job of their dreams. These women have worked too hard to attain middle-class respectability to accept the role of "baby mama."

They strive to sidestep the assumption that others are inclined to make. When Chicago resident Sheila Jackson got pregnant during the second year of her marriage, she refused to take her wedding band off, even as it grew uncomfortably tight over the course of her pregnancy. "I was always certain to wear my ring," she tells me, "because I didn't want people to think I wasn't married." After her baby's birth, she once left her ring at home during a visit to the grocery store in her South Side neighborhood. As she balanced the baby on her hip and unloaded her grocery cart, the cashier asked, "Do you have your WIC [Women, Infants, and Children] card?" "No!" she emphatically responded. "I'm not on WIC," she said, at once dispirited and angry to be mistaken for a low-income, typically unmarried woman dependent on a government program. The clerk wasn't the only one to make that assumption. As she left the store, another customer tried to sell Sheila *her* WIC coupons—at a discount, of course—so the woman could get cash for cigarettes. Such encounters rankled Sheila. She wasn't poor, she wasn't unmarried, and she wasn't irresponsible. She had strived to be, as she puts it, "the antithesis of that portrayal of black women."

I heard stories like this from women I spoke with around the country, including a friend who recalled going solo to her daughter's suburban elementary school one day to meet with her child's new teacher. The teacher tried to strike what she thought was a sympathetic note. "I know how difficult it can be for children from the city to adjust to the suburbs," she said. As the teacher prattled on, it became clear that she assumed she was talking to a single mother. My friend, an adjuster for a major insurance company, made clear—as politely as she could—that, no, her daughter was *not* bused to the school from the inner city, and that her husband couldn't make the meeting because he was at work, thank you very much. But while the teacher's assumption irritated her, she can also understand it. After all, she acknowledges, "Most of the black kids at the school *are* from poor single-parent families."

Marriage . . . Without the Shotgun

When Annelise found out she was pregnant, "there was no indecision," she says. "We both knew that we were getting married." Her husband didn't propose—a lapse that would become a bone of contention later—but neither was there an ultimatum from her. "To me, it seemed like the natural thing to do."

They didn't have much time to waste. "The most important thing at that point," she says, "was getting married soon so that this child would be born to a wedded union." Annelise wanted to wed in a Catholic church, but was told they would need six months of lessons first since her husband wasn't Catholic. "I don't have six months," she told the priest. "If we couldn't find a church, we'd have been down at city hall. One way or another, we were getting married before that baby came." Eventually, they convinced the priest at her childhood church, where her parents were still active, to marry them without the lessons. She was "married in the church with a bouquet of flowers hiding my big stomach," she says. "We didn't have a honeymoon."

After four years and two more children, Annelise filed for divorce. As much as she wanted the father of her children to be her husband, she couldn't make the marriage work. She was finally prompted to file for divorce when, after enduring the death of a loved one, she realized that if she were on her deathbed, her husband was the person whose eyes she'd least want to gaze into. "I know that sounds bad," she acknowledges, "but that's what I felt."

The irony of Annelise becoming a single mom is not lost on her. She feels she still gets the same looks as she did at that doctor's office in Beverly Hills. But now she takes comfort in the fact that, although the marriage didn't last, her children at least "all have the same dad" and "all have their dad's name." Divorce was not what she planned, but she'd prefer it to having never married at all. As expressed by another woman with the same preference: "At least I could say we started out as a happy, loving couple. How you start out matters."

Missing Fathers

After Annelise's divorce, the children remained with her. Their father saw them regularly at first. But as time passed and the parents moved on—to new careers, neighborhoods, relationships—the children's father became less of a presence in their lives. Even though Annelise's ex-husband doesn't fit the image of an unwed black father—after all, he did marry their mother, he worked consistently and earned a good income, and he showed in many ways that he cares about his children—he might still become another black father missing in action.

No group of parents has been as reviled, condemned, and criticized as black fathers. Poor unwed fathers have been denigrated by the likes of Bill Cosby, who accused them of trying to "run away" from their parental roles.[188] Even presidential candidate Barack Obama, during a 2008 Father's Day speech at a Chicago church, urged, "We need fathers to realize that responsibility does not end at conception. We need them to realize that what makes you a man is not the ability to have a child—it's the courage to raise one."[189] He charged that "too many fathers . . . have abandoned their responsibilities, acting like boys instead of men." The implication of both President Obama's and Bill Cosby's assessment is that black fathers are uninvolved with their children because they are unconcerned about them.

But these criticisms are misguided and misleading. Although men disappear from their children's lives for many reasons,[190] one crucial factor is the father's relationship with the mother. Here, as with unwed mothers, the problem cannot be reduced to deficient values. Unwed fathers lose contact with their children for the same reason that Annelise's ex-husband might: because they're not married to the children's mother.

Simply put, a father's involvement with his children depends crucially on his relationship with the children's mother. Marriage links a father to his children, as captured in the aphorism: "A mother's a mother for life; a father's a father only with a wife." Even in intact families mothers typically mediate the relationship between father and children. This may be less true now than in ages past, as more fathers have become active and involved parents. But it is still the case that women perform the bulk of child care in our society and, as a consequence, have more durable and intimate relationships with their children than men do. So when parents separate, then, the question is whether the mother will continue to facilitate the father's relationship with their children.

The acrimony of separation, whether it involves divorce or simply the ending of the relationship, can leave some women disinclined to do so. A turning point often comes when the father enters a new relationship with another woman. Consider the experience of a friend of mine, who birthed a child by a man she hoped to marry. When she later discovered that her man was seeing another woman, she began keeping the child away from the father on weekends; "I don't want my child around that woman." By getting involved with someone else, the man had dashed the hopes of his baby's mother, who wasn't about to reward that "no-good cheater" by allowing him to spend time with her precious child. Suddenly the baby became, in my friend's view, *her* child. Almost by reflex, she had written the father out of her child's story.

And if the father is not permitted to see his child, he may well become less inclined to support the child financially. Worse yet, what if the mother, as many unwed mothers do, has a child by another man?[191] This puts the father in the position of knowing, or at least suspecting, that any financial support he offers will go to some other man's child.

Women who have children by multiple men stand less chance of getting significant financial support from any of them as compared to women with a single "baby daddy."[192] A growing body of research describes these dynamics in the relationships of unmarried parents; the research identifies a constellation of conflicts, loyalties, and jealousies that, however understandable they are, ultimately make victims of the children.[193]

It's true that too many black fathers are missing in action. But it's often not because they don't care about their children. Black fathers lose contact with their children for many of the same reasons that white fathers do. Black fathers are less likely than white fathers to have a relationship with their children, in part because black fathers are less likely than their white counterparts to be married to the child's mother. The absence of black fathers from their children's lives, then, is yet another cost of the marriage decline.

Childlessness

Annelise has her children, even if she no longer has a husband. But other black women who share her aversion to having a child without a husband often end up with neither. Monica Wilson is one such woman.

"I thought by now I'd be married, 2.4 children, the car, the house, the dog—that whole thing," says Monica, the forty-eight-year-old D.C. church administrator. "I would like to have children with a husband. The two go together. I'm not married, so I don't have children."

Monica fleetingly considered having a child by a sperm donor, but decided against it. "If I'm having the baby," she explains, "I want to be able to say, 'This is Daddy.' If I do it on my own, where's Daddy?" She worried about having to say to her child, "'Well, honey, your daddy is

#396 from a tube and I went to this place and they put in some sperm . . .' " Without completing the statement, she adds, "No. I don't want to do it that way. I want to do it the old-fashioned way."

By deciding not to have a child without being married, Monica envisions her life as many college-educated black women do. In my interviews, I was struck time and again by the cultural conservatism exhibited by many of the women, which inclined even the most financially secure and mature women against having a child without a husband. For some women, finding a husband may feel less like the goal and more like the means to a coveted end. "I flirt with kids in a way that I can't flirt with a man," says investment manager Rachel Lewis from Chicago. "I love children. I even used to tell people I'm looking for the father of my unborn children."

As one corporate professional in Atlanta told me, "I want children, but I don't want to have children outside of marriage." When I asked this thirty-eight-year-old woman whether she would have a child on her own, she responded, "My thought is that I'll cross that bridge when I come to it. I don't need to think about it yet." And then after a pause, "I think it's totally possible that I will find someone who I want to have kids with before the time comes when I can't have kids."

Here again, black women share the same hopes as women of other races. Unwed childbearing has increased most dramatically during the past few decades among poor women; affluent, highly educated women of all races, in contrast, tend to delay having a child until they have a husband. Thus, ironically, the women who are best able to support a child on their own continue to treat marriage and children as a package deal.

But for black women the package is not so readily available. Not only are college-educated black women twice as likely as their white counterparts not to marry, the longer they wait the more likely they are to confront an unanticipated obstacle: infertility. Accurate measures of the incidence of infertility are elusive, but some evidence suggests that the infertility rate among black women has been increasing,[194] and that it now may exceed the infertility rate of white women.[195] One potential contributor is the incidence of sexually transmitted diseases to which man-sharing relationships expose women. Black women who delay childbearing until after they have a husband thus confront two distinct risks: that the husband will never arrive, or that infertility will.

Some women satisfy their desire to be a parent without compromising their belief that they shouldn't have a child without being married. Many single black women adopt a child on their own. Although none of the women I interviewed had adopted, nearly all had considered it, and viewed it as preferable to giving birth to a child without a husband. "Adoption is not about bringing another fatherless child into the world," reasons Lauren, a middle-age, aspiring author from Cleveland, "as much as embracing a parentless child who's already here." Because adoption records are maintained by states, there is no reliable national data about the racial characteristics of adults who adopt children. But anecdotal reports by adoption agency personnel suggest that black women comprise nearly half of the single women who adopt children.[196] The moral logic of these women's inclination is clear: While having a child on one's own might seem irresponsible, providing a home for a parentless child contributes to the solution rather than exacerbate the problem; adoption helps the black community rather than compounds its disadvantage.

But most childless black women will not adopt. Census data

confirm that among women with professional or graduate degrees, black women are nearly twice as likely as their white counterparts to remain childless.[197] Twice as likely. As Lauren describes her own and many of her friends' experiences, "You do what you're supposed to do, take responsibility, get educated, manage your life, all in the hope that you'll eventually find the right person to have children with. And then when you don't, what can you do? Take the loss. That's what it turns out to be: a loss."

The loss falls on these women, and on the next generation as well. The advantages that their white counterparts will transmit across generations will for these black women stop with them. They have excelled in the race of life, only to find that there is no one to whom they can pass the baton. The pain of this realization is reflected in odd ways, like the regret that I heard from a middle-age graduate of Harvard and Yale. She used to imagine children who would follow in her footsteps, thanks in part to the admission preferences that Ivy League universities extend to the offspring of graduates. But now, she says, "There's no one who can benefit from my legacy status. It amounts to nothing."

Abortion

Annelise avoided a consequence of the marriage decline that is less visible than either childlessness or unwed motherhood: abortion. Years of national abortion statistics reflect troubling racial disparities. Black women have a disproportionate number of abortions in the United States,[198] as a black woman is four to five times as likely as a white woman to have an abortion in any given year.[199] According to data from the Centers for Disease Control and Prevention, African Americans, who constitute 13 percent of our nation's female population, have more than one out of three abortions.[200] Each year black women abort half a million fetuses. That figure exceeds the annual number of African Americans who are sent to prison, drop out of high school, or are victimized by violent crime.

As with the racial gap in marriage, racial disparities in abortion extend beyond the disadvantaged. Even among college-educated women, African Americans have more abortions than their white counterparts.[201] Nor are racially disparate abortion rates confined to teenagers. Among women in their late twenties or thirties, black women have a disproportionate number of abortions.[202]

One factor that contributes to black women's disproportionate number of abortions is the marriage decline. Most abortions result from unplanned pregnancies, which are more common among African American women,[203] who often lack the health insurance necessary to obtain the Pill and the IUD, the most reliable forms of birth control.[204] But not all unplanned pregnancies are resolved by abortion. In fact, fewer than half of unplanned pregnancies culminate in abortion.[205] A significant factor in whether a woman decides to go forward with her pregnancy is whether she is married. A married woman surprised by a pregnancy is more apt to adjust her plans and begin shopping for maternity outfits. A single woman with an unplanned pregnancy is about twice as likely as a married woman to abort.[206]

It's easy to see why. Two factors unquestionably associated with marriage—a supportive partner and the ability to provide for the child—might, and should, weigh heavily in a woman's decision. A prospective father is more likely to support the woman's decision to have the child if he is married to her. And the couple is more likely to be economically stable if they are married. For many women, being alone no doubt tips the balance between aborting a fetus and raising a child. Black women thus may have so many more abortions than other groups in part because they are so much less likely to be married.

There's an irony here: Although black women as a group have a disproportionate number of abortions, the evidence suggests that single black women, when confronted with an unplanned pregnancy, are less likely to abort than are other groups of single women. Sociologist Averil Clarke has found that among single college-educated white women, for example, nearly four out of every five pregnancies end by abortion.[207] That is a considerably higher figure than for similarly situated African American women—fewer than half of those pregnancies are ended by abortion.[208] How, then, could black women have more abortions if among single women, the group most likely to abort, white women choose abortion at a higher rate? The answer is that black women are much more likely to be single than white women. Some portion of the racial disparities in abortion are yet another cost of the marriage decline.

CHAPTER 6

Power Wives

After graduating as a top student from a Detroit public high school, Cecelia Edwards excelled at the University of Michigan and then entered a management training program at General Motors. Her understated intelligence, her agreeable manner, and her high standards and work ethic served her well. But professional success was not enough. She craved a greater intellectual challenge. Her parents—a factory worker and a nurse's aide—had always stressed education, and as their child, Cecelia valued it too. She decided to return to school to earn her law degree.

A few years after law school Cecelia attended a friend's family reunion and met her future husband. Two things were immediately clear: "He was smart and he was funny, funny as hell; that's what drew me in. If you're smart and you're funny, I'm done. He was both." They lived in different cities—he in Denver, she in New York—but were unwilling to let that stand between them. "We would have these three-hour phone conversations about anything and everything," she recalls. "I was impressed with how intelligent this man was, even though he never went to college. He was the classic underachiever." He has potential, she remembers thinking at the time. A man that smart and funny could go far.

After months of long late-night phone calls, they decided to see if they could make a relationship work. As a corporate lawyer, Cecelia was well established in her profession. As a construction worker, Daryl could go anywhere. Cecelia explains, "It came to a point where I said, 'I don't do long-distance relationships. If we like each other, then somebody needs to move, and I'm not moving to Denver.'" So Daryl moved to New York and lived with Cecelia in the brownstone she had purchased a few years earlier. Less than a year later, they were married.

Marriages, like Cecelia and Daryl's, in which the woman earns the bulk of the family's income, are more common among African Americans than among any other group. Black women are also more likely than any other group of women to be better educated than their husbands.[209] As with the general population, the education advantage of black women has been growing; African American wives are more likely to be better educated than their spouses now than they were in 1970.[210]

For college-educated black women, in particular, the educational gap is stark. As I mentioned earlier the majority of married, college-educated black women have husbands who did not graduate from college.[211] The outcome is consistent with the gender imbalance in the African American college population.[212] Recall that African Americans graduate college at a ratio of two women to every one man, every year. Thus, if a college-educated black woman marries a black man, chances are good that he'll be less educated than she is.

Degree-holding black wives put their education to use. In black families, college-educated wives often assume the conventional economic role of the husband. According to one study, married, college-educated black women earn more than 60 percent of their household income, approximately the same percentage earned by the average white husband.[213] College-educated black women are sometimes the sole earners in their family, as more than one out of ten married, college-educated black women have a husband who is unemployed.[214]

White Follows Black (Again)

Although most common among African Americans, relationships in which wives earn more than their husbands are increasingly prevalent among other groups as well. Over the past few decades, women have become more likely to marry a man who earns less than they do. The proportion of wives who earn more than their husbands has increased from approximately one in twenty in 1970 to more than one in five now.[215]

The changing relative economic positions of husbands and wives reflects changes both outside marriage and within. What has changed within marriage is the frequency with which wives work for pay. In the last forty years, there has been a massive entry of married women into the paid workforce. Half a century ago it was unusual for a married woman to work outside the home. Now, married women without children are nearly as likely to work as their single counterparts. And married women no longer drop out of the labor force completely when they have children. Six out of ten married women with young children continue to work at least part-time.[216]

Here again, the historical trend is one in which white follows black. Black women have always worked more than other groups of women.[217] Whereas in the 1960s and '70s most white wives stayed home, in the decades since, they have followed black women into the labor force. White wives are as likely to work for pay now as black wives were in the 1970s.

What has changed outside marriage is that over the past several decades, as discussed in Chapter 3, the relative economic positions of men and women have shifted. Women's earnings have increased far more than those of men, a repositioning that reflects two changes. One is that women have surpassed men in college completion and also gained ground in graduate education. The other is that the economic benefits of advanced education are greater than at any time since the mid-twentieth century.

The educational advantage that women now enjoy is apparent in couples. It used to be that when spousal education levels differed, the husband was the better educated of the two. Today, it's more often the wife.[218] Between 1970 and 2007, the relative educational positions of husbands and wives flipped, with wives claiming the educational advantage that belonged to husbands forty years ago.[219] College-educated women—white and black—are more likely now than their counterparts were four decades ago to marry a man who is less educated than they are.[220] And just as the earnings of black wives have been bolstered by increased education and labor market shifts, so, too, are wives of other races earning a greater percentage of family income than ever before.

The significance of wives' increased earnings may have been accentuated by the recent economic downturn, dubbed a "mancession" by some commentators because more men lost their jobs than did women. In many families women became the top earner only temporarily; when the husband finds another job he will once again assume the role of primary earner. But in other families the wives' earnings advantage will endure. Some wives, particularly those with advanced education, will earn more than their husbands for the simple reason that her skills are more valued in the marketplace. For these families, the recession has magnified a long-term trend in the shifting economic fortunes of men and women.[221]

Most wives still earn less than their husbands. But with women outpacing men educationally and with education becoming more valuable economically, one wonders how long husbands' economic dominance will last. For some commentators, the question of whether wives will overtake husbands is best framed not in terms of "if" as much as "when." At any rate, if or when wives do, then white will once again have followed black.

The Blue-Collar Brother

For African Americans, relationships between middle-class women and working-class men have figured prominently in popular culture. They are a staple in much of the work of the most popular and commercially successful filmmaker in black America: Tyler Perry.

Consider Perry's first big cinematic hit, *Diary of a Mad Black Woman,* in which Kimberly Elise is rejected by her wealthy, self-centered husband, only to find unexpected solace with the truck driver who comes to remove her belongings from their mansion. The truck driver is a tall, handsome, understanding, and sensitive Christian man who is there when she needs him. Elise eventually begins to see that he offers a love that her rich and successful husband could not. As their romance takes root, he assures her: "I know you don't believe in fairy tales, but if you did I'd want to be your knight in shining armor." "I may not be able to give you all that he used to," the truck driver acknowledges, "but I do know I can love you past your pain." Which he does.

The same theme appears in *Why Did I Get Married?,* a movie in which four affluent couples—an author, a doctor, and a business owner among them—meet at a mountain cabin for a couples retreat led by one of the wives. Another of the wives (played by Jill Scott) is horribly mistreated by her husband, who never misses an opportunity to berate her for her weight and even has a brazen affair with her friend during the retreat. Scott finds a haven in the form of the local sheriff, who initially provides food and shelter after she's stuck in a snowstorm on the way to the cabin. Later, when she expresses dismay at being overweight and says she doesn't feel confident enough to work out, the sheriff says, "Baby, if you don't like how you look, I'll work out with you." The good ol' sheriff—a hardworking man in a uniform—wants only what's best for her. As her relationship with her husband dissolves, the sheriff provides a shoulder to cry on, an ear for her troubles, and a heart ready to connect to hers.

But it is *Daddy's Little Girls* that offers the most pointed commentary on race, class, and romance. Idris Elba plays Monty James, an auto mechanic raising his three daughters alone while fending off a custody challenge from the girls' mother. Gabrielle Union plays Julia Rossmore, the workaholic Ivy League–educated corporate professional that Monty meets when he takes a job as a limo driver to make extra money.

Julia is overbearing, impatient, and rude, especially to working-class guys like Monty. When Monty describes his custody battle over his children, she thinks he has some ulterior motive. "What are you getting out of this?" she asks. "Why do you want your daughters back so bad? You getting a check for them, some sort of government assistance?" For all her success, she seems rather pitiful and doesn't have much of a life. When Monty suggests, "You ought to get out and have some fun," she responds, "What's fun? All I do is work."

Julia complains, "Because I make six figures, I can't find a decent man to save my life." But Tyler Perry's point is that there's a decent man right in front of her. Monty is a good man, a salt-of-the-earth brother with big dreams. "I want to open my own shop," he tells Julia. He's fallen short of that dream only because he had to use his savings for his children. "It was worth it, though," he sighs, and then observes, "You know parents, sometimes they have to give up their dreams so their kids can have one."

Although devoted to his children, Monty also gives Julia all she needs. "Why you go on them blind dates?" he asks her at one point. "Why you need that? You so beautiful." "It's really hard to meet a nice black man," she explains, "when you're in corporate America like me." Monty responds with a smile, "Well, I love me some black women."

All that stands between Julia and this black man ready to love her is her own elitism and narrow-mindedness. When Julia complains about not being able to "find a decent man to save my life," one of her friends counsels her: "It's possible if you'll just relax your standards a bit. I think you're too hard on some of these guys. Relax."

"I have standards."

"The pope can't meet your standards."

Some of Julia's other friends are even more snobbish than she. One gives her a hard time about dating Monty. "The driver?" the friend says. "Oh, hell no. Are you out of your mind? . . . He's supposed to be driving you, not you riding him. What could you two possibly have to talk about?"

Then another friend adds, "Three children? All by the same mother? Don't fall for this guy, he will ruin your credit."

In time, Julia transcends her pettiness and superficiality. As the movie ends, Monty has the kids, gets the girl, and even opens the auto shop he dreamed of. The credits roll as a soothing song, "Family First," plays in the background.

In these movies, the heroes are working-class guys who enable successful yet superficial black women to understand what really matters. These movies hilariously and sometimes melodramatically mine a populist, down-home sentiment that runs through black popular culture: that the bonds of race transcend any divisions of class; that black people, by virtue of their race alone, are more alike than different. The message is that professional black women should abandon their highfalutin ways and go for the guy driving the bus or repairing the car. Black women undermine their own chance for happiness, these movies suggest, by insisting on a man who makes as much money as they do or is as well educated as they are.

These sentiments pervade popular culture. For example, in the 2010 *Nightline* segment on unmarried black women that I mentioned earlier, comedian-turned-relationship-guru Steve Harvey reminded four accomplished and single black women in their thirties not to overlook lower-achieving black men. "If you're a corporate executive," he asked, "does he have to be a corporate executive?" He raised his eyebrows as if to say "That's your requirement?" Harvey's approach fit perfectly with a question that ABC News had used to frame the segment about single black women: "Are they asking for too much?"

Harvey told the women that a man "doesn't have to be 'on your level' for you to date him. This is not hiring somebody for a job."

Similar advice issues from the pages of *Essence* magazine, by far the most popular publication targeted to black women. One article describes a nurse with a master's degree whose husband is a janitor, who at times "misses the mark when it comes to subject-verb agreement." The wife says that she delayed their marriage because she "had to do a lot of inner work around the fact that he hasn't been exposed to many things and hasn't finished college."[222] Note here that the problem, in the wife's view, is her attitude or expectations, a perspective shared by the author of the article, who advises black women to look "beyond money and status" in choosing a man. The author urges women to value a man's "affection, loyalty, nurturing, willingness to pull extra weight as a parent or the fact that he'll just plain have our back." The author counsels professional women with working-class husbands that "Feeling embarrassed by your spouse occasionally is a trifle to pay for true love."

And if the woman can't accept the man as he is, the best option, according to this ethos, is not to reject him, but to change him. This sentiment is embodied in the advice that a friend of mine gave to a group of young professional black women at a career development workshop: "Y'all can't expect to find a man with all these great qualities," she told them. "Don't think you can buy the floor model. They don't come set up and ready to go. Assembly is required. You have to put some time into it." Or as a relationship counselor advised during a discussion of black male-female relationships, "If you want Superman, you got to be willing to start out with Clark Kent." The messages are all around us, as pervasive as the advertising that blends into the background. Black women are encouraged—by magazines, by so-called relationship experts, by network news shows, by blockbuster movies, and by some pastors—to find one of those "good men" who would have made something of themselves if only they'd had the chance, men who are now only a woman's loving touch away from success.

The message of this chorus is that if black women are alone, it is their own fault: Their standards are too high. They'd be happier if they relinquished their snobbishness and elitism, and stopped insisting that their man be as accomplished as they are. If successful black women only became more willing to partner with working-class men, the argument goes, single black women would find the fulfilling relationships they seek.

In fact, college-educated black women are already following the advice with which they have been bombarded. Black women more frequently marry less-educated and lower-earning men than any group of women in our nation. However much black women value economic stability in a partner, they haven't let that stand in the way of their relationships with black men. Examination of the personal ads placed by black women gives a clue. The criteria that many ask for set a very low bar: no drugs, no jail, employed. Black women are not holding out for the guy with the pristine résumé. As I heard from Lauren, the middle-age, aspiring author from Cleveland, "My friends and I have been open-minded about dating a guy who didn't have what we had, the working-class guy who is still a good guy. I don't know a woman who hasn't tried it." During the two-plus decades of Lauren's dating life, she has rarely excluded men simply because they weren't as successful as she. "I've dated men with no car," she recalls, "no checking account, no job."

Monica Wilson, the never-married D.C. church administrator, has also cast her dating net wide. No one could accuse her of clinging to standards that are absurdly high or unreasonable. "I just want your average Joe Blow," she explains. "Go to work, come home, watch a movie." These were not the men she found. One boyfriend, she learned some months into their relationship, had sold drugs and spent time in jail. Monica stayed with him after these discoveries because he vowed he would change. But as it turned out, change didn't come so easy. "He had a temper," she soon realized. "He couldn't keep a job because he would get mad and walk off the job." Then, when he got another job, he'd call in sick, and tell Monica "I didn't feel like going to work today."

Money Matters

For Cecelia and Daryl, their relationship didn't unfold the way many do on the big screen. Three children and five years after saying "I do," they divorced. From early on they had had conflicts about a common source of marital disagreement: money. After Daryl relocated to New York, it took him the better part of a year to find work. "It was a huge strain on the relationship," Cecelia says. *She* didn't mind his being out of work, but he did. "He was uncomfortable living off me," Cecelia says. "It came to a point where I said, 'If you're this unhappy being unemployed, go get a job doing whatever. But stop being so picky and go get a damn job.'"

Eventually, he did, but steady income didn't solve the problem. "After he found work," Cecelia explains, "the dynamic shifted from 'I don't have a job' to 'I'm not making anywhere near your income, so I still feel inadequate and inferior.'" Now, several years after the divorce, all she recalls about his job is that it was "at a small factory somewhere in Brooklyn and he was basically doing whatever, putting together whatever the company made. I don't even remember anymore."

Cecelia recalls that "he felt less than a man because my income ran the household." They fought about the money. Given her ample income, the problem wasn't a lack of funds as much as who would control it. Cecelia says she didn't want to take advantage of the fact that she accounted for most of the family's income—"I didn't feel like I was lording it over him that I made more money"—but they both knew whose paycheck was bigger.

Daryl wanted to consolidate their assets, but Cecelia resisted opening a joint bank account. She repeatedly delayed and deflected discussion of it, claiming that she didn't get around to opening the joint account because she couldn't find time to get to the bank, or didn't want the hassle of changing account information or the difficulties of coordinating two people using the same account. He became frustrated by what he saw as Cecelia's refusal to give him a straight answer. In hindsight, she owns up. "At some level it was my income," she recalls, "and I did want to keep that control." "As part of this whole wrestling-for-control thing that we had going on, I think he didn't want to have to ask me for extra money," she explains. Cecelia never rejected any of Daryl's requests for money, but she did always want to know how the money would be spent. "Those discussions were clearly very uncomfortable to him," she recalls. She thought it was reasonable to ask why he needed the money and why he was coming to her. He thought she was treating him like a child. "He was upset about the very idea of having to ask," she says, and felt that she was giving him, as he put it, "the third degree. "

And at the root of Cecelia's unease was a corrosive belief: a fear that she couldn't trust him, that he might squander her hard-earned cash. She explains: "There was only so much I was willing to contribute to whatever nonsense I thought he might be getting himself into."

Cecelia and Daryl's situation is emblematic of some of the difficulties that can arise when the wife supports the family and the husband is unable to do so. Sometimes, the husband feels less of a man. He hasn't fully relinquished the view that as the man, he should be the primary earner, and that if he's not, he has somehow fallen down on the job. And then to have to ask your wife for money, and even worse, to have to explain what you need it for—well, that just reminds the man in a humiliating fashion of his own failure to fulfill the role of the husband.

"I Tried to Help"

But not all men married to higher-earning wives share Daryl's feeling of inadequacy. And not all woman start off wanting to control the money as Cecelia did.

When Carla, a human resources manager in Atlanta, married the man she loved, she earned nearly twice what he did. Neither had a problem with that. The more money she made, in fact, the happier he became.

Yet only months into their marriage, problems emerged. The source of the recurring conflict: gas and the car.

Carla's husband had totaled his car and was driving hers. Though it meant that she sometimes had to catch rides with co-workers, the arrangement was one she could live with. "Until," she explains, "he brought my car back on empty." She had planned to drive it to the gym one Saturday morning and could barely make it to the gas station. He told her he had just forgotten to gas up—his car got better mileage than hers, and he hadn't adjusted, he said, to her car's need for more frequent refueling. For Carla, this wasn't just about the gas. "It's not about you bringing back my car empty," she told her husband. "It's about you looking out, making sure that I'm taken care of." In her parents' decades-long marriage, she scarcely recalled her mother ever having to put gas in the car. Dad took care of that. Carla didn't expect her husband to do everything for her that her dad did for her mom. But still. Gas in the tank? It was a small thing. If he was going to use her car, he should make sure that an empty tank didn't leave her stranded. Over the following weeks, it became apparent to Carla that her husband wasn't simply forgetting to refuel the car, and he eventually confirmed her suspicions. "I never bring up the fact that you make more money than me," he told her, "but that fact is, I don't have enough money for gas. You pay for it."

Carla thought she was doing him a favor by letting him use her car. It inconvenienced her, but he needed it more, so she thought it was worth the sacrifice. What did she get in return? No appreciation. What galled her was his sense of entitlement, an attitude she interpreted as "She has the money, so she can pay." Worse, his expectation wasn't limited to the car. For all manner of expenses he thought that, as Carla puts it, "because I made more, I should pay more." He seemed all too content to limit his contributions to what he felt he could afford. When the bills came due, "You can handle that" seemed to be a frequent refrain.

Carla didn't have a problem with paying more, not in the abstract. After all, she did make more money than he did. The issue of the empty tank need not have become a fight, Carla reflects: "If he had come to me and said, 'I don't have enough money. I'm sorry. I apologize for not putting gas in,' that would have been acceptable." Instead, he disclaimed responsibility.

So that her husband would no longer find himself short of funds, they established a joint bank account—in her name, because her husband had, as she says, "credit issues." That worked for a while, until he overdrafted the account and then denied it. He insisted that there was some mix-up, or that maybe Carla had made a mistake. "No," she says to me, as firmly as I imagine she said it to him. "What happened was he spent too much money. Yet he kept insisting it wasn't his fault." She paid the fees and then closed the account. "No more joint accounts," she announced. End of conversation.

Working Without a Script

In Carla's marriage, as in Cecelia's, the partners were cast in the roles of husband and wife but without the shared script that guided prior generations. Whatever the drawbacks of the conventional role-divided marriage, one virtue is that everyone knows their job. Roles, if constricting, are at least understood: The husband provides economically, while the wife cares for the home and the children. When a wife outearns her husband, the couple cannot conform to that conventional male-breadwinner model. Rather than adhere to predefined roles, they have no choice but to improvise, to attempt to fashion their own model of a relationship as they patch together expectations developed during their own coming of age.

Many husbands find it difficult to accept a subordinate economic role in the family. They know they don't earn the bulk of the income, but they might still feel that they should. Daryl, Cecelia's husband, felt inadequate and resented his wife for having usurped his role. Even if the man doesn't care who earns the most, he knows that other people do. Friends, family, and co-workers might think to themselves that "he's living off her," a sentiment rarely if ever directed at a wife. And even if his wife thinks no less of her husband, it is difficult for him not to think less of himself. However sexist those values might seem, they constitute the social and cultural context within which many adults were raised.

Even those of us who disclaim any adherence to the traditional model probably haven't freed ourselves fully from it. A woman who stays home with her young children is viewed as a devoted mother. But when a man does so, it is difficult not to wonder: When will he get a job?

These sentiments reflect an enduring cultural script. For most of our nation's history, the law explicitly accorded only men the obligation to support the family. In most states, a husband was required by law to support his wife, but the wife had no reciprocal obligation to support her husband. He was designated the head of the household, she the dependent spouse. If the couple divorced, the obligation to pay alimony was one that by law could only be imposed on the husband. It wasn't until the 1970s that wives could be obligated to support their former spouse.

Neither Cecelia nor Carla had completely relinquished traditional gender roles. Cecelia says it didn't bother her that her husband earned a lot less than she did. But the more I talked with her, the more it seemed that in some basic way she did think less of him for it. It was as though he hadn't earned the right to make financial decisions.

Cecilia, like other primary-earning wives, operated on a model in which her earnings were secondary, additional income—what women of another era would have called "mad money" or "pin money." This sensibility appears to underlie both Cecelia's and Carla's expectation that their husbands should ask them for money and be thankful when they get it. Although each of these women earned substantially more than their husband, neither had a sense that their earnings went into one big pot from which either partner could freely draw. For each of these women, her money was just that: not his, not joint, but *hers*. These women shared with their husband to the extent that they chose, but they didn't feel obligated to do so. The idea of turning their money over to their spouse to manage, as many husbands have done when they earned the money, was unthinkable for these women. Had the roles been reversed, and a higher-earning husband refused to freely share his income with his wife, he would have been roundly (and rightly) condemned as an oppressive patriarch. Yet Cecelia and Carla each thought that her approach was reasonable.

Other women no doubt share their view. A 2010 report issued by the Pew Research Center, "Women, Men, and the New Economics of Marriage," found that when the husband is the primary earner, each member of the couple is equally likely to have the final say about how money is spent; but that when the wife is the primary earner, she is more than twice as likely as her husband to have the final say about financial decisions.[223] It seems that if the husband earns the money, it is assumed to belong to the family. When the wife earns the money, it is more likely to be viewed as hers.

Adding Insult to Injury

Cecelia's treatment of Daryl could only have compounded his sense of failure and inflamed his resentment of her. Imagine how Daryl must have felt having to come to his wife whenever his income fell short. Cecelia would question whether he needed as much money as he thought, whether the expenditure was a prudent one, whether it was a cost that she should bear. "The third degree," he thought, and he was probably right.

Yet Cecelia found it difficult to relinquish control. Many women may be unwilling (understandably) to do so. Today's adult women grew up being told that they could and perhaps should pay their own way. They expect to complete higher education and to compete for high-status jobs. They expect to earn salaries commensurate with their responsibilities. They even hope to have it all—career, family, marriage. But they haven't planned on being the sole support for their family. For them, working and earning is a way to avoid dependence, not a means of fulfilling a responsibility. And they don't want to jeopardize their hard work by opening their pocketbook to a less responsible partner.

I suspect that these sentiments are particularly strong among black women. In my interviews I found a striking consensus about money. Women who had never met spoke as though their mothers had been friends and formed some pact about how to raise their daughters. The chorus went like this: "My mother always told me, 'Have your own money. Don't be dependent on a man.'" These words did not surprise me. Black women are more likely than their white counterparts to work, even when their economic need to do so is no greater than that of white women who stay home and raise children.[224] The stereotype of the strong and independent black woman, my interviews suggest, has more than a grain of truth to it. These women intend to earn their own way, and many of them do.

When the parties don't share the same script, misunderstandings mount. Carla didn't mind paying most of the expenses, but she didn't want to feel like she had to. She viewed her willingness to shoulder more of the financial load as a choice, not an obligation, a favor for which her husband should be grateful. Her husband, on the other hand, thought that paying the bills was the job of whoever had the money; since Carla did, she should pay, simple as that. Carla, meanwhile, attached special significance to the fact that the man who didn't refuel her car was her husband. His dollars-and-cents decision was, for her, fraught with emotion, an oversight by a man she loved that spoke volumes about their relationship.

These tensions about gender roles no doubt help to explain the empirical finding that marriages in which the wife earns substantially more than the husband seem to be more likely to dissolve than marriages in which the husband is the primary earner. I wouldn't find it surprising if such marriages are more conflict ridden. However enticing improvisation may seem, it often produces discord. I expect that in the long term—in, say, another generation—people will become less wedded to traditional gender roles. Then it will matter little which spouse earns the most. But marriages are not negotiated in the long term. The couple has to work things out in the here and now, with expectations and associations that began forming in childhood.

While some couples do fine when the wife supports the family and the husband cannot, other couples, like Cecelia and Daryl, cling to an old script to which their current economic positions do not conform. When the old script no longer applies and a new script has yet to be written, couples will struggle and will bear many of the costs—confusion, uncertainty, resentment—that often come with social change.

CHAPTER 7

Mixed Marriages

Cecelia and Daryl's conflicts about money went beyond their struggle with gender roles. What divided them became apparent to Cecelia in retrospect. "Absolutely different values," Cecelia says, explaining their inability to make it work. "That was the crux of it."

Conflicts over values arise in many marriages, but they may be especially pronounced when the partners have attained starkly different levels of education. Cecelia presumed Daryl hadn't finished college due to obstacles beyond his control—trouble with financial aid, a professor who didn't like him. Only later, after their marriage had ended, did she realize that her husband hadn't finished college because he didn't want to. It just wasn't important to him. He didn't value education as much as she did. And because he never fully invested himself in the college experience, it didn't broaden his perspective and shape his life goals the way college had for Cecelia.

Their differing values became apparent in those disagreements about how to spend money. "He wanted me to display my income in a way that was uncomfortable to me," Cecelia recalls. "He couldn't have this wife who went to Columbia Law School and who is a partner at a law firm without having some stuff to show for it." He wanted her to buy a Mercedes. He didn't share her priorities—to put the children in private school, pay the mortgage, fund a retirement account—"because you couldn't *show* those things," she explains. "You can't drive those things around town and have everybody see them." Eventually she relented and bought an Acura as a concession.

Their values gap went beyond money. Cecelia recounts a story that Daryl was fond of telling about his early adulthood. "It was about a friend of his who he freely described as a killer," she says, "a dude who got off on killing people, if that's what the situation called for." Cecilia recalls a particular scene to which Daryl always returned. "Daryl and his friends were out drinking one day with this killer guy," she recounts, "and he flicked open his switchblade, and it was so full of crusted-on blood that the blood splattered into their drinks."

Cecelia regarded this story as "brutal and horrible" and interpreted it as an indictment of Daryl's friend. "I thought he was telling me about some of the characters that he dealt with in his youth. I was expecting these stories to be part of his explanation for 'this is why I'm here in my forties and haven't done more with my life.' "

It wasn't until years later that Cecelia began to understand Daryl's fascination with these stories. They were tales of his "glory days," a glamorous past that, truth be told, he still missed. "I didn't really understand that those stories were part of his identity," she says. The ruthless killer was not the villain in Daryl's mind; he was the hero. "Eventually," Cecelia explains, "it dawned on me that he liked his association with this guy. In some weird way, he admired him."

Now, in retrospect, Cecelia knows that her experience, though extreme, is not unusual. She has seen many other professional single women struggle through doomed relationships with blue-collar men. "I think a lot of black women wind up in these situations," she surmises, "because we remember that dude from middle school we had a crush on who now drives a UPS truck and who is still a good dude. Why would you turn down a good dude just because he didn't get a chance to go to college like you did?"

For Cecelia, describing the logic also reveals its flaw. "You start believing that the background matters more than the values that led you each to make the choices that you made." Her husband was academically capable, but he was more attracted to the street life than to studying. "The fact that we might have grown up in the same type of 'hood is not enough," she concludes. "What's going to sustain the relationship is who you are now."

Cultural Divide

Cecelia and Daryl shared a racial identity, but theirs was a "mixed marriage" nonetheless. Race was only part of who they were. Beyond race, their life experiences were entirely different. So different, in fact, that, as Cecelia has concluded, they inhabited different cultures. Cecelia assumed that their racial commonality dictated shared cultural values. She was wrong. They had contrary outlooks on life, the result of their distinct upbringings and their divergent experiences as young adults.

A difference in values or cultural orientation is not something that a couple can or should "get over." Our cultural values are part of who we are, an expression of what we deem important in life. They influence how we want to spend our time and our money, how we intend to raise our children.

Such a dramatic difference in perspective poses obvious challenges. And those challenges are accentuated by the expectations that people today bring to marriage. I explained earlier how many of the traditional functions of marriage—a way to manage property, express sexuality, raise children—have diminished in importance, and that as a result, what had been a marginal aspect of the marital relationship has now assumed primary importance: emotional fulfillment and understanding. People want a partner who understands them, with whom they can share their deepest hopes, aspirations, and fears. Divergent interests and sensibilities imperil a relationship today in a way they would not have a hundred or even fifty years ago.

In the case of Cecelia and Daryl, neither was solely to blame for their partnership's demise. They are both good people. They are just not good for each other. Cecelia and Daryl were mismatched.[225] How could he understand the importance his wife placed on their children's education if he had never aspired to graduate college, much less law school? How could she share in the memories of his youth if he idealized the urban world that she had strived to leave behind?

These sorts of relationships are mismatches for reasons of education and cultural orientation rather than income. It's one thing for a woman to earn more than her husband. It's quite another for her to have been to college and graduate school while he's content with his high school diploma. Or for her to have traveled the world when he's never boarded a plane. Cecelia valued education more than Daryl did; that's why she summoned the discipline to finish college and law school. Whatever the reason for that difference—family background, peer influences, lack of role models—it shaped their decisions and was magnified by their experiences in school and after. As she studied for chemistry exams and debated legal issues, he moved from one job to the next, hustling to get ahead. They each worked hard, though in different settings. Years later, no matter how alike they may have seemed back in third grade, they had evolved in ways that left them unsuited for each other.

These sorts of mismatched relationships are much more common among African Americans than any other group. Among whites, when the wife earns more than the husband, it is usually because she is, say, an administrative assistant, and he is a construction worker or a truck driver who is temporarily unemployed. And her educational advantage over her husband might be the two years of junior college in which he saw no economic benefit. With African Americans, in contrast, the gap between spouses is often much more substantial. Recall that a majority of college-educated black wives have husbands who didn't graduate from college. These professional women and their working-class husbands often embody different cultural orientations. The women, increasingly, are part of an educated American mainstream. The men, increasingly, are part of a group of deeply disadvantaged African Americans. The black middle class—understood in terms of income, education, and sensibility—is becoming more female, and the black poor disproportionately male. As the educational and economic gap between black women and men continues to widen, they will become ever more culturally dissimilar. Over time, barring a dramatic change in either the labor market or public policy with respect to education, many black men will seem more and more alien to those black women who have moved ahead.

As women surpass men educationally, couples from other ethnic groups will confront some of the same issues with which so many black couples already struggle. But the cultural divide is less of an issue for couples of other races because the educational and economic gulf between men and women is not so pronounced.

Hope over Reason

How do such mismatched relationships come about? Let's consider Monica Wilson, the never-married church administrator with the former boyfriend who couldn't keep a job. She had remained with him so long for a simple reason. "When I asked him what made him stop dealing drugs," she recounts, "he said that one day he was in jail and decided he was just tired of living like that."

How that declaration must have resonated with this good-hearted Christian woman who is in those pews every Sunday and who believes in redemption. She saw in front of her a man who had set himself on what the pastor would have called the "path of righteousness." And Monica was there at his side, holding his hand on that walk. She believed he could change, and wanted him to do so. She had faith, in the Lord and in him. "Hate the sin, love the sinner." It was an injunction by which she lived. He had committed crimes, but she didn't want to label him a criminal.

Faith in redemption is a principle of Christianity. No one is beyond the reach of the grace of God. It is never too late to start on a new and better path. This spiritual orientation, while common to all Christian denominations, is especially salient in black churches. As so many black communities struggle, the vision of a better tomorrow is the hope that many pastors offer. "I ain't what I need to be, but I'm better than I was." That sentiment sustains many people. They cling to its realization in their own lives. For African Americans in particular, the mantra of change may well be a means of sustaining oneself in a society that seems in so many ways to depict black people as pathological, incorrigible, unwilling to change.

Cecelia, like Monica, believed in redemption. Cecelia concludes, in retrospect, "There was a part of me that wanted to rescue him. All the stuff that went wrong for him just seemed to me to be silly high school foolishness. 'We can fix that,' I thought, 'this guy's smart.'" She couldn't separate her vision of who her husband could become from who he actually was.

Years of marriage finally taught her that "he was good with who he was. He wasn't really interested in being rehabilitated, because he didn't think he needed rehabilitating. You shouldn't want to raise your partner, but we end up doing it. That's what we women do."

It is natural, loving even, to want to help a struggling man improve, polish him, smooth the rough edges. Whether the woman can succeed in that task is another matter, as is whether the man wants and appreciates that help. There is a fine line between improving a man and controlling him. And there is a big difference between seeing a partner's promise and trying to remake him into what you need. What many women intend as much-needed help may be experienced by many men as unwelcome control.

For black women, this challenge is far greater than what most women of other races will ever face. To a unique extent, black women confront a pool of men who are in need of uplift—changes that go far beyond a more refined sense of style or improved social graces, changes that are both more daunting and less likely. Working-class black men have borne the dual burdens of the contraction of labor market opportunities and the expansion of incarceration for those who enter the illicit market of drug dealing. However laudable the desires that lead black women into troubled relationships, the tendency to trust hope over reason can lead to not just heartache, but to danger as well. Sometimes the problem is not simply that the couple is mismatched, but that the man is unsuitable for any woman.

Tonya Hunter-Lyons lived in Cleveland.[226] A black woman in her early forties who had a master's degree and was in the process of earning her Ph.D., she had achieved a lot in her life. She taught college classes, had been featured on local radio programs, and wrote articles for a Cleveland-area magazine. She owned her home and also some rental property.

Tonya believed that people could change. That belief was at the core of her professional identity. After earning her degree in social work, she eventually started her own counseling service. "I realized that a lot of people have problems," she had explained, "and I was a problem-solver. So the best job for me was to be a social worker." Those who knew her say her goal was to become the Dr. Phil of Cleveland.

The need for change was apparent in the man she chose to be her husband, Maurice Lyons, a convicted felon with criminal records in Missouri, Illinois, and Ohio who had served years in prison for violent crimes. He may have told her he wanted to change, but his efforts to do so weren't successful. He continued using drugs after they married. Less than a year into their marriage, he was convicted of domestic violence against Tonya.

When Tonya and her husband appeared in court together in connection with the domestic violence case, the judge told her, in very blunt language, to leave him. Tonya resisted that advice. "Maurice is a good husband," she told the judge. "He really is." Tonya took comfort in the fact that he had started to go to church with her, which in her mind portended better days. She saw promise, and she wanted "to work on the marriage," as she told the judge.

Four months after Tonya had insisted to the judge that "Maurice is a good husband," she was found dead in the garage at her home, stabbed seventeen times. According to news reports, Maurice Lyons reportedly killed his wife after she refused his demand for money. Although not yet convicted, Lyons reportedly covered his wife's body with plastic and took her car and credit cards, which he used at a drugstore and gas station before being arrested by the Cleveland police. This was the second murder in three weeks in Cleveland of a professional, college-educated black woman, both allegedly by a husband who was a convicted felon.

In the aftermath of these murders, one local blogger reflected on her own tendency to date less successful men. "I reasoned that everybody hasn't had the opportunities I've had," she wrote, "and maybe if the guy had someone who believed in him for once in his life, he might be able to do better. . . . [But] it never turned out that way. It always ended with 'Bitch, you think you better than me!' and one time, I was even kicked in the stomach. You'd think that would have put an end to my Sister-Save-A-Brotha days, but it didn't. Loneliness will make you invite the devil himself in for tea."[227]

Loneliness is no doubt part of what leads black women into relationships with troubled men. Partnering with such men may seem like an understandable response to the man shortage. But in addressing one problem it may exacerbate others. When women enter relationships with men who have drug or alcohol problems, who are inclined to violence, or who are unable to hold a job, those relationships often falter. Sometimes, as with Tonya Hunter-Lyons, the result is much worse.

A Missing Piece of the Puzzle?

Successful black women marry down when they partner with a man who is lower earning and less educated than they are. Black women marry down more frequently than any other group of women. The prevalence of marry-down relationships may constitute a missing piece in many puzzling aspects of the marriage gap, a means of explaining empirical findings that have confounded researchers. Most obviously, the high incidence of African American marry-down relationships may contribute to racial disparities in divorce rates. African Americans may divorce so frequently in part because the educational and cultural gap between the spouses renders them incompatible as mates. Marry-down relationships are more prone to dissolve, and African Americans are more likely to have marry-down relationships.

Marry-down relationships may also contribute to a lesser-known aspect of the marriage gap: There is a racial gap not only in the frequency and durability of marriages but in their quality as well. Surveys of married couples indicate that, on average, African Americans have less satisfying marriages than other groups do. According to some studies, marriage does not boost the well-being of African Americans as it does for other groups. An obvious explanation for this anomaly is that African Americans more often find themselves in dysfunctional marriages. The low level of marital satisfaction among African Americans is also reflected in the high infidelity rates that I mentioned in Chapter 4. The research suggests that married black men are more than twice as likely as other groups of men to have affairs.[228]

By lowering the average quality of African American marriages and boosting the divorce rate, marry-down relationships contribute to further suppressing the marriage rate among African Americans. In contemplating marriage, single people talk to their married friends or at the very least observe what they can about the marriages of those around them. Whether they decide to join the club depends in part on the experiences of those who are already in it. The fewer happily married couples one knows, perhaps, the less likely one is to marry.

Most sobering of all, the gap in marital quality burdens children. Some research suggests that black children raised in a two-parent family do not fare substantially better than black children raised in a single-parent family. For example, one study by sociologists at Cornell University and the University of Utah suggests that African American children who grow up with a single parent actually do just as well, both academically and socially, as black children in two-parent homes.[229] This is a puzzling finding. Even putting aside the obvious economic benefits of being raised in a two-parent family, one might expect two parents to provide more of the nurturance, stability, and advice that children need.

An easy explanation for the lack of difference between black children raised in a single- versus two-parent family is that black children benefit from the support of an extended family. According to this view, an assortment of relatives—uncles, aunts, grandparents, cousins—contributes to child rearing when needed and thereby buffers the effect of a missing parent. I wonder, though, if this puzzling research finding can instead be explained on the basis of another difference between African American and white families: that black relationships are often so conflicted that they don't deliver to the child the benefits associated with two parents. Put simply, parents are less likely to meet their child's needs if they are failing to meet each other's. This explanation fits with evidence that the much-heralded benefits of marriage depend almost entirely on the quality and stability of that marriage.[230] Functional marriages benefit children, high-conflict marriages do not. In black marriages that are high-conflict, neither the adults nor their children are well served.

CHAPTER 8

Beyond Race?

Tyrone, like every other man Patricia Pullman had dated, is African American. "I always liked black men," she says. "Dark, big, bulky, unmistakably black men." Throughout her college years in the late 1980s at UCLA, this Los Angeles native maintained her relationship with Tyrone, the high school boyfriend whose formal education ended at graduation. After college, when her white co-worker tried to set Patricia up with her brother, she initially resisted. Eventually she agreed to go out with him as a favor. One time only.

But the date went so well that Patricia wanted to have another one. The interaction between them was "easy." "I can't describe it any way other than that," she says. "We were both comfortable. He's smart. We had similar interests in travel, similar outlooks on life." She says the story is so drama-free it's boring. Their relationship "naturally progressed" she says, as it became clear how well-suited they were for each other. And although Patricia had not once in her life thought of white men as attractive, when she looked at this particular man, really looked at him, she could see that he was. With his dark wavy hair and broad shoulders, the sex appeal was there. It still is. They've been married more than a decade.

Intimate Segregation

As a black woman, Patricia is an exception. As I mentioned earlier, black women are among the least likely of all groups to marry across racial lines.[231] According to recent data, roughly one in twenty black wives is married to someone of another race.[232] Recent marriages are more likely to be interracial, but even black women who have wed recently are unlikely to have a nonblack husband. In 2008, fewer than one in ten black female newlyweds married across racial lines, which makes them less than half as likely as black men to marry someone of a different race.[233]

Black women are also less likely to intermarry than are other minority groups. Asians and Latinos are as much as three times as likely as black women to wed across group lines.[234] Commentators sometimes compare the low intermarriage rate of black women to that of Asian men; these groups are thought to be disadvantaged in the relationship market by stereotypical images depicting Asian men as soft and effeminate and black women as strong and masculine. But even Asian men intermarry at considerably higher rates than black women.[235] Asian American men born in the United States are three or more times as likely to marry interracially as are black women.[236]

Perhaps the starkest evidence of the intimate segregation of black women emerges not in contrast to other minority groups as much as in comparison to whites. Usually, the smaller a group, the more frequently its members intermarry. This is a straightforward matter of numbers. For members of smaller groups there are more potential spouses outside of the group than in. The situation is reversed for members of the largest groups. Thus, in the United States, whites have long had lower intermarriage rates than members of any minority group. Now as more whites intermarry, that may be changing. By some measures the intermarriage rate of black women is now no higher than that of whites. This is an extraordinary development, and one that bolsters the conclusion that black women are more segregated in the intimate marketplace than any group in American society.

An Historical Surprise

Black men now intermarry more than twice as frequently as black women, but that gender gap is not long-standing. It developed during the same period as the racial gap in marriage.[237] During the middle decades of the twentieth century, black women were as likely as black men to marry across racial lines.[238] Granted, the numbers were low for both groups, as interracial marriage remained illegal in some states. But interracial marriage rates were no lower for black women than for black men. In fact, according to United States Census data, in 1960 there were slightly more interracially married black women than interracially married black men.[239] Then, over the next few decades, as rates of interracial marriage increased throughout society, an interracial marriage gap developed between black men and women. That gap has widened with each decennial census. Now, there are more than half a million interracially married black men, and only two hundred thousand interracially married black women.

The widening gender gap in African American intermarriage is a puzzling phenomenon. There are a number of reasons the intermarriage rate for black women should have increased dramatically during the 1960s and '70s. The Supreme Court's 1967 decision in *Loving v. Virginia*—a case involving the marriage of a black woman to a white man—invalidated the prohibitions of interracial marriage that remained on the books in more than a dozen states.[240] After *Loving,* interracial marriage became legal throughout the United States.

The intermarriage rate for black women should also have been spurred by the fact that black women were much more likely than black men to interact with members of other races at school or work. College is a setting ripe for interracial relationships. College takes people from neighborhoods and home environments that are often segregated and places them in more racially diverse university settings, where students are inculcated with values typically hospitable to intermarriage. The fact that black women attend college at higher rates than black men should have led them to intermarry more frequently than black men, not less.

The intimate segregation of black women is a striking phenomenon, yet it has been taken for granted by many people. Consider again the most popular and widely discussed depiction ever of successful black women and their difficulty in finding a man. *Waiting to Exhale,* the best-selling book and hit movie, chronicles the romantic hopes and frustrations of four middle-class black women friends in Phoenix. At the emotional center of the story is Savannah, an attractive, successful television producer (played by Whitney Houston) who seems to have it all—except for a man. In one scene, when she walks into a black nightclub, the men light up at the sight of her while the women throw daggers with their eyes. She thinks to herself as she sits down, "I'm single and desperate. As soon as one of you turns your back, I'm going to flirt my butt off and take your man."

The story showcases the strengths of the four friends and the bond that they share. But by story's end, all but one remain alone. If they can exhale, it's because they've learned to live without a man rather than because they've found one.

What is remarkable is that for all these women's frustrations with black men—who are presented as married, gay, or unwilling to commit—and even as they live in a city where African Americans are only 5 percent of the population, the story never provides any indication that any of these women have ever considered dating a man who is not black. There are white women who enter the picture—one of the women catches her son having oral sex with his white girlfriend, another's husband leaves her for a white woman—but no white men, much less Latinos or Asian Americans. These women bemoan their intimate isolation (and the reader or viewer is expected to empathize with their plight) even as they leave unexplored 95 percent of the male population. Four attractive, accomplished black women seek a life partner in a southwestern city in which blacks are a small fraction of the population, and not one of them ever suggests that perhaps the time has come to consider a relationship with a man of another race. More telling still is that the underlying assumption that these black women could only partner with a black man received virtually no attention, much less criticism. No one decried the movie as unrealistic, as having unjustifiably circumscribed the women's options, as leaving the women at the mercy of black men. No, the book and the movie struck a chord with black women precisely because it seemed to capture their own experiences in a way that no other popular culture product had. The movie relied on a pervasive assumption, one that viewers accepted all too readily.

In the course of writing this book, I have encountered a wide array of self-styled experts ready with advice for black women: Look for older men, younger men, previously married men, less-educated men, men in other cities, men in different parts of town. Black women are given all manner of advice, from all types of folks. But rarely, it seems, are they given the advice to look beyond their race.

The Consequences of Not Going "Out"

Black women marry down because they don't marry out. The pool of college-educated black men is small, but the pool of college-educated men of other races is quite large. If more college-educated black women dated men of other racial groups, they'd be more likely to partner with men who are their peers in terms of educational and professional attainment. Increased outmarriage would leave fewer black women with men who share their race but not much else. Fewer black couples would be mismatched.

More outmarriage would yield another benefit: Fewer black women would be alone. Just as some black women marry down rather than marry out, other black women remain unmarried rather than partner with a man of another race. Again, there is a shortage of men only if black women remain confined to a segregated market. Black women who marry a man of another race could bypass many of the hazards of the single life—unsatisfying and nonmonogamous relationships, the increased risk of sexually transmitted diseases, abortion, single parenthood.

Despite the fact that black women are the most likely to be unmarried and the most likely to marry down, they are also the least likely to marry out. Why? What is it that keeps black women in a segregated relationship market even as other groups, including whites, mix ever more freely?

Typically, the intimate segregation of black women is taken for granted, assumed to be, if not desirable, then at least inevitable. Over the past few decades, as the marriage rates for black women have declined, commentators, including researchers, have tended to assume that even the most successful black women—those with college degrees and good jobs, and who seem to navigate comfortably in mostly white professional environments—must marry black men, if they marry at all. For these women, no less than for their less-educated counterparts in disadvantaged urban areas, the troubles of black men have left them with no viable candidates for marriage. Or at least many commentators have so assumed.

Status, Stereotypes, and the White Standard of Beauty

That assumption is animated by another one: that nonblack men are not open to marrying black women. If men of other races don't want to marry black women, the question is why? Social scientists have considered a number of reasons why nonblack men might be disinclined to partner with black women. The explanations have to do with group status, stereotypes, and the white standard of beauty. The "group status" argument is that African Americans are disfavored as potential spouses because black Americans as a group are devalued in American society.[241] Some black men can, to a limited extent, overcome the stigma of blackness by trading their high professional status for the higher racial status of a white wife. Black women less frequently marry interracially, the theory goes, because that sort of trade is less available for black women, for whom beauty rather than education or earning capacity is a metric of value in the eyes of potential spouses.[242]

Another explanation is that black women are disadvantaged in the relationship market by long-standing and unflattering stereotypes. Sometimes black women are viewed variously as sexually loose and promiscuous; big, aggressive, and strong; or as an asexual, motherly caretaker.[243] Each of these stereotypes is at odds with the conventional feminine qualities that men are thought to desire.[244] Again, there is little doubt that these stereotypes have circulated throughout American culture. Some psychological research, for example, finds evidence that African Americans as a group are viewed as more masculine than other groups, a perception that could easily constrict black women's romantic prospects.

The third common explanation has to do with the white standard of beauty. The idea here is that the characteristics that make women beautiful, and hence more desirable in the relationship market, are features associated with white women: light complexion, narrow noses, long straight hair. Although the significance of the white standard of beauty is difficult to measure precisely, there is little doubt that it has powerfully shaped the relationship market. The white standard of beauty is the reason why the black women who are widely recognized as beautiful are often black women whose features approximate those of white women.

The Story Internet Dating Reveals

While these impediments to intermarriage by black women have been discussed for decades, the rise of Internet dating has finally allowed researchers to assess the actual preferences with which individuals enter the relationship market. The information collected by Internet dating websites is far from perfect—after all, people self-select into one site or another, and the variety of Internet dating websites is astounding and constantly changing—but still, the trove of information that these sites collect makes it more possible than ever to study people's racial preferences and behaviors in the market for intimacy. This evidence allows us to begin to answer the question: Among nonblack men, is there a market for black women?

Practically every study of Internet dating has found that black women are disfavored in the market for intimacy. The empirical data attest that when it comes to romance, Americans are far from colorblind. Much of this research seems to confirm the intuition that African Americans are the least desired romantic partners.[245] In one study using data from Yahoo!'s dating site, only 49 percent of whites were willing to date African Americans.[246] A 2009 study conducted by researchers at the University of California, Irvine, found that white Internet daters accorded race more importance than education or religion in their selection of a partner. White men, for example, were more than twice as likely to state a racial preference as they were a religious preference.[247] The same study found that black women specifically were the least preferred racial group for white men.[248] In this study, when Internet daters were allowed to explicitly *exclude* certain groups, more than 90 percent of white men who stated racial preferences excluded black women.[249]

The most consistent source of research about Internet dating has been the website OkCupid, whose operators have performed their own analysis of their data and published the results on the website's blog. In one study, OkCupid found that 40 percent of white men prefer to date white women.[250] Moreover, the website found that black women sent the most messages and received the fewest replies of any group. This disparity existed even after the study excluded men who had explicitly declared that they weren't interested in dating black women, and even after the site took into account the so-called compatibility of particular users. Based on the website's analysis, white men write back to black women 25 percent less frequently than they should based on the compatibility scores the site calculates (men reply 32 percent rather than 42 percent of the time). This evidence confirms that black women are disadvantaged in the relationship market.

Explaining the Preferences

Yet it is also important to understand that the preferences expressed on Internet dating websites are opaque. Researchers know the boxes that users checked, but they don't know why they checked them.

Some white men may be afraid to express interest in a black woman. One black woman I interviewed from St. Louis dated a white man who told her he had often been attracted to black women before, but had never dated one. The reason? "I was afraid," he told her, "I thought I'd get beat up. Beat up by the white guys, beat up by the black guys." He even worried, in the Southern town where he grew up, whether the white girls would date him anymore once he crossed the color line, giving new meaning to the old saying, "Once you go black, you never go back."

Moreover, some of those white men who exclude black women on the Internet dating website likely do so for the simple reason that they don't think black women would be attracted to them. A number of the women I interviewed were familiar with that assumption. One woman suspected that a number of white college classmates were attracted to her, but that the relationship "often stayed in the friendship zone, because they didn't know if [she'd] be attracted to them." Some even asked her, "Do you date white guys?"

A white male friend who lived in Chicago for a few years tells me that he regularly encountered appealing black women, but that he had never asked any of them out. Not one. "I just assumed they weren't interested in white guys," he explains. He attributes their supposed lack of interest to "family pressures, how they grew up." He knew that this generalization, like all stereotypes, didn't apply to all black women. The problem was that he didn't know which were which, and he had little confidence in his ability to discern between them. Like many men, he didn't want to put himself "out there" if rejection was likely. My friend embodied a truth that social psychologists have empirically confirmed: We tend to like people who we think will like us.

One of the women interviewed for this book said much the same thing: "I've had white guys express interest in my black girlfriends," she said. "But they seem unsure of what to do because they get mixed signals about black women. I think they hear that [black women] only really like black guys or they don't date outside their race, or they aren't allowed to do so or the culture tells them not to. They aren't sure how to navigate those waters."

Some men may exclude black women from their pool of Internet dating matches for reasons of efficiency rather than dislike. The 2009 study by researchers at the University of California, Irvine, found that the white men who exclude black women from their pool of potential partners are also more likely to express a body-type preference.[251] Some men may exclude black women because they do not want to date an overweight woman and they believe (correctly so, based on national data) that black women are more likely than other groups of women to be overweight. Some men might use race as a proxy for weight because it's difficult to know in online dating whether a woman is overweight. Photographs may be dated; self-descriptions may not be accurate. And black women are likely, given their social and cultural context, to describe their body type as "average" when in fact they are overweight, as determined by national standards. Men who state a racial preference when their real concern is weight might in fact be open to dating a black woman who is not overweight.

The Other Part of the Story

The lack of demand for black women cannot be the sole explanation for their intimate segregation. The conclusions that many commentators draw from the Internet dating research underestimate black women's prospects for intimacy in an integrated market. To begin with, many of the studies look only at the preferences of white men and ignore the multitude of Asian, Indian, Middle Eastern, and Latino men who now populate many major urban areas. In some cases, including these men would yield a much more optimistic picture of black women's intimate possibilities. Consider the OkCupid study that emphasized that white men do not reply to messages sent by black women as often as they should (based on the website's calculation of compatibility). In that study, Latino, Middle Eastern, Indian, and Native American men all responded to black women at rates substantially higher than did white men. In fact, some of these groups of men responded to black women at higher rates than did black men!

Another reason that existing studies understate black women's options is that researchers typically talk in terms of the percentages of men willing to date black women, when the actual dating opportunities available to individuals depend much more on absolute numbers. Black women are a numerical minority in the relationship market. They constitute only 13 percent of the female population in the United States; nonblack men account for roughly 87 percent of the United States male population. Even if, say, two-thirds of nonblack men refuse to date a black woman, there would be at least two or three times as many nonblack men willing to date black women as there are black women.

Researchers and journalists also overstate the impediments faced by black women by describing empirical findings selectively. I mentioned a study above in which 90 percent of white men who stated a racial preference explicitly excluded black women. That's the finding that the researchers emphasized and that received a great deal of media attention. That 90 percent figure is what people who hear about the study will likely remember. But that 90 percent figure is grossly misleading. What descriptions of the study often left out was how few white men stated a racial preference at all. In that study fewer than 60 percent of white men stated *any* racial preference. A more positive and no less accurate description of that same study would have been that nearly half of white men expressed openness to dating a black woman and that, by extension, there were more white men willing to date black women than there are single black women.

This study highlights a more general point: Women, including black women, face fewer barriers to interracial dating than do men, for the simple reason that women are much more likely than men to express racially restrictive preferences. While researchers' findings differ, most Internet dating studies have found that men are much more open than women to interracial dating.[252] Women are more likely to exclude men on the basis of race than men are to exclude women on the basis of race.[253] In one recent study of Internet dating, for example, 64 percent of white women stated a preference for a white man, while only 29 percent of white men stated a preference for a white woman.[254] In another study, only 22 percent of white men registered a preference for dating white women.[255] While the particulars of these studies vary, they all converge on the same conclusion: Dating pools are limited more by the racial preferences of women than by those of men. One implication of this fact is that black women, according to Internet dating studies, have greater opportunities to date across racial lines than do black men.[256] White men are more likely to be open to dating black women than white women are to dating black men. Yet black men outmarry more than twice as frequently as black women. Thus, any satisfying explanation of black women's intimate segregation must look beyond the preferences of non-black men. We must examine the desires of black women themselves.

CHAPTER 9

Desire

Black women are less willing than black men to enter an interracial relationship. One recent study of the preferences of Internet daters, for example, found that black women were between three and four times as likely as black men to say they wanted to meet only other blacks.[257] Studies in the 1970s and '80s suggest that many African American professional women refused to date white men despite a dearth of professional black men.[258] As recently as 1988, 67 percent of black women at a Southern university said they would rather remain single than date outside their race.[259] More recent research has found that many black women continue to prefer black men.[260]

In their disinclination to form intimate interracial relationships, black women are no different from women of other races. As I mentioned in the previous chapter, the available empirical evidence suggests that women are more wary than men of entering an interracial relationship.[261] One study of Internet dating, for example, found that 38 percent of women preferred to date someone of the same race, while only 18 percent of men expressed such a preference.[262] One explanation for this finding is that women tend to invest more emotionally in their romantic relationships, and might avoid interracial relationships because they see them as risky.[263] Another explanation favored by some researchers is that women are more concerned than men are with the strength of the couple's relationships with family and friends.

The fact that black women strongly desire black men is only the beginning of the inquiry. To fully understand this desire, we need to look at the motivations that lie behind it.

"I Didn't Think He Was Interested . . ."

Just as some white men think that black women are not interested in them, some black women assume the same of white men. For both groups, then, their own apparent lack of interest may simply reflect their mistaken beliefs about the desires of the other group.

Some black women are oblivious to romantic interest expressed by nonblack men as a result of messages absorbed since childhood. Even those black families that never prohibit or even discourage interracial dating might nonetheless prime their daughters' expectations. As one black woman from Chicago explains: "My mother and grandmother gave me the impression that only black men know how to appreciate a black woman. I'm brown-skinned and my grandmother would say that 'only black guys can really appreciate that,' that 'they're the ones who will see that beauty.'"

The assumption that only black men want black women is a common one. Its most vehement proponents include some black men. As I researched this book, I was surprised to hear so many black men state without the least bit of doubt or equivocation that only black men are attracted to black women. If my discussions with black men are any indication, many black men believe that black women have no choice but to remain with black men. This assumption, which can leave black women feeling powerless, is continually buttressed by the public dialogue about black women and marriage. Consider, for example, that studies of Internet dating preferences emphasize, as I discussed earlier, the impediments that black women encounter in dating or marrying across racial lines. So, too, do reports of black women's low rates of interracial marriage typically imply or assume that black women remain segregated because nonblack men don't want them. Many liberal social scientists take for granted that black women's intimate isolation is determined by forces beyond their control. Psychologists emphasize pervasive stereotypes, and sociologists an inescapable racial hierarchy, each of which casts black women as powerless victims of a racially rigged market.

One problem with black women assuming white men are not interested in them is that they overlook those who are. A number of the fortysomething black women I spoke to realized belatedly that during their young adulthood they had had more white men interested in them than they ever could have imagined. One woman recalls a business school classmate (one she might have described at the time as a "nondescript white guy") asking her about a case their professor had just discussed in class. They chatted for a few minutes and went their separate ways. A class or two later, he did the same thing, wanting her opinion about a different case. Always trying to help, she answered his questions as best she could. That he might have been interested in something more than corporate strategy she considered only later, at her friend's nudge, "Girl, he was interested in you."

So, too, did Tina Ingram, the still-single lawyer, overlook what in retrospect were unquestionably romantic overtures. When a white law school classmate asked her to his student group's annual formal dance, she went and they had a nice time. But she never imagined he wanted to be anything other than friends. He had paid more than a hundred dollars for the tickets and rented a tux for the biggest social event of the year, and Tina thought it was all just a friendly gesture.

Consistently overlooking expressions of interest from white men leads to more than missed opportunities; it also contributes to a potentially vicious cycle. Because, as I've discussed, people tend to like others who they think like them, black women might not be attracted to white men because they don't think that white men are attracted to them. White men, in turn, might not approach black women because they don't think their interest would be reciprocated. Social psychologists have a name for such situations: pluralistic ignorance. Even if substantial numbers of black women and white men are open to interracial relationships, those relationships will not form as long as each side underestimates the other's interest. I view the outcome for black women as "desire by default"—they remain with black men because they don't see an alternative.

The Black Track

For other black women, though, there is more to the picture. These black women love them some black men. As Annelise, the divorced mother of three, admits, "I've had some great dates with white men, storybook dates." But as great as those dates were, she never wanted more from the relationship. "I can look at a white man and think he's good-looking," she explains, "but feeling that deeper level of attraction is a whole 'nother matter." Annelise is accepting of interracial marriage, but she doesn't want one of her own. Her reaction to interracial couples is simple: "There but for the grace of God go I."

Some of the women I interviewed left open the possibility of dating a white man, but as one college admissions officer from Atlanta says, "He would have to be better than any black man I could ever have." She tried for months to make a relationship work with a black man who had a personality disorder. "Had he been white," she says, "I would have cut him loose immediately."

For some black women, black men are a habit they can't shake. One woman I interviewed had tried. Brothers had put her through so much, she explains, that she wanted to give them up. Yet she recognizes, "I've been on the black track so long, I don't know that I can get off." Her friend seemed more adamant. "Black men been acting up," she says. "I'm putting them on the bench." Still, she eventually found herself calling them back into the game.

For many black women, their desire for black men begins with physical attraction. "I don't do pale," one woman told me. No blond hair or blue eyes for her. But a swarthy Mediterranean man? Well, she had married one of them. Still, she'd say, "I'm not attracted to white men." She doesn't think of her husband as white. Another friend offered a different limitation: "I can't do one of the ones with no upper lip," she said, pursing her lip as if to mimic what she found so distasteful. These women erected no categorical bar against white men. They just didn't encounter many who made their skin tingle.

For still other women, virtually no white men meet their standard. As one woman told me, in a tone that she might have expected to end the conversation, "I'm not attracted to white men." I couldn't take her at her word. "Brad Pitt?" I asked. "Tom Cruise? George Clooney?" I pressed for at least one exception. She kept shaking her head. "John Travolta? Antonio Banderas?" I offered, switching from the pretty boys to the gritty boys. And then my favorites: "How about Nicolas Cage? Sean Penn? Tom Brady?" No, no, no. The head kept shaking. There were no exceptions: black men only. She insisted that she never would, never could, date any man who wasn't black.

What did these men lack that many black men had?

Swag

The single-syllable answer I got from many women was that ineffable quality more easily felt than defined: swag. Women know it when they see it. Will Smith has swag; Brad Pitt does not. LeBron James has swag; Tom Brady does not. But swag is not limited to athletes and entertainers. Barack Obama has swag; George Bush does not. Although unquestionably associated with race, swag is not, strictly speaking, limited to black men nor possessed by all black men. Bill Clinton has swag, but, according to some women at least, Denzel Washington does not. Unless he is in *Training Day.*

While swag may seem to come naturally to black men, to white men it does not. One woman in Atlanta describes a common look among young white men: "Dockers or khaki shorts, colored polo shirt, Oakley sunglasses." Another woman calls it the "frat boy look" and acknowledges that such a look may count as "a white guy's swagger" but it didn't do it for her.

What, then, is swag? Many women associate it with confidence, brashness, bravado, charisma. Swag, women emphasize, may begin with appearance, but it is a matter of style and demeanor as well. A woman in D.C. says she met an Asian man she really liked, but then realized, "He didn't have enough backbone. He was asking permission for things and wasn't willing to take charge." Definitely not a man with swag. A man with swag leads rather than follows. And he's not afraid to let others know it. Swag embodies a model of black masculinity that, it seems to me, is part leader and part outlaw. The man with swag is one who sets his own agenda and refuses to abide by anyone else's.

Swag may have gained prominence in recent years thanks to a culture saturated with black rappers and athletes, men whose physicality embodies and expresses their masculinity. But I suspect that the roots of swag go deeper into black identity and further into the past. Swag recalls black folk heroes who were bloody but unbowed. Swag connotes a certain authority or genuineness; the man who has swag is "keepin' it real." And for middle- and upper-middle-class black women in particular, especially those worried that their own racial bona fides might be questioned, that assurance may be precisely what they need.

But even swag might not be enough if it doesn't come in the right color package. Carla, the human resources manager in Atlanta, recalls the relationship she couldn't bring herself to pursue with the man she describes as "the hippest white boy I ever met." He was from Oakland, California. "He was fly as all get-out," she said. "A cool-ass white boy. If you look up *swag* in the dictionary, you'll see his picture."

Yet Carla "waffled," as she put it, about whether to have a relationship with him, caught in what she describes as a "crazy dilemma." Of all the reasons that she had ever concocted to stay away from white men—that he wouldn't accept her, that he wouldn't be cool, that he had never been around black people, that he lacked swag—none of them applied. Her head said yes, but her heart said no. "I couldn't do it," she reflects, frustrated with herself for, as she puts it, "acting the fool."

Culture Preservers

When I asked one woman in D.C. whether she limited herself to black men, she responded immediately and enthusiastically.

"Yes, Lord. I love my father." For her, that said it all. It was her love for her father that made her, as she puts it, "a connoisseur of black men." "Every single trait that I look for in a man," she says, "comes from my father."

Other women I spoke with also traced their desire for a black man to their love for their father. As Annelise explains, "If I love black men, then I need to love a black man." It was just that simple. "I loved my father," she tells me. "I loved my grandfather." These men inspired Annelise. She recognized them as honorable, hardworking men who were devoted to their families. "I want a guy like my dad," she says. "I want a guy like my grandpa."

Of the white men she had dated before she met her husband, a number were both hardworking and devoted to family. But these qualities, even if complemented by other virtues, were never enough. Speaking of her father and grandfather, she reflects, "I can't separate the essence of their goodness from the essence of their blackness."

Annelise's desire for a black man is not simply about the appeal of the familiar. For her, the choice of an intimate partner carries a broader significance. "I don't think who you marry is just about that person. I think this is an opportunity to exercise a choice that is really emblematic of what you value."

What Annelise values is black culture, identity, and history. She's a race woman. Her marrying a white man would, in her view, betray her father and grandfather, dishonor their legacy, and demean herself. "Everything that made me me, my identity as a black person," she explains, "was about my loving black men." And what if she loved and married a man of a different race? "My black heart," she says, "I would need to turn it in."

Annelise doesn't want this racial consciousness to end with her. Just as it stretches back to her father and grandfather, she hopes her children will carry forward a strong black identity, and that they will reaffirm it through their own choices of spouses. But as a parent of children whose environment is multiracial and diverse, she can't quite bring herself to say that she would oppose a marriage across racial lines, much less attempt to forbid it. "I want my children to be happy," she says. "But I would be happier if they were happy with a black person."

I admit that during the course of my interviews for this book I was taken aback by the depth of this desire among many women. One interviewee had married her white college sweetheart and then began to rethink their relationship as the prospect of having children became more concrete. Because she lived and worked in predominantly white environments, she felt that establishing a black identity in her future children would take some effort. She began to doubt if her white husband would make that effort. "If there was anything we were doing that had to do with black culture," she says of their relationship, "it was always me organizing it." The effort to find a black church or black friends, that all fell to her. She didn't want to blame him for his lack of interest and initiative, but neither did his apathy bode well. "I began to feel that if we had children I would be on my own in making sure they had exposure to black culture and black people." What she didn't want was for her children to think, "We only do the black stuff with Mom." She wanted her husband to buy into the black identity preservation project. But he hadn't. A few years into their marriage, for this reason among others, she filed for divorce.

For black women who embrace this sort of culture preservation project, the personal is political. They see partnering with black men as a means of fighting racism. As one forty-year-old married black woman from Oakland implores, "We should never give up on our black men. Never. We have to support them. We know it's a struggle, but we women got to stand by the black man. If we don't, who will?"

When I asked her why she felt that way, her answer always came back to the same issue. "If you know your history, how can you not support black men?" She spoke of the past as though she had lived through it. "We saw our black man beat down, lashed by the slave master, punished for running away. If we can make it through that time together, how can we give up on them now?"

For many black women, partnering with a white man has a troubling historical resonance. As the black feminist scholar Patricia Hill Collins has memorably written, "Freedom for Black women has meant freedom *from* White men, not the freedom to choose White men as lovers."[264] During the 1960s and '70s, black power advocates explicitly accused African Americans involved in interracial relationships of "sleeping with the enemy."[265]

This accusation still resonates powerfully among some black women. Those black women who are best positioned to intermarry—graduates of racially integrated universities who hold white-collar jobs in professional environments—are also the most likely to feel the tug of racial solidarity, the nagging sense that finding love with a man of another race is selling out. As black women move ahead, many of them aim to make a black man part of that success.

Successful black men haven't been as committed to bringing black women along, even as they laud the importance of solidarity. One of the black women interviewed for this book recalls from her time in college: "I always heard that dating outside your race is a betrayal of the race. Funny thing is that I would always hear black men telling black women that; and those same men would be going out with white women." Another woman relates a scene from her college days in the late seventies. "There was a fire alarm in the middle of the night," she says, and "all these people came running out of the dorms. Instant bust. You saw brothers running out of white women's rooms"—the same men who had always extolled the primacy of black unity and proclaimed the glories of black women.

Black men, it seems, escape parallel accusations of "sleeping with the enemy." Because black men are disadvantaged by racism and white women by sexism, their union can signify the joining of two disempowered people, committed to resisting the related evils of racism and sexism. No such narrative can frame the relationship of a black woman and a white man. In loving a white man, a black woman, supposedly, is not fighting the power so much as joining it, betraying not only herself but her group.

Rebutting Inferiority

Black women's commitment to black men was bolstered by social pressures that intensified during the civil rights era of the 1960s and '70s.

During that period, forming a family with a black man became a way not only to sustain the culture but also to rebut accusations of racial inferiority. Let me explain. Debate about racial inequality has always pivoted on whether African Americans are inferior; whether the group has been wrongly disadvantaged or instead whether they've brought misfortune on themselves and somehow deserve their plight. Prior to the middle of the twentieth century, many commentators asserted that African Americans were disadvantaged because they were genetically inferior. After the Holocaust "gave racism a bad name," as my former colleague George Fredrickson put it, arguments based on alleged genetic inferiority became taboo. Efforts to blame blacks for their economic disadvantage focused instead on their supposed cultural deficiency. And arguments that invoke cultural deficiency almost invariably point to the family, the primary means of socializing children and transmitting culture from one generation to the next.

So during the tumult of the 1960s and '70s, debate swirled around the role of the black family in either ameliorating or exacerbating black disadvantage. This simmering debate was inflamed by the 1965 publication of the Moynihan Report. Officially titled "The Negro Family: The Case for National Action," the controversial report by Daniel Patrick Moynihan, the future senator and at the time a Labor Department official, made the case for providing jobs and social services to struggling African American families. Moynihan hoped to generate the political will to address black poverty. Yet the way in which he made that case proved so inflammatory that it almost completely overshadowed Moynihan's liberal agenda of supporting black families. Drawing the harshest criticism was Moynihan's characterization of single-parent black families as a "tangle of pathology." Moynihan reasoned that while the black family's troubles may be traced to slavery and economic inequality, the tangle of pathology had perhaps become so entrenched as to be self-perpetuating.

Many interpreted Moynihan's report as an effort to blame African Americans for their own disadvantage. The "tangle of pathology" language in particular made it seem as though single-parent black families were deeply and somehow fundamentally deficient, and that if African Americans didn't fare well it was because their families hadn't raised them right. Within this discourse, as Professor Candice Jenkins has observed, black disadvantage was attributed to "a degenerate domestic sphere,"[266] in which dysfunctional families impede group advancement. Many of Moynihan's critics branded him a racist.

Although black men were the missing characters in the African American family, it was black women who became associated with the failures of the family. The supposed pathology of the black family was embodied in the domineering figure of the black matriarch.[267] Perhaps, the imagery suggests, black women have driven black men from the family. Moynihan, of course, never blamed black women for the problems of black men or of black families. But women's roles are so deeply identified with the family that black women were implicated nonetheless. Thus did the civil rights era intensify some black women's commitment to joining with a black man in the hope of establishing a strong black family that, by its very existence, would rebut accusations of cultural deficiency and racial inferiority.

Black popular culture since the civil rights era has emphasized the need for black women to remain loyal to black men. Former *Essence* editor in chief Susan L. Taylor's monthly letter to readers often mined the theme of black love. In one, Taylor urged black women to commit to loving black men, even though "loving a Black man in America can be like welcoming home a war veteran." She asked her readers, "Who will be allies to Black men in their personal development if not us? Choose a man you can love and work with him. See him as your brother."[268] In another essay (published in the National Urban League's annual report, *The State of Black America*), Taylor discussed how "racism has exerted its crippling force, undermining the prospects for all African Americans, but for black men particularly."[269] To counter that racism, according to Taylor, black women need black men. "All the mighty forces arrayed against us would be rendered powerless in the face of mutual black love."

This sense of group solidarity is not limited to black women. Religion, ethnicity, nationality, all are sources of identity and culture that people want to sustain. A primary way to do so is through the family. The need to maintain group identity is often felt most acutely by those who have been historically marginalized or stigmatized. Having been disadvantaged on the basis of one's identity—as in the case of slavery, Jim Crow, or the Holocaust—can lead people to cling to it ever more fiercely. What sets black women apart from others is that their commitment to the race takes a greater toll, in all the ways this book has examined.

CHAPTER 10

Fear

Let's return to Cecelia and her life before she met Daryl. Years earlier, there had been another smart, funny man in her life. He was a law school classmate. She relished his jokes and admired his intellect. Their relationship progressed from hanging out after class to studying together to late-night meals to sexual intimacy. All went well until they confronted that familiar question: What does this relationship mean? Where is it going?

"I don't want to just have sex. I want to be a couple." That's what he told her.

She responded: "I'm not interested in being a couple. Sex, hanging out, fun—that's all this can be."

The problem? He was white. And Cecelia couldn't imagine "bringing some white dude to Detroit to sit up in my parents' house." She even told him, "I'm not bringing you home to meet my momma."

When her best friend later asked why the relationship had ended, Cecelia explained matter-of-factly, "He tried to get all serious on me. Had to let that go."

Only in hindsight, nearly twenty years later, does Cecelia recognize why she ended it: fear. She worried about whether their relationship would be accepted—by her family, by his family, by their communities. She worried about the biracial children they might have. So there was a part of her she never let him reach. Had he been black, she says, "I would probably have been in love with him."

Fear emerged as a theme in my conversations with many black women, and although nonblack men hail from many different racial groups, that fear almost always centered on the black-white divide.

Will His Family Accept Me?

One long-standing and justifiable fear has been that the white partner's family will not accept the interracial couple. My own family history attests to the virulence of white opposition to interracial couples and what was once called miscegenation. My maternal grandfather was born in Alabama in the late nineteenth century, the child of a white woman and a black laborer who worked her farm. The townsfolk might have accepted a white man fathering a child by a black woman, continuing, as it were, a long-standing practice of white men taking sexual liberties with black women. But a white woman who had a black man's child? That upset the social order on which Southern society was based. Townsfolk threatened to kill both father and son. The threat was credible enough and legal protection meager enough that my great-grandfather left town, and my great-grandmother placed her mixed-race son in a shoe box and smuggled him to an out-of-state relative with whom he remained for several years until the furor died down.

Even more recently, white families who thought of themselves as nonracist attempted to control and punish their daughters' intimate choices, pressuring them to maintain the so-called purity of the race. When Deidre Strickland, a sixty-five-year-old school administrator, announced her intention to marry a black college classmate in the late 1960s, her father—a white pastor of a progressive Northern church that promoted interracial understanding—almost lost his job. Church members resigned, some church leaders called for his resignation, and her parents received hateful and harassing phone calls in the middle of the night—calls so menacing that Deidre hesitates, even forty years later, to relay the specifics.

Deidre's parents were among the most racially liberal people she knew, yet her father told her bluntly one day, "You shouldn't do this. It's not good for you." When she persisted, her parents eventually resigned themselves to her marriage, but didn't embrace it. When it came time to shop for china and silver—a symbolically significant event for a young wife in the 1960s—Deidre's mother didn't take her; her piano teacher did. It was also her piano teacher, not her mother, who bought Deidre a nightgown for her wedding night. Many of Deidre's family members boycotted her wedding. Some didn't speak to her after she married. Some family members who had been close beforehand remained cold and distant for years, until Deidre's first child brought about a much-needed thaw.

For years into Deidre's marriage, many people never recognized them as a couple, so ingrained was the assumption that spouses share a race. On one occasion, Deidre felt ill and asked her husband to drive her to the hospital. After dropping her off at the emergency room, he went to park the car, but when he returned, Deidre was nowhere to be found. Frantic, he ran through the halls looking for her. He asked orderlies, desk assistants, and doctors if they knew where his wife was, but no one could help. Meanwhile, Deidre's condition worsened, and the doctors began to prep her for surgery. As she descended deeper and deeper into an anesthesia-induced wooziness, she remembers looking toward the door of the operating room and seeing the vague outline of a figure moving frantically past, first in one direction, then the other. She knew from the fleeting profile that it was her husband. She could hear him asking, "Where's my wife? Where's my wife?" Deidre wanted to scream "Here!" but was too drowsy to do so. Although the hospital personnel knew a woman was in the operating room, they didn't connect the two—they couldn't imagine that this black man was looking for his white wife.

Many white families may have looked the other way when their sons had sexual relationships with black women, but when those relationships progressed from casual to committed, familial opposition was often no less vigorous than it was when it came to their white daughters. Consider the experience of Bill and Sondra. He's white and she's black, and they began dating in college in the mid-1980s. The relationship became serious within months, but Bill concealed that fact from his family for years. He didn't tell his family when he and Sondra started living together. As Sondra explains, "He knew they would hate it." And they did. His wealthy white family threatened to disown him. When they eventually did marry, Bill's grandmother, along with other family members, refused to attend the wedding. She died having never forgiven her once favorite grandson for his "betrayal." Bill's mother didn't forgive him, either, until she was diagnosed with terminal cancer and realized that she didn't want to die without having reconciled with her son.

As these stories suggest, white opposition to interracial relationships is long-standing. As recently as 1970, nearly four out of five whites were willing to tell a pollster that they would object to a member of their family marrying a black person. A majority of white adults at that time still thought that interracial marriage should be prohibited by law. Many white people from the generation that came of age in the 1950s never came to accept interracial marriage. I talked with one black woman who has been married to her white husband for more than twenty years—and has never met his mother. The mother lived twenty minutes from them and talked with her son often. But she had absolutely no interest in forming a relationship with her black daughter-in-law. She died having never met her son's wife.

These sorts of stories, more social history than isolated experiences, leave many black women wary, inclined to expect the worst. One young black woman explained her view toward her white boyfriend's family. "I operate under a racial generalization," she says. "I expect that his family won't like me because I'm black. I assume that if you're white you hold racist views. That is my presumption. Rebuttable. But still a presumption."

Can He Come to Dinner?

Yet opposition to interracial relationships doesn't only come from the white side of the racial divide. Maya, a divorced prosecutor from D.C., grew up in an integrated neighborhood and her family had friends of all races. She didn't think it would be a big deal when she decided to go to her senior prom with a Japanese American classmate.

She was wrong. "They made jokes, called him names, ridiculed us as a couple," she recalls. When Maya protested, they claimed it was all in fun. It wasn't. Maya knew that. What should have been a joyful occasion became the most anguished time of her high school career. Her family's veiled hostility toward her prom date distanced her from them. And she didn't want that. Ever.

And so in college, when she met a man who seemed to have all the qualities she sought, she told him after two weeks of dating that she couldn't see him anymore. He was white. She imagined, hoped, that in time she'd find that level of emotional intimacy again, but with a black man. She hasn't.

Some black parents have explicitly told their children as they ventured out into the world: "Don't bring home a white person." One black woman I interviewed remembers her mother giving her and her brother these very instructions when they started college. The mother worried most about her son and urged him, "If you love your mother, bring home a black girl." (He rejected her injunction; the daughter who abided by its spirit remains single.)

Often the worry is not about outright rejection as much as whether a white man would fit in with the woman's family. Rachel Lewis, the Chicago investment manager, met a guy online who was tall, in shape, and a high school teacher with a Ph.D.—all qualities that her socially conscious, health-food-oriented family would appreciate—but she was hesitant to start a relationship. "When I looked at him I just thought, 'I can't bring him home to my family.' I come from a black nationalist family. We celebrate Kwanzaa." Her elders hadn't told her explicitly not to bring home a white man; "They acknowledged that they would deal with it," she says. "But it wouldn't be anyone's first choice. That weighs on me."

Remember Tina Ingram, the happily single lawyer who manages the career of a celebrity? She explains quite frankly that while she has dated plenty of white men, she would never bring one home. "My immediate family would be fine," she says, before pausing and then shaking her head. "But my extended family? Some are more ignorant than others, and who knows what they might say?"

These women aren't just worried about cultural fit. The problem is more basic, and more difficult to surmount. Remember the black woman who hadn't met her mother-in-law? Well, her husband hadn't met his father-in-law either. Her family remained in Mississippi, which she had left for California as a young adult. She regularly returns to Mississippi to visit her parents and has even taken her husband. But her parents, and particularly her father, weren't eager to welcome a white man into their family. The reason was simple: Her father didn't like white people. "White people put my father through too much," she explains.

In my interviews with black folks throughout the country, I again and again confronted this unmistakable marker of continuing racial division: Many black parents don't want their child to marry a white person because they don't like white people. As one black woman in her midthirties says: "My mom doesn't trust 'em."

Truth be told, lots of black people don't trust white people. They may maintain cordial relationships with white co-workers and neighbors. They may want to live in an integrated neighborhood and are fine with their young children having playdates with white classmates. But as integrated as their lives are, many blacks don't feel as comfortable with whites as they do with other blacks. They harbor too much bitterness and resentment to feel the sort of closeness with white people that the notion of "family" connotes.

What fuels African Americans' distrust of whites is a painful past. One need not look far for examples. My own parents had ample reason to feel unsettled if any of their children had married a white person.

My father's family left Georgia for Cleveland in the 1920s to escape death threats against his older brother, who had the audacity to wear a new suit into town, causing the white boys to taunt, "The nigger thinks he's better than us." On my mother's side there's the story of my uncle being forced to leave Alabama in the 1930s after retaliating against white boys who had harassed his sisters. For my mother and father's families alike, living under Jim Crow didn't mean simply separation. It meant the threat of violence and the reality of degradation every day. While some commentators recall fondly the cohesive and segregated black community, living in the South subjected African Americans to the caprice and cruelty of whites who could act with impunity. Life in Cleveland, where my family ended up, was better than it was in the South, but the conditions were racially oppressive nonetheless. Blacks were consigned to the most dilapidated housing and the worst jobs.

These corrosive experiences did not end with the demise of Jim Crow and the passage of civil rights laws. African Americans who grew up as recently as the seventies carry with them bitter memories of their interactions with whites, experiences that evoke shame and anger even decades after the fact.

One fifty-year-old black man recalls that as a teenager he took a liking to one of the girls in the white suburban Detroit neighborhood his family had helped to integrate. Her parents told him, "I don't want you seeing her," and, "Don't come around here." He moved on. Then the same thing happened with another girl. He found it galling. "I had excellent grades, I was a good athlete, I never caused trouble," he tells me. After starting college at the University of Michigan he began to date black girls and, after earning graduate degrees in both law and business, married one. But he still hasn't forgotten how unwilling his white neighbors were to let him, an honor student bound for success, date their daughters. Now the father of a ten-year-old girl, he is already "working hard to make sure that [his daughter] is exposed to black men."

The Exotic Adventure?

Another fear that many women expressed had less to do with family and friends and more to do with the man himself. Some black women worry that white men see them as an exotic adventure. They suspect that the white men who approach them have a "thing" for black women or are indulging a curiosity that will soon pass, just as one might sample exotic food with no intention of making it part of one's daily diet.

When Maya, the prosecutor from D.C., first started dating Bill, a sports agent, he seemed really cool. They got along well, and she liked that he seemed so into her. But over time her view of him changed. Bill represented a lot of black athletes and often took Maya to celebrity gatherings. She enjoyed meeting sports figures whom she had before only seen on television. But after a while, she began to feel that he was showing her off. When he paraded her around his black clients and buddies, "he even *talked* differently," she recalls. "I started to feel that he thought he was better off with the black athletes because he was dating a black woman. I started to wonder whether he thought having a black girlfriend could raise his status in the eyes of his clients." Eventually, Maya ended the relationship. "It just wasn't about me, you know? He's one of those guys who has a thing for black women."

As Maya's experience suggests, some white men do want to date black women for the wrong reasons. One woman I spoke with summed up the worry of many: "With white men, it's almost like they want to possess me rather than have a relationship with me."

For some women, it is difficult to shake the suspicion that a white man's desire for a black woman—*any* white man's desire for *any* black woman—is somehow sordid or degrading. Many black women associate white men's attraction to them with the twisted sexual relationships that often developed between master and slave. One woman from New York says that when she visited rural Virginia to work on the Obama campaign, a white man there expressed interest in her. "But I didn't think it should be taken as complimentary," she says, "because throughout Southern history there were all these white slave masters who took black mistresses." She felt that appreciating his attraction to her would somehow perpetuate that pattern, as if he regarded her not as a potential wife, but as something akin to a concubine.

A number of the women I interviewed can relate. As one woman explains, "I do see white men as the oppressor. Even within my own family," she says, "black women have been the victim of sexual violence by white men. I think it's still very prevalent, this desire for white men to want to conquer or tame exotic women."

In some cases, though, this suspicion on the part of black women does them a disservice. When a white businessman she had dated a few times told Tina Ingram early in their relationship, "You remind me so much of my ex-girlfriend," it set off alarms for her. She didn't want to be one in a string of black girlfriends, nor part of some perverse racial dynamic. Just as she was about to end the relationship, she happened to see some pictures of his ex-girlfriend. She wasn't black, but Tina could see immediately what linked them in his mind: their sense of style and flair. "There were all these quirky little outfits that I wore," Tina explains, "and I could see from the pictures that she liked them too." She felt bad for having assumed the worst.

Will He Understand?

Just as women worry about white men who have a fetish for black women, they also worry about white men who don't know anything about black women. As one woman says, "I worry that with a white guy I won't be able to be myself. That I could never really relax, that I'd always have to explain myself to him."

Indeed, some of the women I interviewed did have to explain themselves to men who weren't black. One thirty-one-year-old schoolteacher in D.C. told me she dated an Asian man once who was nice but just didn't "get it." Simple things. "I was putting my scarf on before going to bed one evening," she recalls, and he said, 'What are you doing to your hair?'" As she recounts the story to me, she rolls her eyes and cocks her head, just as I imagine she did with him. "I was like, 'Hon, let's have a little talk.' I told him I cover my hair at night, every night." To his puzzled "Why?" she responded, "Because it stays where I put it, and if I don't cover it, I wake up and it's all over my head."

He understood, but it was a conversation she would rather have skipped. "It's easy to date a black man," she told me, "because he knows about my hair. He knows I don't wash it every day. He knows I'm going to put the scarf on."

Many of the black women I spoke with don't want to have to explain themselves to their partner. They don't want to have to educate some man about black women, much less black culture. Even if he were open to learning, the mere fact of needing to have a conversation about, say, hair care, is a problem. Among some of the women I interviewed, just the thought of having the "hair talk" made them tired, emblematic as it was of so much else they'd have to teach. Much better to have someone who already understands.

Another source of tension among practically every interracial couple I spoke with, was that the black woman saw racism where the white man did not. Whenever Sherie, an African American chemist, attributed mistreatment by a restaurant server or a store clerk to race—the clerk didn't approach her because he assumed she wouldn't buy anything, or the waiter was surly because he thought she wouldn't leave a tip—her white husband, Michael, would counter, "Oh, maybe they were just in a bad mood." Which irritated Sherie even more. "She thinks I'm not considering her point of view," Michael explains in his defense, "when I was just trying to bring a different perspective." Michael, an immigrant from Europe, admits that he doesn't have much experience with race. "I have a hard time seeing things from her point of view," he concedes. "I may have been naive in some cases."

Though Michael has become more open to acknowledging racism, Sherie and many other black women would simply prefer that their intimate partner "get it" without having to be educated about race. As one black woman in her late twenties explains, "It sure would be nice to have a black man so that I don't have to explain what I mean when I say someone looked at me funny."

What I observed in the couples I interviewed was captured by the

2006 movie *Something New,* which stars Sanaa Lathan as Kenya, an attractive, professional black woman seeking her "IBM"—Ideal Black Man.[270] After a friend sets her up on a blind date with a white man named Brian, Kenya begins an improbable relationship, fraught with repeated disagreements about race. When Kenya complains that clients stereotype her at work and assume that she shouldn't be handling their multimillion-dollar accounts—a pervasive skepticism she refers to as the "black tax"—Brian asks whether she's paranoid. When she complains about another race-related slight, Brian implores her, "Could we just not talk about race all the time?" Kenya responds angrily, "Well, you don't need to think about race 'cause you're white. You don't even know you're white until you're in a room of black people. Well, for me, that's what I face every day, a bunch of white people who refuse to believe that I'm qualified." In time, though, they surmount these hurdles. Brian apologizes for dismissing Kenya's complaints and pledges, "Even though I may not always understand, I promise always to listen." They agree on one point: "It'd be a shame to let something so superficial get in our way." By the end of the movie, they're married. The film is typical Hollywood—unlikely couple overcomes obstacles, finds true love, lives happily ever after—but it mirrors the experiences of many interracial couples I spoke with.

All these recurring disagreements about racism didn't seem to threaten the relationships of the interracial couples I spoke with. They didn't view their differing perspectives as superficial, but neither were they a deal-breaker. These couples each told me variations of the same story: "We disagree about this, we wish we didn't, it can be irritating that we do." But when all is said and done, it just isn't that big of a deal.

Amid all the things to bicker about, disagreements about race are more a bump in the road than a roadblock.

And other bonds hold these couples together. For Angela and Robert, an interracial couple in their midtwenties, disagreements about race are intractable; they agree to disagree. But the bond that holds them together is their faith. Angela, a black woman, is a Seventh-Day Adventist, and she wanted a man who shares her particular faith—not simply a spiritual man or even just a Christian man, but an Adventist like her. Adventist practices differ from mainstream Catholicism or Protestantism—Adventists treat Saturday as the Sabbath, for example—and having a man who shared that faith mattered to Angela. Yet even when she discovered that Robert, a white man, was Adventist, Angela doubted how close that would make them, since Adventist churches remain de facto segregated. She took for granted that Robert knew only about the white churches. "I think I'm going to spit some knowledge," she told me, "so I tell him about one of the prominent black pastors in the area." To her amazement, Robert didn't miss a beat. "Yeah, I go to him often," he said. "He's a good pastor."

Beyond their shared faith, their lives overlapped in other ways. They both grew up in California, both became accountants, and both embraced the same political beliefs. As Angela said, "He wouldn't have been interested in me if I were white and I didn't have my other qualities, and I wouldn't have been interested in a black version of him who didn't have all the things that he has. Racially we're quite different, but culturally we're very similar."

Well, not in every way. Straightlaced Robert didn't understand much of the black slang Angela used. Once when she referred to a "'round the way girl," he laughed with her but had no idea what she meant. After a while they both tired of him asking her to explain. So Robert did what any self-respecting, technologically proficient, clueless boyfriend of a slang-talking black girl would do: He bookmarked Urbandictionary.com on his Internet browser. Angela was thrilled. "I love that he did that," she exclaims to me. "I completely appreciate that I can speak the way I speak when I'm with him. That lets me be comfortable."

But while some barriers are easily overcome, others present greater challenges for interracial couples. Prior to her marriage and divorce Annelise Hemphill was working at what she describes as a "little hoity-toity women's boutique" in 1995 when the jury pronounced O. J. Simpson "not guilty." When the verdict came down, all of her white co-workers and all the customers, "these rich white women," in Annelise's words, "were just crestfallen, talking about how horrible this is, this travesty of justice." Annelise wasn't hoping for O.J. to go free, but the verdict didn't upset her. One black man wrongly going free, Annelise thought, paled beside much greater injustices: the untold numbers of poor black boys locked up for years for petty crimes, the murders of black people ignored by the police and media, the rich and guilty white folks whose expensive lawyers got them off for offenses that would have meant hard time for the poor black people who grew up where she did. These were the problems that bothered her, pervasive injustices of which the white women in that boutique were blissfully ignorant. Let one black man get off, she thought, and they act like the world is about to end.

As the boutique's white customers and her co-workers condemned the verdict, Annelise felt the anger swelling within her. As much as she needed to vent, she dreaded seeing her boyfriend that evening. He was white too.

When the two of them discussed the verdict that night, "He said all the right things." He was, as Annelise describes him, "very liberal and as open and understanding of black people as any white person could possibly be." But somehow that wasn't enough. Thinking and saying the right things "is not the same," she tells me, "as feeling the right things." Her white boyfriend could never experience life as a black person. And for Annelise that meant he could not experience the Simpson verdict as she did. "I could not get over his whiteness," she concludes.

Worse, the response of the women in the boutique rekindled every bit of anger toward white people that Annelise had ever felt. "How do you reconcile that if you're married to a white person?" she wonders. "Do you go home and say, 'These damn white people.' Can you even think these things if your partner is white?" Annelise admits, "There are some days when I don't even feel like being around white people. If you're married to a white person, how do you deal with that?"

What seems to underlie Annelise's anxiety is a sense of vulnerability. There's a sense of shared predicament and perspective, of being in this together, that leads black people to assume that other black people will understand when they recount some race-related slight—being stopped by the police, or followed around a store, or not treated as though they belong at some high-status establishment. There's a whole array of experiences that black folks, for the most part, don't need to explain to one another—like the salesclerk whose "May I help you with anything?" simultaneously suggests that the salesclerk does not in fact want to help you, and more likely wonders what you are doing in the store, and would prefer that you left. These shared understandings—the fruit of our own experiences, and those of friends, and stories passed down through family—mean that black people expect one another to "get" their grievances. Black women and their white partners don't share that same sense of solidarity.

What About the Children?

That's a question voiced by generations of white racists, often more a rhetorical means of fomenting opposition than a search for truth. It's also a question that, to my surprise, black women ask themselves. Remember Cecelia's reluctance to initiate a serious relationship with a white law school classmate because she couldn't imagine him "sitting up in her parents' house in Detroit"? She also couldn't imagine herself birthing his children. "I wanted chocolate babies," she explains. I knew better than to ask whether white chocolate would suffice. She can confront now what wasn't so clear then: "I was reluctant to get into a serious relationship with a white man because I was concerned about being able to raise biracial children." Cecelia has a milk-chocolate complexion herself, and her green eyes and curly hair betray the mix of peoples in her ancestry. She worried, given how "mixed up" her own genes were, that a biracial baby might come out looking white.

Many of the black women I interviewed raised this issue. Lighter-skinned women in particular were concerned that if they married a white man their children wouldn't be "black enough." One light-skinned woman went so far as to joke with her white fiancé, "If we have twins, one dark and one light, we're putting the light-skinned one up for adoption." Although the suggestion was clearly in jest, it reflects a very real anxiety.

My mother felt this anxiety as well. The most lightly complected of all her siblings, she could almost have passed for white. As we leafed through photos of her old boyfriends and noticed that they were all dark-skinned men, like our father, she explained, "I didn't want no buttermilk babies."

Their concerns about complexion led a number of the women I spoke with to be more open to a man who was neither black nor white. One woman from Atlanta said she could never allow herself to have a child with a white man. But a Latino? "I could do that," she asserts. "A lovely African American Latino baby. He would still be brown." Other women say they'd be OK having a baby with an Asian man as long as he wasn't pale." "Vietnamese, Filipino, East Indian?" one woman asks. "I could work with that."

For Cecelia, as for many of the women I interviewed, race is filtered through the prism of the black-white divide. Cecelia wanted chocolate babies because she wanted her children to identify as black. "I wasn't interested in having some little white girl telling me what she was and wasn't," she says. Down that path, Cecelia thought, lay a whole heap of trouble.

Cecelia's fear stemmed in part from the experience of an older cousin whose life Cecelia regarded as a cautionary tale. The child of Cecelia's aunt, this cousin was half white; her hair turned nearly blond in the summer and her eyes had a hint of blue. The cousin never found a place within their family. No one was outright mean to her, but she was always on the periphery, an outsider in an otherwise tight-knit clan. As an adult, this cousin "semipassed," as Cecelia explains, and became engaged to marry a white man. The marriage was called off when his family discovered that the girl's mother was black. Cecelia didn't want a life like that for her own children.

Cecelia wanted chocolate babies for another reason: so that no one would ever question whether they were hers. With biracial children she feared that she'd be mistaken for the nanny, a worry far from unfounded. Award-winning author and freelance journalist Veronica Chambers wrote an essay about precisely this dilemma.[271] Chambers thought she and her daughter looked so much alike that they could only be perceived as mother and child. She was wrong. "When I took cupcakes to Flora's school for her birthday," she writes, "another mom said within earshot, 'I hate when these working women send their nannies for their kid's birthday. I mean, really.'" Even worse, this was a mom she had met, on more than one occasion, though she evidently had neglected to specify that she was the mother, not the babysitter.

Chambers developed a snappy comeback to these impertinent assumptions. When some stranger would exclaim, "Oh, what a beautiful baby! How long have you been taking care of her?" she'd deadpan, "Since I almost died giving birth to her," a reference to a pregnancy-related illness that had threatened them both.

Some women might laugh off being mistaken for the nanny. But for many black women, a faux pas like this one conjures a long history in which poor black women cared for the children of affluent white families. These women—who live on in the popular imagination as the mammy figure—were of an era when the social order formally subordinated blacks to whites, and black women were permitted to care for children or clean houses but not much else. The error of the white mother at the preschool birthday party was to symbolically, even if unintentionally, relegate the educated and professional Veronica Chambers to the role of mammy, eclipsing her achievements, denying her success.

Other women worried less about perception and more about rejection—the potential censure of their children for being neither wholly black nor white. Popular mythology envisions a mulatto child torn between two races and never finding a home in either. Historically, there's some truth to that characterization. My own mother endured the difficulties of having to straddle the divide between black and white. Although her parents were both African American, as a light-skinned child in the 1920s and '30s in rural Alabama, she was taunted and teased by her dark-skinned classmates. Even in my own childhood, we ridiculed the only biracial child in our otherwise all-black elementary school class. How heartless we were. Black folks have long victimized anyone whose racial bona fides could be called into question. One of my interviewees recalls: "[I remember] years of being treated like I wasn't black enough because I am light-skinned."

Assimilation Anxiety

Black women also worry about whether biracial children would help to perpetuate black culture. One woman shared a prediction she'd read, "that in twenty or thirty years everybody is going to look alike. We're all going to be roughly the same complexion. There's going to be a whole lot of interracial dating, marriages, and babies. We'll lose our race, so to speak, our culture." She paused. "I don't want to lose it," she said. Women like her are committed to cultural preservation, and having black children is one way to ensure it. Another added: "I strongly identify myself as a woman of color, and I've always assumed that my kids will see themselves in that same light. I've always thought that my offspring would identify as black." What if her children don't embrace that identity?

That question resonates across generational boundaries. In her 2007 book *Blue-Chip Black,* Karyn Lacy recounts her discussions with middle-class African Americans about the possibility of their children marrying outside the race.[272] One mother seemed unhappy over the prospect of any of her children marrying a white person: "I wouldn't encourage it, but I would accept it," she explained. "I guess psychologically, I would want little black grandkids. I'm not sure how to explain it. I just would prefer that."

Recall Monica Wilson, the never-married church administrator in D.C. She took it upon herself to provide some lessons in racial identity for her nieces, the daughters of her brother and his white wife. "She does the best that she knows," this woman says of her white sister-in-law, "and I can't fault her for that. But my nieces need to be a little bit more aware of their black side. I'm not pushing it on them," she told me. "I just want them to know where our people came from." A few months earlier, around Martin Luther King Day, her niece kept talking about black people in the third person. It made Monica cringe, hearing about "the black people this, the black people that." When Monica couldn't take it anymore, she asked her niece directly, "What are you?"

The little girl looked her in the eye and, without a bit of hesitation, announced, "I'm a Wilson." Her niece's answer was not what Monica wanted but neither was it one with which she could quarrel.

For some women, the concern over a child's racial allegiance extends beyond their particular child to the broader community. A black female law student told me some years ago that if women like her married white men it would accelerate a trend toward a black America where the elite were light and half white, and the poor were "just black." That wasn't a future she desired, and she didn't want to play a role in helping to create it. More comically, one woman "promised" a family member concerned about the future of the black race, "If I marry a white guy, I'll adopt. If I marry a black guy, I'll give birth."

The anxiety that black women feel about having biracial children may have been exacerbated by social and cultural changes that we rightly regard as progress. For most of American history, the question of whether a black woman's children would be black was a nonstarter. Of course they'd be black. That was the work done by the so-called one-drop rule, more formally known as the "rule of hypodescent." According to this principle, reflected in social practice and law alike, "one drop" of black blood was sufficient to make a person black. In the infamous 1896 case of *Plessy v. Ferguson*, for example, the fact that seven out of Homer Plessy's eight great-grandparents were white was not sufficient to allow him to sit in the white railroad car in segregated Louisiana. As with the railroad law, segregation laws throughout the South applied as forcefully to those with one black parent as to those with two. Now the relaxation of that coercive system means that children with one black parent and one white parent will have unprecedented freedom to define their own racial identity. The same freedom that allows people to fashion their own identity compounds the anxiety of African Americans in particular, who worry that if people can exit, perhaps they will. It is the very openness and fluidity of identity, the prospect that one might be able to *choose* whether to be multiracial or just black, that leaves some black women so concerned about their children.

But just as the relaxation of the one-drop rule intensifies anxiety, it also underscores the futility of placing our children into boxes and hoping they'll stay there. The opportunity for the next generation to choose their racial identity is apparent more now than ever, and increasing numbers of people are taking advantage of that opportunity. Children become adults who make their own choices, and many will fashion identities to which their parents may find it difficult to relate. Better to acknowledge that reality than to cling to a certainty that is illusory. Our children will exercise their autonomy to choose a racial identity no less than any other aspect of their selves. The only question is whether we, their parents, will embrace or resist that inevitability.

It is no more possible for me to control my children's self-conception than it was for my parents to make their identity mine. My mother came of age in a rural town in Alabama, and I grew up in the inner city of Cleveland. The suburbs of northern California are the only home my children have ever known. If identities are a matter of one's surroundings, then these three generations of my family are destined to think of themselves in quite different ways. This is no less true because we are all black. To regard oneself as an African American is not to answer the complicated question of what it means to be one, much less how prominent a role one accords race.

Hallmarks of my childhood will have no meaning for my children. The sound of "Lift Ev'ry Voice and Sing," also known as the Negro National Anthem, still makes my skin tingle. But the song will mean nothing to my sons, one of whom asked me curiously, as we listened to jazz saxophonist Charles Lloyd's stirring concert rendition, "Is that the song where you had to stand up in school?" Even if we teach them this song, it will never mean to them what it did to me. It is a song of my childhood, not theirs.

Change

The fears that keep black women segregated in an increasingly integrated relationship market are not irrational. But they should not be allowed to foreclose the chance of happiness. The basis for many of these fears is less substantial now than ever. According to a Pew Research Center Report from January 2010, 64 percent of white respondents said it "would be fine" with them if a member of their family told them they were going to marry a black person.[273] More than three in four American adults agree with the statement that it is "all right for blacks and whites to date each other."[274] This is an extraordinary change from the middle of the twentieth century when virtually all Americans—94 percent, according to one 1958 poll—disapproved of interracial marriage,[275] a view embraced by half the adult population as recently as 1983.[276]

The growing acceptance of interracial marriage is likely to continue for the simple reason that opposition is most entrenched among those older Americans who are nearing the end of their lives. People born in, say, the 1930s and '40s came of age in an era in which the norms of racial segregation prevailed. More than a dozen states legally prohibited interracial marriage until the Supreme Court's 1967 decision in *Loving v. Virginia.* Interracial marriages were so rare as to seem nonexistent. Younger generations, in contrast, cannot recall when interracial marriage was illegal. They may learn about miscegenation statutes in history books, but they never lived with them. They see and know too many interracial couples—from work, church, school, the neighborhood—to regard them as pathological. The effect of these social changes is apparent in survey data about attitudes toward interracial unions. Among Americans born after 1976—in other words, people who are now in their twenties or thirties—more than 90 percent find interracial dating acceptable.[277]

The shift in attitudes about interracial marriage is apparent in popular culture as well. Consider, for example, the comedic remake of the classic movie *Guess Who's Coming to Dinner.* The original pivoted on the ambivalence of the ultraliberal white father and mother, but the remake, which stars Bernie Mac as the black father whose daughter wants to marry Ashton Kutcher, lampoons the girl's father's opposition to their union. So fundamentally has the social context changed that most viewers cannot sympathize with a father opposed to his daughter's boyfriend's race. In another film, *Lakeview Terrace,* Samuel L. Jackson plays a law enforcement officer who terrorizes the interracial couple who moves next door, an obsession that stems, we learn near the end of the movie, from his own unsettled trauma: His wife died in an auto accident with her white boss, with whom she was having an affair. These days, the assumption is that it is the *opposition* to interracial relationships that is pathological.

One woman I interviewed thought that the stigma of interracial marriage had dissolved so completely that her white husband benefited socially from having a black wife. "People are pleasantly surprised when they realize he's married to a black woman," his wife says. "A look, a nod, a smile, as it dawns on them. Among whites *and* blacks. Particularly in liberal environments," she explains, "when people find out he is married to a black woman they think more highly of him. They see him as more liberal, more progressive, more open-minded, more sensitive." She describes him as "the beneficiary of tremendous respect" because of their marriage. "People think things like 'You're a good person because you married a black woman,' or 'You're a more complicated person.' 'You're a better person.'"

At the core of many black women's fears, I suspect, is the sense that there is a divide between blacks and whites that cannot be bridged. But in fact some white people may be able to relate to the black experience—particularly the sense of being an outsider—more than the primacy of race would lead many people to think. Consider Michael and Sherie. As an Italian who grew up in the German-speaking part of Switzerland, Michael knows what it is like to be an outsider. Italians were looked down upon in Switzerland. No one could tell by looking that he was Italian, Michael explains, "But when you speak," he says, "you do stand out." He remembers his mother not allowing him to talk when they were in public. "She felt a little bit—not ashamed—but overly conscious about me speaking Italian when we were on a public bus or tram," he recalls.

Consider as well Jason O'Grady, a white man who grew up in Boston, and Stephanie Jones, a black woman who grew up in Mississippi. They are married. He laughs loudly and tells raucous stories. She listens and speaks softly. They seem to have nothing in common. As I talk to Jason one day, I can't help but wonder what had brought them together. They certainly seem an unlikely couple. He is only too happy to explain, and begins by talking about their daughter, a toddler sitting in a stroller next to us. "My daughter was just shy of two years old when Barack Obama was elected," he says. "I was just shy of two when John F. Kennedy was elected." Then he makes the parallel explicit. "I'm Catholic, and for my family, the world changed when Kennedy was elected—he was the first Catholic in the White House. Now we've had a monumental shift again. It's kind of like my daughter is in the same position now that I was then." As a Catholic man from a working-class Irish family, he, too, had occupied the role of outsider.

If fears of interracial intimacy keep people separate now, it is because those fears embody the echo of the past. Many of us continue to act out the roles we first began to inhabit long ago. We scarcely stop to consider that we might change the script.

CHAPTER II

Saving Black Marriage

Joe Lehman and Teresa Johnson are married; he is white and she is black. They differ along many dimensions. He was born and raised on the Westside of Los Angeles and played basketball at UCLA before embarking on a successful business career. She was born in Louisiana and had two children by different fathers before making her way to California as an adult. Their personalities contrast too: She's boisterous, he's not. He's cerebral and contemplative, she's not. She's stylish and flamboyant, he's not. He's rich, she's not. As improbable as their relationship may seem, it is also emblematic of some of the challenges and benefits that await black women who open themselves to interracial intimacy.

They met by chance in the late 1990s, when Teresa rang Joe's doorbell one day. Joe was remodeling his home and his building contractor had recommended Teresa as an interior designer. Teresa came to examine the project. She showed Joe some swatches of cloth and samples of wood grains, and described, in detail, the array of possibilities he should consider. But all Joe had on his mind was her. He can still remember, these many years later, exactly what she was wearing: tall black boots and a knee-length skirt that, as Joe describes it, billowed in the wind and left her leg exposed just above the boot. "I wasn't seeking a black woman," Joe explains. "It just happened."

It is true that Joe wasn't seeking a black woman. When he registered with an online dating service some months earlier and selected the characteristics he preferred in a partner, Joe checked "white." But he didn't check the "white" box because he was adamantly opposed to dating a black woman, much less out of any antipathy toward African Americans. He checked the "white" box as a reflex. Growing up in a predominantly white environment, he had always dated white women, as had his friends. "There are so many reasons relationships don't work out," he reflects. "Why not try to make it so it does work out? The more things you have in common, the better."

On his first date with Teresa, Joe wanted to make a good impression. "I took some flowers from the backyard before I went to pick her up," he recalls. Teresa lived in a working-class, minority neighborhood that Joe had only glimpsed from the freeway. When he arrived at her town house, he felt more than a little out of place. "I had pants that were probably a little too short," he recalls, certain that people had immediately pegged him as "a goofy white guy" from another part of town.

Things got worse. "I knocked on her door, and these big black boys answered." There were four of them—Teresa's two sons and their two friends. They were watching a boxing match on television, Joe remembers, and they were "rowdy and loud, wrestling, hitting each other." They were, as Joe says, "black and scary."

"I'm sitting on the couch waiting for Teresa with my pants too short and my little bouquet of flowers, thinking, 'Where am I? This is not my world.'"

Teresa didn't quite fit into Joe's world either. Joe's best friend, a man he'd known since their college days nearly three decades ago, didn't accept Teresa. Throughout their decades-long relationship, this friend never had a problem with any woman Joe dated until Teresa—Joe's only black girlfriend. At Joe and Teresa's wedding, his best friend came to shake his hand and said, "If you're happy, I'm happy." He meant to offer congratulations, but to Joe it didn't feel that way. "It felt like he was saying, 'You're kind of crazy to marry this woman, but if you're happy . . .'" The friend later told Joe, "I'll see you at the weekly poker games. But I can't see you with her. I don't want to do things as couples." Joe pauses as he tells me this. "That was pretty ugly," he concludes. For a while, they did see each other at their weekly poker game, but then Joe stopped going. "I gave him up," he says, a loss that Joe describes as "shattering."

In talking with Joe about this episode, it struck me that, for Joe, the decision was simple: If his friend could not accept Teresa, then Joe could no longer accept his friend.

To this day, Joe and Teresa disagree about why his friend rejected her. Teresa concludes succinctly, "He lives in a lily-white world, and I didn't fit in with the color scheme."

Joe offers a different explanation. "It wasn't that Teresa is black," he says. "It was just a personality clash. It had nothing to do with race." He prefers to believe that they didn't get along because his friend—a widely known, and far from modest, cardiothoracic surgeon—expected people to defer to him, which Teresa refused to do. Their personalities clashed in another way. "He is Birkenstock people," Joe explains, "Teresa is high-heel people. They just didn't mix well."

I have never met this friend, but I admit I am inclined to favor

Teresa's account; she hadn't drawn a hasty conclusion. "I try not to make things about race," she says, "but at the end of the day, after I do the checklist of everything else that could have gone wrong—then I say, 'It's race.'" Her husband refuses to accept that possibility. Joe cannot bring himself to think that the man he expected to be his lifelong friend was a racist.

But such disagreements about racism don't threaten their relationship. There is too much else that draws them together. They complement each other. Teresa is everything Joe isn't—stylish, emotionally expressive, forthright—and he appreciates those things about her. He knows that he can learn from her, that her example might prompt him to develop certain aspects of himself.

And Teresa appreciates that Joe both accepts her and encourages her to grow. With other men, she hasn't always felt that way. "With black men," she says, "I've often felt like I had to stifle my growth so as not to outshine my man." She mimics the criticisms she'd heard so often: "Why you got to be so smart? You just a show-off." After years of relationships with men whose own personal and professional failings left them too insecure to support her, Teresa realized that she needed a man like the one she eventually found, one who is "not intimidated at all," she says. "In fact, he'll tell me, 'Why don't you push yourself?'"

Going Natural

On that first date when Joe picked Teresa up from her town house, she wore her hair long and straight, as she always had. Now, five years into their marriage, this regal, dark-skinned black woman wears her hair in twists, what some people call "sister locks." She explains, "I wear my hair natural now. I used to relax it, blow-dry it, flatiron it, curl it." Teresa, along with untold numbers of black women, had always spent long hours at the hairdresser, enduring harsh chemicals and straightening combs, and always attentive to the first sign of needing a "touch-up."

Struck by the contrast between the woman standing before me and a picture of her from before she met Joe, I ask, "What made you switch?"

"He did," she says, gesturing toward her husband.

From the beginning, they'd had issues about hair, as when Joe asked, "Is that your hair?" and Teresa responded, without missing a beat, "Yeah, I bought it, I got it in my head, it's mine."

Joe had never dated a woman with a weave. Once, when he gently pulled on Teresa's, it gave her pause. "A brother would know not to pull the weave," she thought to herself. But she tried to be patient. Whatever Joe asked, she answered.

Still, he remained, in her view, clueless. "I like real hair," he told her. "It's as simple as that."

Teresa couldn't imagine going without extensions, much less not straightening her hair. She had straightened her hair throughout her entire adult life. Her mother had straightened her hair during her childhood.

A few months after their conversation about Teresa's weave, Joe asked a seemingly innocuous question. "What's that burning?" he said. There was no cause for alarm, at least not as far as Teresa was concerned. She was just doing her hair, the old-fashioned way.

"Once I explained to him how I did my hair," Teresa recalls, "he pleaded with me, 'Stop it, just stop it. Don't do it anymore.'" She thought to herself, "Oh, my gosh, can I go out of the house with natural hair?"

Teresa had always wanted to have "good" hair, a term widely used among African Americans even today. But Joe didn't know what "good hair" was. "It was just icky to me," he says of what she went through to keep her hair straight. "It wasn't her. It just wasn't right."

Still, he didn't push a natural hairstyle on Teresa. "He said, 'I love you,'" Teresa recalls. And then he asked her, "Try it. Just try it for me."

And so she did.

Teresa's story is not atypical, at least not based on the interracial couples I interviewed. Sherie, the black chemist who argues about racism with her white husband, Michael, tells a similar tale. She, too, had "locked" her hair after Michael encouraged her to stop straightening it, a practice he called "absurd." He pointed out how great it would be to be able to take a walk in the rain, or to swim when they were on vacation. As it was, she spent her life trying not to get her hair wet.

Once she decided to go natural, Michael supported her fully. "When you first start locking your hair there's always a point where it looks bad for a long time," she explains. "When I said, 'I don't think this is working. I'm going back to relaxing,' he was like, 'Nooo.'" When she took a class in hair-locking techniques, she discovered that nine of the ten black women in her class had boyfriends or spouses who were not black.

Sherie concludes that black women who are willing to date a nonblack man are also unconventional enough to wear a natural hairstyle. She also wonders whether nonblack men who partner with black women are especially open to those women wearing locks. Might these men be more encouraging of a natural hairstyle than black men typically are?

Teresa thought during her young adulthood that a partnership with a black man would rest on a foundation of commonality and understanding that would invariably nurture her well-being. But as she reflected on her relationships with black men, she began to think otherwise.

"I never had permission from any black man I dated," she tells me, "that it was OK to be natural. No black man I ever went out with suggested that I wear my hair short." She says she heard from one black man after another: "Wear your hair straight and long, baby." The black men she had dated had wanted her to have "good hair."

Teresa's experience may be extreme; after all, not all black men prefer long straight hair. But enough do that I heard other women report similar pressures. One woman's former boyfriend still encourages her to let her hair grow long and not to "lock it." Given that their relationship ended years ago and, even worse, that he's married, she told him, "You don't get a vote." Another woman I interviewed, a lawyer, expressed to her boyfriend, "You don't have to like my hair, but *you* making a decision about what I do with it?" She paused. "No. You have no jurisdiction over the hair."

For Teresa, letting her hair go natural brought a newfound sense of freedom. Having gone natural, she doesn't think she'll ever go back. Joe's ignorance about race may have irritated her, but it also liberated her. It was only because Joe didn't know anything about "good hair" that Teresa was able to leave it behind.

As Teresa and I talk, Joe sits nearby at the kitchen table eating a sandwich. He almost doesn't seem to be listening. But he is, and at a breach in our conversation adds, "I have no interest in making Teresa be more white. Zero."

Teresa echoes his comments. "He accepts me how I am. He never, ever, ever says that I don't look good. I can look in the mirror and know I don't look good. But he just loves me right where I am. Just loves me." She walks behind him, puts her arms under his, and squeezes.

Dark but Pretty

Teresa may have benefited in another way from her willingness to cross the race line. Teresa is dark-skinned. While some black women worry about having childern who are too light, many black men don't want a wife who is too dark.

That preference is reflected in popular culture, as in a line from Stevie Wonder's classic 1970s song "Living for the City": "His sister's black, but she is sho'nuff pretty." *But* is still the conjunction that commonly connects *dark* and *pretty,* an expression of an underlying premise so widely accepted as to escape scrutiny.

This preference is also reflected in the experiences of many dark-skinned women, including some of the women with whom I spoke. One Atlanta woman, whose radiant clear skin is so dark it shines, recounts men saying to her when she was younger: "Dark-skinned girls are cool, but I just have an attraction to lighter skin." Some men even tried to compliment her by saying, "You're cute to be so dark. If you were lighter . . ."

The salience of complexion among African Americans is starkly presented in Spike Lee's late 1980s movie *School Daze.* Set at a black college, the film highlights the various lines that divide the black community, with skin color prominent among them. The membership of one of the two sororities at the school is exclusively light-skinned, while the other consists solely of dark-skinned women. Complexion not only divides the community, it also plays a large role in determining whether or not a woman is considered attractive, with the lighter-skinned sorority sisters usually finding more favor with the men on campus. These sorts of depictions are controversial precisely because they resonate with the actual social history of black sororities, and with standards of beauty within black communities.

In all these cases, the preference for light skin is a form of "colorism," a legacy of the privileged status accorded to light-skinned blacks during and after slavery. Colorism within black communities nurtures an anxiety that one of my interviewees says trailed her throughout her young adulthood: "Am I light enough?"

The worry is justified. As it turns out, recent research by economists using sophisticated statistical analysis has documented the effect of colorism in the African American marriage market. The researchers found that the lighter a black woman's complexion, the more likely she is to be married.[278] Moreover, the researchers found that among married women, lighter-skinned black women marry higher-earning black men than their darker-skinned counterparts. In the African American marriage market, complexion counts. While colorism is a long-standing phenomenon, the researchers suggest that the current scarcity of successful black men makes those men more able to act on their color preferences than they might have been able to do in generations past. For college-educated black women, who outnumber college-educated men two to one, colorism operates with a vengeance.

For dark-skinned black women in particular, then, might an interracial relationship provide an escape from a color hierarchy in which many black men are invested? Teresa's experience leaves me wondering if interracial marriage indeed allows black women to opt out of this black communal norm that is more oppressive than comforting. As Teresa describes the irony, "I can be blacker with my white husband than with any black man I've ever dated."

Black women benefit from interracial marriage in other ways as well. In the past, interracial marriages may have well been more likely than same-race marriages to dissolve. But the conditions that undermined interracial relationships in decades past—lack of familial support and societal rejection—have changed. Interracial couples encounter fewer barriers than ever. Recent research suggests that black women may be less likely to divorce when they marry outside of the race than when they marry within it. Such research counters any assumption that, for black women, an interracial marriage is fraught with peril.

The Paradox

But we've seen that the arguments against interracial marriage that resonate most powerfully with many women are not about simply their own relationships; they are about the black race too. And at the center of concerns about the race are black men. Black men struggle. We lack jobs, we lack education. We fill the prisons.

Black women witness these struggles and many of them do not want to abandon black men. As they succeed, they want to help. Even in their intimate relationships, they want to lift as they climb. And those black men who surmount the obstacles that overwhelmed others? Well, they inspire admiration and black women want them even more. So black women remain with black men. They are perhaps one of the most loyal groups of women in the world. Some imagine that by allying themselves with black men they can bolster the race.

But here's the rub: The same scarcity that is a mark of black men's disadvantage is also a source of power. Let's revisit the idea of the relationship market. We've seen that the central fact shaping the relationships of black men and women is the numbers imbalance. Recall that relationships are negotiations and that, as in any negotiation, which party prevails depends on the power that that person can bring to bear. One important source of power is the set of options that each party has outside of the relationship. The better one's options outside of the relationship, the more power one has within in. Because black men, successful ones in particular, are scarce and black women are not, black men wield greater power as they negotiate relationships with black women.

We have already seen that for African Americans the numbers imbalance contributes to a whole slew of racial disparities: herpes, HIV, unwed childbearing, abortion. And, of course, there is the central fact that animates my inquiry: that African Americans are now the most unmarried people in the nation. We marry less and divorce more. We have fewer enduring and committed relationships than any other group. The most blameless, our children, bear the consequences. Even middle-class black children lag far behind their white counterparts.

Black women's response to this state of affairs? Some black women redouble their commitment to black men. They hope to build a strong black family, to bolster the black community, to rebut lingering accusations of racial inferiority. What Annelise says for herself seems to capture the sentiment of many: "If I love black men, then I need to love a black man." It's a stirring call to action.

But the strategy hasn't worked so well. We remain unmarried, at odds with one another, our relationships crippled by a distrust that can only be described as extraordinary. More, the "stand by the black man" approach may worsen the very problems it intends to solve. To the extent that the problems of the black family stem from the numbers imbalance, black women's commitment to black men can actually undermine the black family that women hope to salvage. The more that black women limit themselves to black men, the more power black men gain.

So what would happen if more women followed the lead of Teresa and opened themselves to a relationship with a man outside of the race? In other words, how do women like Teresa shape the African American relationship market?

The first thing to see is that as black women marry men of other races, the numbers imbalance among single African Americans diminishes. For every one Teresa who marries outside of the race, the black gender imbalance becomes a little less severe. And as the imbalance shifts, so, too, does the power. Teresa's openness to exiting the segregated market, then, shifts the balance of relationship power, ever so slightly, in favor of black women. Even those women who remain committed to black men benefit from Teresa's willingness to cross the race line.

We arrive now at the paradox that is at the heart of the story I have told: If more black women married nonblack men, more black men and women might marry each other. If black women don't marry because they have too few options, and some black men because they have too many, then black women, by opening themselves to interracial marriage, could address both problems at once. For black women, interracial marriage doesn't abandon the race, it serves the race.

AFTERWORD

This book is the result of an intellectual journey that began not long after I joined the Stanford Law School faculty in 1998. My first substantial piece of legal scholarship, published that same year, examined the role of race in the adoption of children, and in particular how governmental policy undermined the welfare of black children by discouraging white couples from adopting them. That article joined two long-standing interests of mine: racial equality and discrimination on one hand, and families and children on the other. The article adhered rigidly to the norms of legal scholarship. It reviewed judicial decisions, explained the relevant statutory framework, assessed the research literature about transracial adoption, and then made a recommendation for policy reform.

When I began to plan this book, I knew I wanted to focus on the marriage decline among the black middle class. The near disappearance of marriage among the black poor had already attracted the attention of scholars and other commentators, but the middle-class marriage decline had received little attention. Part of my interest was intellectual and professional. But part of it was, admittedly, personal. After all, I am a member of the black middle class, and have witnessed firsthand the decline and fragility of marriage among that group. I couldn't help but wonder: Why? Why are affluent professional black men less likely than their white counterparts to be married? And why are black couples so much more likely than whites to divorce?

Eventually, the desire to make sense of the marriage decline among the black middle class began to overtake my desire to analyze and prescribe policy. The need to design effective government policy is important, but what I wanted to understand is how marriage is changing in the lives of black people. At this point, I think I was still planning to rely on the research literature, which emphasized the shortage of black men. After a couple of years of research, I had assembled a structure for the book. Interviews were not part of the plan; the voices that law professors usually listen to are those of judges, policy makers, or, of course, other law professors.

I began to interview people almost by accident. I had some vague sense that personal stories might enliven the text and broaden its appeal, but I didn't act on that impulse until some of the people to whom I mentioned this project—specifically black women—responded with an intensity of interest that startled me. Some of the women I spoke to seemed to want to tell their own story. The topic of the marriage decline among the black middle class seemed to strike a deep chord, to raise issues about which they had already given some thought. One woman told me that it sounded like this book would speak to her life in a way that none other had. So I began to conduct a few interviews.

I later decided to embark on an ambitious interview agenda. I wanted to interview middle-class black men and women across a wide age range, from young adulthood on up. Once I decided to interview people, it wasn't difficult to find participants. Interviewees came disproportionately from schools that I had attended, and more of them were lawyers than a random sample of the United States population would have yielded. I interviewed people from New York, Oakland, San Francisco, Los Angeles, Washington, D.C., Chicago, Cleveland, Atlanta, and Philadelphia. Nearly all of the interviews were in person. Most people were interviewed individually, although I did conduct some focus groups (two for women, and one for men) of four or five people at a time. Interviews lasted anywhere from thirty minutes (in only a few cases) to several hours (in most cases). Most interviews occupied an entire afternoon or evening. Interviews often occurred over the course of a meal, sometimes lunch or brunch but more typically a dinner. With a number of people, I conducted follow-up telephone interviews, usually to fill in a story or a thought that I realized they had not completed in our initial conversation. In total, approximately one hundred people were interviewed, some of them more than once.

Nearly all of the interviews were recorded and then transcribed. Any quotes that appear in the book are the actual words of the interviewees. The only liberties I have taken are those that are appropriate to convert spoken language into written language (e.g., "ums" and "ahs," and sentences that restart before finishing, have been eliminated). For the sake of readability, I don't use the ellipsis to indicate when language has been removed. In the text, I have also changed interviewees' names and any identifying details so as to preserve their anonymity, my promise to them in exchange for their willingness to share so freely and honestly the intimate details of their lives.

I initially planned to interview a comparable number of men and women, but it soon became clear that the women had much more to say about the topics I wanted to discuss. Men would answer questions, but women would answer and then elaborate at length. It seemed that for women the questions were ones they'd already been thinking about themselves. Maybe the women heard a biological clock ticking, while the men did not, or maybe the women were more comfortable than the men about opening up to a male interviewer about intimate aspects of their lives. Whatever the reason, women were much more forthcoming. I also found that the interviews with women in their late thirties and older were richer and more nuanced than interviews with younger women. Thus, I began to focus my interviews, and the book, on black women in their thirties and forties. As a result, the voices of men and of younger women are not well represented.

I cannot overstate the significance of the interviews in the evolution of this project. My conversations with black women transformed my vision for this book, as did their willingness to rethink their own lives. Their sense that their story had not been told was palpable. It was as though, for all their success, their lives remained invisible. I began to think of this book as a small effort to remedy that. No longer a social science project designed to evaluate alternative causes of the marriage decline, or even to systematically assess the consequences of the marriage decline, the book became more of an effort to illuminate a set of experiences that had been obscured, a casualty of attention that oscillates from the black poor to everyone else but rarely settles for long on the black middle class.

I hired two student assistants—one female African American law student, and one male African American undergraduate student—who interviewed their contemporaries. I discussed with my interview assistants a list of questions to ask and topics to cover. I told them to describe the project to interviewees just as I did, by saying that I was writing a book about the decline in marriage among African Americans and that I wanted interviews from people to learn about their dating experiences and views for potential inclusion in the book. For interviewees, we described the puzzles the book engages—why marriage has declined so much among African Americans and why black women, faced with a dearth of available black men, don't marry men of other races.

None of the interviewees were compensated (other than by my paying for the meal), although a few did joke at the end of our meeting, "How much do I owe you?"—a reference to their feeling that our discussion seemed more like a counseling session. I smiled and nodded, thinking that my wife was wrong that I wouldn't have been a good therapist (my career goal when I entered college). There was no checklist of information that I wanted to obtain. My goal wasn't to get specific questions answered. My questions were more open-ended, along the lines of "So, how do you feel about interracial dating?" or "What led to the end of that relationship?" or "Have you ever thought about . . . ?" I asked broad, open-ended questions because I wanted to give people a chance to explore issues and to feel free to talk at length. This was for my benefit—I wanted to get a sense of the person, not only their manner and demeanor, but how they saw the world. I didn't realize at the time how beneficial that opportunity was to my interviewees. They appreciated the opportunity to talk about matters that are crucially important in their lives but about which they don't feel as though they have space to talk. But the benefits of our discussion, for at least some of my interviewees, went beyond the chance to unload. For some, the interview was an opportunity to reengage with some issues that they had closed off; to think about some issues that they had not allowed themselves to confront in the deep and sustained manner that they did in our conversation. The best interviews were the ones in which the interviewees reexamined their own lives and discovered things about themselves in the course of the conversation. In these interviews, the women—who were typically in their late thirties or forties—weren't providing me with information as much as they were grappling with their own lives, reassessing past turning points that maybe hadn't appeared to be as important at the time. It was satisfying, I admit, to see people begin to step outside of the scripts that their younger selves had accepted unquestioningly but that now, and perhaps then, didn't fit their lives.

A number of the issues discussed in this book came directly from the interviews and were not initially a part of my project: marrying down, the stigma of unwed motherhood, the success gap between black women and men, the anxieties about having biracial children. These issues are featured in this book, but prior to my discussions with the women I interviewed, they were issues to which I was either oblivious or whose significance in the lives of black women I just didn't understand. These women transformed my views of the lives led by black women. As I heard similar stories from women who had never met one another, I began to see themes in their perspectives, to hear resonances across stories. I began to connect their experiences into a new story, one very different from the template with which I had started. Or more accurately, I allowed myself to accept the insights and growth that they were reaching themselves, the fruits of their own self-assessment. The stories that made it into the book are those that I heard from more than one person—not in their particulars, of course, but in their underlying substance—and that seemed to capture especially well a broader truth about the experiences that these women have had. Indeed, it was a revelation for me that stories that are unique are also universal, shared among women who confront a similar social and cultural terrain.

My primary goal in this book has been to try to understand and convey some of the truth of the lives of black women, to capture their life as they experience it. This is not a book where I supplement with personal stories the insights gleaned from the research literature. That's the way the project began, but it's not the way it ended. Instead, this is a book constructed from the bottom up, and from the top down. The social science evidence generated some of the questions I asked—for example, why don't black women intermarry as much as black men do, or what are the consequences of the marriage decline—but the women's stories provided a way to answer those questions from the ground up. I hope that the final product fuses those two sources of insight, and that it also highlights the interplay of social constraint and individual choice.

In keeping with the centrality of personal stories to this project, I invite readers to join an online conversation that explores further some of the many issues touched upon in these pages. Readers are welcome to share their own experiences, as well as to learn from those of others. Join the dialogue at www.ismarriageforwhitepeople.com.

ACKNOWLEDGMENTS

Although this book bears my name alone, I could not have completed it alone. Many people contributed, in varied ways, to my work on this project.

Stanford Law School has provided intellectual and material resources that have helped to bring this project to fruition. I have benefited from the leadership of three extraordinary deans—Paul Brest, Kathleen Sullivan, and Larry Kramer—and from a group of faculty colleagues who have unfailingly enriched and deepened my own thinking. Beyond the law school, I also received substantial support, intellectual and financial, from Stanford's Michelle R. Clayman Institute for Gender Research, under the able direction of Londa Schiebinger and, more recently, Shelley Correll. Stanford's Research Institute for Comparative Studies in Race and Ethnicity also provided a stimulating environment in which to discuss the issues explored in this book.

One of the greatest assets of Stanford University is the staff of the Robert Crown Law Library, under the direction of Paul Lomio. When I arrived at Stanford, I was awed that I could stop by the law library, request an obscure source with only the vaguest of information about it, and then find it in my e-mail by the time I reached my office. While the entire staff is exemplary, Erika Wayne, George Wilson, and Rich Porter deserve special thanks. Their expertise, cheerfulness, and willingness to help are unmatched.

I was fortunate to teach two courses devoted specifically to the intersection of race and marriage, one at Stanford Law School, and the other at the University of Virginia Law School at the invitation of Kim Forde-Mazrui, then the director of the Center for the Study of Race and Law. I also presented parts of this project at a number of institutions other than Stanford, including the University of Virginia Law School, the University of Michigan Law School, and the University of Minnesota Law School.

Prior to my arrival at Stanford, I was blessed to clerk for Judge Barrington D. Parker Jr., who is as honorable and thoughtful a man as he is a jurist, and to benefit from the intellectual guidance of two of my Harvard Law School professors, Randall Kennedy and Duncan Kennedy, each of whom remains a model of intellectual rigor and integrity.

Many friends and colleagues have helped this project along, by sending me relevant news stories, by offering words of support, or even simply by asking, "How's the book coming?" This group includes: Tom Adams, Allison Aldrich, Jan Barker-Alexander, Paul Butler, Prudence Carter, Eugene Clark-Herrera, Sonya Clark-Herrera, Daniel Coles, Greg Crossfield, Linda Darling-Hammond, John Donohue, Bill Gould, Lani Guinier, Sam Halteh, Jerry Harris, Odette Harris, Bruce Haynes, Chad Hurley, Cathy Clark-Hurley, Amalia Kessler, Mike Klausner, Raquiba LaBrie, Robin Lenhardt, Gary Malone, Hazel Markus, Sharon Meers, John Rickford, Jennifer Sandell, Syma Solovitch, Claude Steele, Dorothy Steele, Larry Stewart, Ewart Thomas, and Joya Wesley. Special thanks as well to the LaBrie family, who on two separate occasions hosted stimulating discussions about this project.

A number of friends and colleagues read an entire draft of this book and shared very useful detailed comments: Michael Wald, June Carbone, Paula England, Kim Forde-Mazrui, Greg Martin, and Rose Marie Krieder. Michael Wald and Kim Forde-Mazrui, in particular, not only helped me to refine specific arguments but contributed to the overall structure of the book. The manuscript benefited greatly from those who took the time to read some portion of it and to offer their thoughts: Anita Banks, Betsy Bartholet Bruce Haynes, Syma Solovitch, Myra Strober, David Hollinger, Deborah Rhode, Cecelia Ridgeway, and the other participants in the gender/race reading group.

One of the luxuries of academia, and of Stanford in particular, is the opportunity to encounter such talented and hardworking young people. Many marvelous students have contributed to this project. They include: Albert Gilbert, Mahlet Seyoum, Lori Wu, Hilary Bergsieker, Reid Shannon, Su Jin Gatlin, Lori Wu, Evan Jones, Jerome Jackson, Miishe Addy, J'vona Ivory, Molly Claflin, Stephanie Rudolph, and Laura Femino. These students amaze and inspire me with their energy.

As helpful as all these students have been, some deserve special mention. Molly Claflin provided extraordinary research and editorial support. Her ability to locate sources and track down information is astounding. She is so talented in so many ways that I remain in awe. Su Jin Gatlin motivated me with her own enthusiasm and conducted the original analyses of census data that first got this project off the ground. Reid Shannon entered toward the end of the process and expertly assembled the bibliography and checked to make sure that all the citations were correct.

Laura Femino provided extraordinary editorial assistance. She has read every word of this book with care. She has spotted gaps, contradictions, and ambiguities that I would have missed, and has consistently offered feedback that is both critical and constructive. The refinement of her editorial sensibility is matched only by her honesty. (I once suggested that her criticism of a portion of the text as "so academic it puts me to sleep" was a little too blunt, and she responded, "You have someone else to lie to you, don't you?")

Some of the people who figure most centrally in this book I cannot thank by name: the men and women I interviewed. Thank you for the hours you spent with me and your willingness to tell your stories. You have inspired me with your courage and candor.

Mary Ann Rundell, who did not live to see the publication of this book, provided superb administrative assistance. She transcribed interviews, cataloged them, and created a first draft of the bibliography. (Not to mention that I probably wouldn't have tenure if it weren't for Mary Ann, as she painstakingly entered changes to successive drafts of law review articles years ago.)

The staff at the United States Census Bureau, especially Rose Marie Krieder, has been more helpful than any citizen has a right to expect, by sending along reports they knew I'd be interested in and guiding me through some of the wealth of data they have collected about the United States population.

I am grateful to my colleague John Rickford for leading me to my agent, Noah Lukeman, who appreciates both the art and the commerce of publishing. I am convinced that there is no better literary agent anywhere than Noah Lukeman. I would have been lost without him. Noah has expertly guided me through what was at times an anxiety-inducing process. I am grateful to Noah for leading me to Dutton, where Brian Tart and Cherise Fisher believed in this book from the very beginning. As a first-time author, I value their support more than they probably realize. My own editorial process has required them to be patient, forgiving, and, importantly, stern. When Cherise was unable to see this project through to completion, Brian Tart assumed the reins and embraced this book as his own. He never lost sight of what this book could be. Thank you, thank you, thank you. Although Jess Horvath entered toward the end of the process, her editorial insight made the book even better. She has been more responsive than I ever imagined an editor could be. Thank you, Jess. In addition, the staff at Dutton has ably shepherded this manuscript to publication and helped to sell it. Christine Ball, Amanda Walker, and Liza Cassity have enabled this book to reach as many readers as possible. I deeply appreciate their efforts.

My deepest and most abiding thanks are for my own family. The Daniel clan is a good one and I am proud and thankful to be a part of it. I cannot imagine a more supportive extended family. Charles Ray Lowery, in particular, has gone to great lengths to help me bring this book into being. It is no overstatement to say that without the Daniel family behind me, I could not have written this book. And without my three sisters, Janet, Anita, and Sandy, I would not have made it this far. Sandy Banks is not only my sister; she is an immensely talented writer, who, even in the midst of her own work as a journalist, found time for this project and provided constructive and critical feedback. Her editorial insight is reflected throughout the book, and helped to make it much more readable than it otherwise would have been.

My wife, Jennifer Eberhardt, remains, even after all these years, the most brilliant and beautiful women I have ever met. She has put aside much of her own work as I completed this project, and patiently done more than her share to care for our children, especially during the many final months that I labored on this project. Not least, every morning, she made sure our three boys arrived at their three schools. She carried the load alone as I traveled the country to conduct interviews. She has also read many drafts of many chapters and provided unfailingly useful feedback. Who would have imagined that an elementary school mate could have become a life partner? My children—Ebbie, Everett, and Harlan—have been understanding as well. They have learned that when Daddy is not around he is probably "working on that book." My oldest son, who read some of the manuscript, has been among my harshest critics. As an eleven-year-old he didn't shy away from telling me, "Dad, why would you write about something so lame as marriage? Who would care about that?"

My greatest regret is that my parents are not here to share in this book's publication. It pains me to think how long they've been gone, but I take comfort that, at times, their spirits feel so near. In our short time together, my mother poured into me enough love to last a lifetime; my father blessed me with his unwavering belief in my abilities and ambitions. They made possible for me opportunities that their lives lacked.

PARTIAL BIBLIOGRAPHY

Books

Allen, Anita L. 2003. *Why Privacy Isn't Everything: Feminist Reflections on Personal Accountability.* Lanham: Rowman & Littlefield Publishers, Inc.

Amato, Paul R., and Alan Booth. 1997. *A Generation at Risk: Growing Up in an Era of Family Upheaval.* Cambridge: Harvard University Press.

Amato, Paul R., et al. 2007. *Alone Together: How Marriage in America Is Changing.* Cambridge: Harvard University Press.

Becker, Gary S. 1981. *A Treatise on the Family.* Cambridge: Harvard University Press.

Blackman, Lorraine, et al. 2005. *The Consequences of Marriage for African Americans: A Comprehensive Literature Review.* New York: Institute for American Values.

Bogle, Kathleen A. 2008. *Hooking Up: Sex, Dating, and Relationships on Campus.* New York: New York University Press.

Bowman, Cynthia Grant. 2010. *Unmarried Couples, Law, and Public Policy.* Oxford: Oxford University Press.

Boykin, Keith. 2005. *Beyond the Down Low: Sex, Lies, and Denial in Black America.* New York: Carroll & Graf Publishers.

Braman, Donald. 2002. "Families and Incarceration." In *Invisible Punishment: The Collateral Consequences of Mass Imprisonment,* edited by Marc Mauer and Meda Chesney-Lind, pp. 117–135. New York: The New Press.

Brand, Peg Z., ed. 2000. *Beauty Matters.* Bloomington: Indiana University Press.

Brinig, Margaret F. 2010. *Family, Law, and Community.* Chicago: University of Chicago Press.

Buchanan, Carla M., Eleanor E. Maccoby, and Sanford M. Dornbusch. 1996. *Adolescents after Divorce.* Cambridge: Harvard University Press.

Buss, David M. 1994. *The Evolution of Desire: Strategies of Human Mating.* New York: Basic Books.

Cahn, Naomi, and June Carbone. 2010. *Red Families v. Blue Families: Legal Polarization and the Creation of Culture.* New York: Oxford University Press.

Canary, Daniel J., Tara M. Emmers-Sommer, and Sandra Faulkner. 1997. *Sex and Gender Differences in Personal Relationships.* New York: Guilford Press.

Carbone, June. 2000. *From Partners to Parents: The Second Revolution in Family Law.* New York: Columbia University Press.

Caron, Simone M. 2008. *Who Chooses? American Reproductive History since 1830.* Gainesville: University Press of Florida.

Chapman, Audrey B. 1986. *Man Sharing: Dilemma or Choice.* New York: William Morrow & Co.

Chase-Lansdale, Lindsay P., and Jeanne Brooks-Gunn, eds. 1995. *Escape from Poverty: What Makes a Difference for Children?* New York: Cambridge University Press.

Chaudry, Ajay. 2004. *Putting Children First: How Low-Wage Working Mothers Manage Child Care.* New York: Russell Sage Foundation.

Cherlin, Andrew J. 2009. *The Marriage-Go-Round.* New York: Alfred A. Knopf.

Cherlin, Andrew J. 1992. *Marriage, Divorce, Remarriage* (Revised and Enlarged Edition). Cambridge: Harvard University Press.

Childs, Erica Chito. 2005. *Navigating Interracial Borders: Black-White Couples and Their Social Worlds.* New Brunswick: Rutgers University Press.

Clarke, Averil Y. 2011. *Inequalities of Love: College-Educated Black Women and the Barriers to Love, Marriage, and Family.* Durham: Duke University Press.

Clear, Todd R. 2007. *Imprisoning Communities: How Mass Incarceration Makes Disadvantaged Neighborhoods Worse.* New York: Oxford University Press.

Cleaver, Eldridge. 1968. *Soul on Ice.* New York: McGraw-Hill Book Co.

Collins, Patricia Hill. 2004. *Black Sexual Politics: African Americans, Gender, and the New Racism.* New York: Routledge.

Collins, Patricia Hill. 1990. *Black Feminist Thought: Knowledge, Consciousness, and the Politics of Empowerment,* 2nd edition. New York: Routledge.

Coontz, Stephanie. 2005. *Marriage, a History: How Love Conquered Marriage.* New York: Penguin Books.

Coontz, Stephanie. 1992. *The Way We Never Were: American Families and the Nostalgia Trap.* New York: Basic Books.

Covington, Jeanette. 2010. *Crime and Racial Constructions.* Lanham: Rowman & Littlefield Publishers, Inc.

Craig, Maxine Leeds. 2002. *Ain't I a Beauty Queen?: Black Women, Beauty, and the Politics of Race.* Oxford: Oxford University Press.

Davis, Peggy Cooper. 1977. *Neglected Stories: The Constitution and Family Values.* New York: Hill and Wang.

DePaulo, Bella. 2006. *Singled Out.* New York: St. Martin's Griffin.

Dey, Judy Goldberg, and Catherine Hill. 2007. *Behind the Pay Gap.* Washington, D.C.: American Association of University Women Educational Foundation.

Diamond, Lisa M. 2008. *Sexual Fluidity: Understanding Women's Love and Desire.* Cambridge: Harvard University Press.

Dornbusch, Sanford M., and Myra H. Strober, eds. 1988. *Feminism, Children, and the New Families.* New York: Guilford Press.

Du Bois, W. E. B. 1908. *The Negro American Family.* Georgia: Atlanta University Press.

duCille, Ann. 1996. *Skin Trade.* Cambridge: Harvard University Press.

Dunaway, Wilma A. 2003. *The African-American Family in Slavery and Emancipation.* Cambridge: Cambridge University Press.

Dychtwald, Maddy. 2010. *Influence: How Women's Soaring Economic Power Will Transform Our World for the Better.* New York: Hyperion.

Dyson, Michael Eric. 2005. *Is Bill Cosby Right? Or Has the Black Middle Class Lost Its Mind?* New York: Basic Civitas Books.

Edin, Kathryn, and Maria Kefalas. 2005. *Promises I Can Keep: Why Poor Women Put Motherhood before Marriage.* Berkeley: University of California Press.

England, Paula, and Kathyrn Edin, eds. 2007. *Unmarried Couples with Children.* New York: Russell Sage Foundation.

England, Paula, Emily Fitzgibbons Shafer, and Alison C. K. Fogarty. 2010. "Hooking Up and Forming Romantic Relationships on Today's College Campuses." In *The Gendered Society Reader,* 4th edition, edited by Michael Kimmel and Amy Aronson. New York: Oxford University Press.

Farley, Reynolds. 1984. *Blacks and Whites: Narrowing the Gap?* Cambridge: Harvard University Press.

Fineman, Martha Albertson. 1995. *Mothers in Law: Feminist Theory and the Legal Regulation of Motherhood.* New York: Columbia Press.

Fisher, Helen. 2004. *Why We Love: The Nature and Chemistry of Romantic Love.* New York: Henry Holt and Co.

Fisher, Helen. 1992. *Anatomy of Love: A Natural History of Monogamy.* Sydney: Simon & Schuster.

Foster, Frances Smith. 2010. *'Til Death or Distance Do Us Part.* New York: Oxford University Press.

Franklin, Donna L. 2000. *What's Love Got to Do with It?* New York: Simon & Schuster.

Franklin, Donna L. 1997. *Ensuring Inequality: The Structural Transformation of the African-American Family.* New York: Oxford University Press.

Franktz, Roger, Jim Gerber, and Harinder Singh, eds. 1990. *Handbook of Behavioral Economics,* Volume 2. Greenwich: JAI Press.

Gallagher, Maggie. 1996. *The Abolition of Marriage: How We Destroy Our Lasting Love.* Washington, D.C.: Regnery Publishing, Inc.

Garcia, Guy. 2008. *The Decline of Men.* New York: HarperCollins.

Gelles, Richard J., and Claire Pedrick Cornell. 1985. *Intimate Violence in Families.* Beverly Hills: Sage Publications.

Giddens, Paula. 1984. *When and Where I Enter: The Impact of Black Women on Race and Sex in America.* New York: Bantam Books.

Golden Marita, ed. 1993. *Wild Women Don't Wear No Blues.* New York: Doubleday.

Graff, E. J. 1999. *What Is Marriage For?* Boston: Beacon Press.

Grossbard-Shechtman, Shoshana. 1993. *On the Economics of Marriage: A Theory of Marriage, Labor, and Divorce.* Boulder: Westview Press.

Gutman, Herbert G. 1976. *The Black Family in Slavery and Freedom, 1750–1925.* New York: Pantheon Books.

Guttentag, Marcia, and Paul F. Secord. 1983. *Too Many Women? The Sex Ratio Question.* Beverly Hills: Sage Publications.

Hacker, Andrew. 2003. *Mismatch: The Growing Gulf between Men and Women.* New York: Scribner.

Hacker, Andrew. 1992. *Two Nations: Black and White, Separate, Hostile, Unequal.* New York: Ballantine Books.

Hanushek, Eric A., and Finis Welch, eds. 2006. *Handbook of the Economics of Education: Volume 1.* Amsterdam: North-Holland.

Hare, Julia. 1995. *How to Find and Keep a BMW: Black Man Working.* San Francisco: The Black Think Tank.

Harford, Tim. 2008. *The Logic of Life.* New York: Random House.

Hattery, Angela J., and Earl Smith. 2007. *African American Families.* Los Angeles: Sage Publications.

Haynes, Bruce. D. 2001. *Red Lines, Black Spaces: The Politics of Race and Space in a Black Middle-Class Suburb.* New Haven: Yale University Press.

Hernandez, Donald J. 1993. *America's Children: Resources from Family, Government, and the Economy.* New York: Russell Sage Foundation.

Hernton, Calvin C. 1966. *Sex and Racism in America.* New York: Grove Press.

Hewlett, Sylvia Ann. 2002. *Creating a Life: Professional Women and the Quest for Children.* New York: Talk Miramax Books.

Hite, Shere. 1987. *Women and Love: A Cultural Revolution in Progress.* Alfred A. Knopf.

Hollinger, David A. 1995. *Postethnic America: Beyond Multiculturalism.* New York: Basic Books.

Hooks, Bell. 2002. *Communion: The Female Search for Love.* New York: William Morrow.

Hooks, Bell. 2001. *Salvation: Black People and Love.* New York: HarperCollins Publishers.

Hymowitz, Kay S. 2006. *Marriage and Caste in America.* Chicago: Ivan R. Dee.

Jayakody, Rukmalie, Arland Thornton, and William Axinn, eds. 2008. *International Family Change: Ideational Perspectives.* New York: Lawrence Erlbaum Associates.

Jencks, Christopher. 1992. *Rethinking Social Policy: Race, Poverty, and the Underclass.* Cambridge: Harvard University Press.

Jencks, Christopher, and Paul E. Peterson, eds. 1991. *The Urban Underclass.* Washington, D.C.: Brookings Institution.

Jenkins, Candice. 2007. *Private Lives, Proper Relations: Regulating Black Intimacy.* Minneapolis: University of Minnesota Press.

Jiobu, Robert M. 1988. *Ethnicity and Assimilation.* Albany: State University of New York Press.

Jones, Edward. 2003. *The Known World.* New York: HarperCollins.

Jones, Stephanie J., ed. 2009. *The State of Black America 2009: Message to the President.* National Urban League.

Jones, Stephanie J., ed. 2007. *The State of Black America 2007: Portrait of the Black Male.* New York: National Urban League.

Jones, Stephanie J., and Julianne Malveaux, eds. 2008. *The State of Black American 2008: The Black Woman's Voice.* New York: National Urban League.

Kennedy, Randall. 2003. *Interracial Intimacies: Sex, Marriage, Identity, and Adoption.* New York: Pantheon Books.

Kimmel, Michael, and Amy Aronson, eds. 2010. *The Gendered Society Reader,* 4th Edition. New York: Oxford University Press.

Lacy, Karyn R. 2007. *Blue-Chip Black: Race, Class, and Status in the New Black Middle Class.* Berkeley: University of California Press.

Lamb, Michael E., ed. 2010. *The Role of the Father in Child Development.* Hoboken: John Wiley & Sons.

Landry, Bart. 2002. *Black Working Wives: Pioneers of the American Family Revolution.* Berkeley: University of California Press.

Laumann, Edward O., et al., eds. 2004. *The Sexual Organization of the City.* Chicago: University of Chicago Press.

Laumann, Edward O., and Robert T. Michael, eds. 1994. *Sex, Love, and Health in America: Private Choices, Public Policies.* Chicago: University of Chicago Press.

Laumann, Edward O., et al. 1994. *The Social Organization of Sexuality: Sexual Practices in the United States.* Chicago: University of Chicago Press.

Lerner, Gerda. 1973. *Black Women in White America: A Documentary History.* New York: Vintage Books.

Lorde, Audre. 1984. *Sister Outsider.* Freedom: The Crossing Press.

Luker, Kristin. 1996. *Dubious Conceptions: The Politics of Teenage Pregnancy.* Cambridge: Harvard University Press.

Mack, Dana. 1997. *The Assault on Parenthood: How Our Culture Undermines the Family.* New York: Simon & Schuster.

Mahony, Rhona. 1995. *Kidding Ourselves: Breadwinning, Babies, and Bargaining Power.* New York: Basic Books.

Mauer, Marc, and Meda Chesney-Lind, eds. 2002. *Invisible Punishment: The Collateral Consequences of Mass Imprisonment.* New York: New Press.

May, Elaine Tyler. 2010. *America and the Pill: A History of Promise, Peril, and Liberation.* New York: Basic Books.

Mayer, Susan E. 1997. *What Money Can't Buy: Family Income and Children's Life Chances.* Cambridge: Harvard University Press.

McAdoo, Harriette Pipes. 2007. *Black Families.* Thousand Oaks: Sage Publications.

McLanahan, Sara, and Gary Sandefur. 1996. *Growing Up with a Single Parent: What Hurts, What Helps.* Cambridge: Harvard University Press.

McMillan, Terry. 1996. *How Stella Got Her Groove Back.* New York: Viking Penguin.

Merida, Kevi, ed. 2007. *Being a Black Man at the Corner of Progress and Peril.* New York: Public Affairs.

Mincy, Ronald B., ed. 2006. *Black Males Left Behind.* Washington, D.C.: Urban Institute Press.

Miller, Ruth A. 2007. *The Limits of Bodily Integrity: Abortion, Adultery, and Rape Legislation in Comparative Perspective.* Aldershot, Hampshire, UK: Ashgate Publishing Ltd.

Moore, Robert M., III, ed. 2006. *African Americans and Whites: Changing Relationships on College Campuses.* Lanham: University Press of America, Inc.

Moore, Robert M., III, ed. 2002. *The Quality and Quantity of Contact: African Americans and Whites on College Campuses.* Lanham: University Press of America, Inc.

Moran, Rachel F. 2001. *Interracial Intimacy: the Regulation of Race and Romance.* Chicago: University of Chicago Press.

Morrison, Toni. 2000. *The Bluest Eye.* New York: Plume.

Morton, Patricia. 1991. *Disfigured Images: The Historical Assault on Afro-American Women.* Santa Barbara: Greenwood Press.

Moynihan, Daniel P., Timothy M. Smeeding, and Lee Rainwater, eds. 2004. *The Future of the Family.* New York: Russell Sage Foundation.

Murray, Charles. 1984. *Losing Ground: American Social Policy 1950–1980.* New York: Basic Books.

Neckerman, Kathryn, ed. 2004. *Social Inequality.* New York: Russell Sage Foundation.

Obama, Barack. 2006. *The Audacity of Hope: Thoughts on Reclaiming the American Dream.* New York: Crown Publishers.

Pascoe, Peggy. 2009. *What Comes Naturally: Miscegenation Law and the Making of Race in America.* New York: Oxford University Press.

Patillo, Mary, David F. Weiman, and Bruce Western, eds. 2004. *Imprisoning America: The Social Effects of Mass Incarceration.* New York: Russell Sage Foundation.

Patillo-McCoy, Mary. 2000. *Black Picket Fences: Privilege and Peril among the Black Middle Class.* Chicago: University of Chicago Press.

Patterson, Orlando. 1998. *Rituals of Blood: The Consequences of Slavery in Two American Centuries.* New York: Basic Civitas Books.

Patterson, Orlando. 1997. *The Ordeal of Integration: Progress and Resentment in America's "Racial" Crisis.* Washington, D.C.: Civitas/Counterpoint.

Perry, Theresa, Claude Steele, and Asa Hilliard III. 2003. *Young, Gifted, and Black: Promoting High Achievement among African-American Students.* Boston: Beacon Press.

Plant, Rebecca Jo. 2010. *Mom: The Transformation of Motherhood in Modern America.* Chicago: University of Chicago Press.

Popenoe, David, Jean Bethke Elshtain, and David Blankenhorn, eds. *Promises to Keep: Decline and Renewal of Marriage in America.* Lanham: Rowman & Littlefield Publishers, Inc.

Posner, Richard A. 1994. *Sex and Reason.* Cambridge: Harvard University Press.

Rainwater, Lee, and William L. Yancey. 1967. *The Moynihan Report and the Politics of Controversy.* Cambridge: MIT Press.

Regnerus, Mark D. 2007. *Forbidden Fruit: Sex & Religion in the Lives of American Teenagers.* New York: Oxford University Press.

Roberts, Dorothy. 1997. *Killing the Black Body: Race, Reproduction, and the Meaning of Liberty.* New York: Pantheon Books.

Romano, Renee C. 2003. *Race Mixing: Black-White Marriage in Postwar America.* Cambridge: Harvard University Press.

Quirk, Joe. 2006. *It's Not You, It's Biology: The Real Reason Men and Women Are Different.* Philadelphia: Running Press.

Schoen, Johanna. 2005. *Choice & Coercion: Birth Control, Sterilization, and Abortion in Public Health and Welfare.* Chapel Hill: University of North Carolina Press.

Schwartz, Pepper, and Virginia Rutter. 2000. *The Gender of Sexuality.* Walnut Creek: AltaMira Press.

Shanley, Mary Lydon. 2004. *Just Marriage.* New York: Oxford University Press.

Shapiro, Thomas M., and Melvin L. Oliver. 1996. *Black Wealth/White Wealth: A New Perspective on Racial Inequality.* New York: Routledge.

Smelser, Neil J., William Julius Wilson, and Faith Mitchell, eds. 2001. *America Becoming: Racial Trends and Their Consequences, Volume 1.* National Academies Press.

Smith, Lillian. 1949. *Killers of the Dream.* New York: W. W. Norton & Co.

Solinger, Rickie. 2005. *Pregnancy and Power: A Short History of Reproductive Politics in America.* New York: New York University Press.

Spickard, Paul. 1989. *Mixed Blood: Intermarriage and Ethnic Identity in Twentieth-Century America.* Madison: University of Wisconsin Press.

Stack, Carol. 1974. *All Our Kin.* New York: Basic Books.

Sullivan, Andrew. 1997. *Same-Sex Marriage: Pro and Con.* New York: Vintage Books.

Taylor, Robert Joseph, James Sidney Jackson, Linda M. Chatters, eds. 1997. *Family Life in Black America.* Thousand Oaks: Sage Publications.

Tommasi, Mariano, and Kathryn Ierulli, eds. *The New Economics of Human Behavior.* Cambridge: Cambridge University Press.

Travis, Jeremy, and Michelle Waul, eds. 2003. *Prisoners Once Removed: The Impact of Incarceration and Reentry of Children, Families, and Communities.* Washington, D.C.: Urban Institute Press.

Trimberger, E. Kay. 2005. *The New Single Woman.* Boston: Beacon Press.

Tucker, M. Belinda, and Claudia Mitchell-Kernan, eds. 1995. *The Decline in Marriage among African Americans.* New York: Russell Sage Foundation.

Tucker, M. Belinda, and Claudia Mitchell-Kernan. 1995. "Trends in African American Family Formation: A Theoretical and Statistical

Overview." In *The Decline in Marriage among African Americans,* edited by M. Belinda Tucker and Claudia Mitchell-Kernan, pp. 3–26. New York: Russell Sage Foundation.

Waite, Linda J., ed. 2000. *The Ties That Bind: Perspectives on Marriage and Cohabitation.* New York: Aldine de Gruyter.

Waite, Linda J., and Maggie Gallagher. 2000. *The Case for Marriage.* New York: Broadway Books.

Wallace, Michele. 1990. *Black Macho and the Myth of the Superwoman.* London: Verson.

Wallenstein, Peter. 2004. *Tell the Court I Love My Wife.* New York: Palgrave Macmillan.

Wallerstein, Judith S., Julia M. Lewis, and Sandra Blakeslee. 2000. *The Unexpected Legacy of Divorce.* New York: Hyperion.

Washington, Elsie B. 1996. *Uncivil War: The Struggle between Black Men and Women.* Chicago: Noble Press, Inc.

Welch, Susan, and John Gruhl. 1998. *Affirmative Action and Minority Enrollments in Medical and Law Schools.* Ann Arbor: University of Michigan Press.

Wilson, James Q. 2002. *The Marriage Problem: How Our Culture Has Weakened Our Families.* New York: HarperCollins Publishers.

Williams, Juan. 2006. *Enough: The Phony Leaders, Dead-End Movements, and Culture of Failure That Are Undermining Black America—and What We Can Do about It.* New York: Crown Publishers.

Wilson, William J. 2009. *More than Just Race: Being Black and Poor in the Inner City.* New York: W. W. Norton & Co.

Wilson, William J. 1996. *When Work Disappears.* New York: Alfred A. Knopf.

Wilson, William J. 1987. *The Truly Disadvantaged: The Inner City, the Underclass, and Public Policy.* Chicago: University of Chicago Press.

Wu, Lawrence L., and Barbara L. Wolfe, eds. 2001. *Out of Wedlock: Causes and Consequences of Nonmarital Fertility.* New York: Russell Sage Foundation.

Zamani-Gallaher, Eboni M., and Vernon C. Polite, eds. 2010. *The State of the African American Male.* East Lansing: Michigan State University Press.

Journal Articles

Adimora, Adaora A., Victor J. Schoenbach, and Irene A. Doherty. 2007. "Concurrent Sexual Partnerships among Men in the United States." *American Journal of Public Health* 97(12): 2230–2237.

Adimora, Adaora A., Victor J. Schoenbach, and Irene A. Doherty. 2006. "HIV and African Americans in the Southern United States: Sexual Networks and Social Context." *Sexually Transmitted Diseases* 33(7): S39–S45.

Adimora, Adaora A., and Victor J. Schoenbach. 2005. "Social Context, Sexual Networks, and Racial Disparities in Rates of Sexually Transmitted Infections." *Journal of Infectious Diseases* 191: S115–S122.

Adimora, Adaora A., et al. 2002. "Concurrent Sexual Partnerships among Women in the United States," *Epidemiology* 13(3): 320–327.

Albrecht, Carol Mulford, and Don E. Albrecht. 2001. "Sex Ratio and Family Structure in the Nonmetropolitan United States." *Sociological Inquiry* 71(1): 67–84.

Amaro, Hortensia. 1995. "Award Address: Love, Sex, and Power: Considering Women's Realities in HIV Prevention." *American Psychologist* 50(6): 437–447.

Amato, Paul R., and Juliana M. Sobolewski. 2004. "The Effects of Divorce and Marital Discord on Adult Children's Psychological Well-Being." *American Sociological Review* 66(6): 900–921.

Amato, Paul R. 2000. "The Consequences of Divorce for Adults and Children." *Journal of Marriage and the Family* 62: 1269–1287.

Anderson, John E. 2003. "Condom Use and HIV Risk among U.S. Adults." *American Journal of Public Health* 93(6).

Andrinopoulos, Katherine, Deanna Kerrigan, and Jonathan M. Ellen. 2006. "Understanding Sex Partner Selection from the Perspective of Inner-City Black Adolescents." *Perspectives of Sexual and Reproductive Health* 38(3): 132–138.

Aral, Sevgi O., Adaora A. Adimora, and Kevin A. Fenton. 2008. "Understanding and Responding to Disparities in HIV and Other Sexually Transmitted Infections in African Americans." *Lancet* 372: 337–340.

Attewell, Paul, et al. 2004. "The Black Middle Class: Progress, Prospects, and Puzzles." *Journal of African American Studies* 8(1): 6–19.

Banks, R. Richard. 2007. "The Aftermath of *Loving v. Virginia:* Sex Asymmetry in African American Intermarriage." *Wisconsin Law Review:* 533–542.

Batson, Christie D., et al. 2006. "Interracial and Intraracial Patterns of Mate Selection among America's Diverse Black Populations." *Journal of Marriage and Family* 68: 658–672.

Bellamy, Nikki D., et al. 2008. "Structural Model Analysis of HIV Risk Behaviors among Sexually Active Minority Adolescents." *Journal of the National Medical Association* 100(8): 914–924.

Bennett, Neil G., David E. Bloom, and Patricia H. Craig. 1989. "The Divergence of Black and White Marriage Patterns." *The American Journal of Sociology* 95(3): 692–722.

Bobo, Lawrence D., and Michael C. Dawson, eds. 2008. "The 'Work' of Race." *Du Bois Review: Social Science Research on Race* 5(1).

Bobo, Lawrence D., and Michael C. Dawson, eds. 2008. "The 'Work' of Race." *Du Bois Review: Social Science Research on Race* 5(2).

Bontempi, Jean M., Eugenia Eng, Sandra Course Quinn. 2008. "Our Men Are Grinding Out: A Qualitative Examination of Sex Ratio Imbalances, Relationship Power, and Low-Income African American Women's Health." *Women & Health* 48(1): 63–81.

Brien, Michael J. 1997. "Racial Differences in Marriage and the Role of Marriage Markets." *The Journal of Human Resources* 32(4): 741–778.

Bulcroft, Richard A., and Kris A. Bulcroft. 1993. "Race Differences in Attitudinal and Motivational Factors in the Decision to Marry." *Journal of Marriage and the Family* 55(2): 338–335.

Bumpass, Larry. 1984. "Children and Marital Disruption: A Replication and Update." *Demography* 21(1): 71–82.

Burnham, Margaret A. 1987. "An Impossible Marriage: Slave Law and Family Law." *University of Minnesota Journal of Law & Inequality* 5: 187.

Buss, David, and D. P. Schmidt. 1993. "Sexual Strategies Theory: An Evolutionary Perspective on Human Mating." *Psychological Review* 100: 204–232.

Butts, Samatha, and David B. Seifer. 2010. "Racial and Ethnic Difference in Reproductive Potential across the Life Cycle." *Fertility & Sterility* 93(3): 681–690.

Charles, Kerwin Kofi, and Ming Ching Luoh. 2010. "Male Incarceration, the Marriage Market, and Female Outcomes." *The Review of Economics and Statistics* 92(3): 614–627.

Chase-Lansdale, P. Lindsay, Andrew J. Cherlin, and Kathleen E. Kiernan. 1995. "The Long-Term Effects of Parental Divorce on the Mental Health of Young Adults: A Developmental Perspective." *Child Development* 66: 1614–1634.

Cherlin, Andew J. 2004. "The Deinstitutionalization of American Marriage." *Journal of Marriage and Family* 66(4): 848–861.

Cherlin, Andrew J. 1998. "Marriage and Marital Dissolution among Black Americans." *Journal of Comparative Family Studies*: 147–158.

Cherlin, Andrew J., P. Lindsay Chase-Lansdale, and Christine McRae. 1998. "Effects of Parental Divorce on Mental Health throughout the Life Course." *American Sociological Review* 63: 239–249.

Childs, Erica Chito. 2005. "Looking behind the Stereotypes of the 'Angry Black Woman': An Exploration of Black Women's Responses to Interracial Relationships." *Gender and Society* 19(4): 544–561.

Chun, Hyunbae, and Injae Lee. 2001. "Why Do Married Men Earn More: Productivity or Marriage Selection?" *Economic Inquiry* 39(2): 307–319.

Clarkwest, Andrew. 2007. "Spousal Dissimilarity, Race, and Marital Dissolution." *Journal of Marriage and Family* 69: 639–653.

Coltrane, Scott, and Michele Adams. 2003. "The Social Construction of the Divorce 'Problem': Morality, Child Victims, and the Politics of Gender." *Family Relations* 52: 363–372.

Crowder, Kyle D., and Stewart E. Tolnay. 2000. "A New Marriage Squeeze for Black Women: The Role of Racial Intermarriage by Black Men." *Journal of Marriage and the Family* 62: 792–807.

Dodge, Brian, William L. Jeffries IV, and Theo G. M. Sandfort. 2008. "Beyond the Down Low: Sexual Risk, Protection, and Disclosure among At-Risk Black Men Who Have Sex with Both Men and Women (MSMW)." *Archives of Sexual Behavior* 37: 683–696.

Doherty, Irene A., Victor J. Schoenbach, and Adaora A. Adimora. 2009. "Condom Use and Duration of Concurrent Partnerships among Men in the United States." *Sexually Transmitted Diseases* 36(5): 265–272.

Dundes, Alan. 1996. "Jumping the Broom: On the Origin and Meaning of an African American Wedding Custom." *The Journal of American Folklore* 109: 324–329.

Dunifon, Rachel, and Linda Kowaleski-Jones. 2002. "Who's in the House? Race Differences in Cohabitation, Single Parenthood, and Child Development." *Child Development* 73(4): 1249–1264.

Eastwick, Paul W., and Finkel, Eli J. 2008. "Sex Differences in Mate Preferences Revisited: Do People Know What They Initially Desire in a Romantic Partner?" *Journal of Personality and Social Psychology* 94(2): 245–264.

Edin, Kathryn, and Joanna M. Reed. 2005. "Why Don't They Just Get Married? Barriers to Marriage among the Disadvantaged." *The Future of Children* 15(2): 117–137.

Family Law Quarterly 41(3). 2007. "The Future of Marriage."

Feliciano, Cynthia Belinda Robnett, and Golnaz Komaie. 2009. "Gendered Racial Exclusion among White Internet Daters." *Social Science Research* 38: 39–54.

Finer, Lawrence B., and Stanley K. Henshaw. 2006. "Disparities in Rates of Unintended Pregnancy in the United States, 1994–2001." *Perspectives on Sexual and Reproductive Health*, 38(2): 90–96.

Fisman, Raymond, et al. 2007. "Racial Preferences in Dating." *Review of Economic Studies* 75(1): 117–132.

Fryer, Ronald G., Jr. 2007. "Guess Who's Been Coming to Dinner? Trends in Interracial Marriage over the 20th Century." *The Journal of Economic Perspectives* 21(2): 71–90.

Fujimoto, Victor Y., et al. 2010. "Racial and Ethnic Disparities in Assisted Reproductive Technology Outcomes in the United States." *Fertility and Sterility* 93(2): 382–390.

Fujimoto, Victor Y., et al. 2009. "Proceedings from the Conference on Reproductive Problems in Women of Color." *Fertility and Sterility* 94(1): 7–10.

The Future of Children 17(2). 2007. "The Next Generation of Antipoverty Policies."

The Future of Children 15(2). 2005. "Marriage and Child Wellbeing."

Gullickson, Aaron. 2006. "Black/White Interracial Marriage Trends, 1850–2000." *Journal of Family History* 31(3): 289–312.

Gupta, Geeta Rao, and Ellen Weiss. 1993. "Women's Lives and Sex: Implications for AIDS Prevention." *Culture, Medicine, and Psychiatry* 17: 399–412.

Hamilton, Darrick, Arthur H. Goldsmith, and William Darity Jr. 2009. "Shedding 'Light' on Marriage: The Influence of Skin Shade on Marriage for Black Females." *Journal of Economic Behavior & Organization* 72: 30–50.

Heaton, Tim B. 2002. "Factors Contributing to Increasing Marital Stability in the United States." *Journal of Family Issues* 23(3): 392–409.

Hill, Mark E. 2002. "Skin Color and the Perception of Attractiveness among African Americans: Does Gender Make a Difference?" *Social Psychology Quarterly* 65(1): 77–91.

Howard, Melissa M., ed. 2001. *The Virginia Journal of Social Policy and the Law* 9(1).

Huddleston, Heather G., et al. 2010. "Racial and Ethnic Disparities in Reproductive Endocrinology and Infertility." *American Journal of Obstetrics & Gynecology,* May: 413–419.

Hummer, Robert A., and Erin R. Hamilton. 2010. "Race and Ethnicity in Fragile Families." *The Future of Children* 20(2): 113–131.

Hunter, Margaret L. 2002. " 'If You're Light You're Alright': Light Skin Color as Social Capital for Women of Color." *Gender & Society* 16(2): 175–193.

Hunter, Margaret L. 1998. "Colorstruck: Skin Color Stratification in the Lives of African American Women." *Sociological Inquiry* 68(4): 517–535.

Ivy, Melissa, Valerie Newsome, and Ola Aroyewun. 2004. "Determinations of Transit from Marriage among African Americans." *Journal of Black Studies* 34(4): 532–547.

Jacobson, Cardell K., and Tim B. Heaton (2008). "Comparative Patterns of Interracial Marriage." *Journal of Comparative Family Studies.*

Jeynes, William. 2000. "A Longitudinal Analysis of the Effects of Remarriage Following Divorce on the Academic Achievement of Adolescents." *Journal of Divorce & Remarriage* 33(1/2): 131–148.

Journal of Blacks in Higher Education 67. 2010. "Vital Signs: Statistics That Measure the State of Racial Inequality."

Journal of Blacks in Higher Education 57. 2007. "African Americans Making Solid Gains in Bachelor's and Advanced Degrees: Black Women Far Out Ahead."

Kelly, Joan B., and Robert E. Emery. 2003. "Children's Adjustment Following Divorce: Risk and Resilience Perspectives." *Family Relations* 52: 352–362.

Kiecolt-Glaser, Janice K., and Tamara L. Newton. 2001. "Marriage and Health: His and Hers." *Psychological Bulletin* 127(4): 472–503.

Kim, Hyoun K., and Patrick C. McKenry. 2002. "The Relationship between Marriage and Psychological Well-Being." *Journal of Family Issues* 23(8): 885–911.

Koball, Heather L., et al. 2010. "What Do We Know about the Link between Marriage and Health?" *Journal of Family Issues* OnlineFirst: 1–22.

Korenman, Sanders, and David Neumark. 1991. "Does Marriage Really Make Men More Productive?" *The Journal of Human Resources* 26: 282–307.

Kurzban, Robert, and Jason Weeden. 2007. "Do Advertised Preferences Predict the Behavior of Speed Daters?" *Personal Relationships* 14: 623–632.

Lane, Sandra D., et al. 2004. "Marriage Promotion and Missing Men: African American Women in a Demographic Double Bind." *Medical Anthropology Quarterly* 18(4): 405–428.

Leichliter, Jami S., and Sevgi O. Aral. 2009. "Black Women in the United States Decrease Their Number of Recent Sex Partners: Temporal

Trends from the National Survey of Family Growth." *Sexually Transmitted Diseases* 36(1): 1–3.

Lester, David. 1996. "The Impact of Unemployment on Marriage and Divorce." *Journal of Divorce & Remarriage* 25(3/4): 151–153.

Lewis, Richard, and George Yancey. 1995. "Bi-Racial Marriages in the United States: An Analysis of Variation in Family Member Support of the Decision to Marry." *Sociological Spectrum* 15(4): 443–462.

Lichter, Daniel T., et al. 1992. "Race and the Retreat from Marriage: A Shortage of Marriageable Men?" *American Sociological Review* 57(6): 781–799.

Lichter, Daniel T., Felicia B. LeClere, and Diane K. McLaughlin. 1991. "Local Marriage Markets and the Marital Behavior of Black and White Women." *The American Journal of Sociology*, 96(4): 843–867.

Loh, Eng Seng. 1996. "Productivity Differences and the Marriage Wage Premium for White Males." *The Journal of Human Resources* 31: 566–589.

Marbley, Aretha Faye. 2003. "'Hey There Ms. Jones!': A Qualitative Study of Professional African American Males' Perceptions of the Selection of African American Females as Partners." *Journal of African American Studies* 7(3): 15–30.

Marsh, Kris, et al. 2007. "The Emerging Black Middle Class: Single and Living Alone." *Social Forces* 86(2).

Massey, Douglas S., and Robert J. Sampson, eds. 2009. "The Moynihan Report Revisited: Lessons and Reflections after Four Decades." *The Annals of the American Academy of Political and Social Science* 621(1).

Newman, Peter A., et al. 2008. "HIV Prevention for Black Women: Structural Barriers and Opportunities." *Journal of Health Care for the Poor and Underserved* 19: 829–841.

Nock, Steven L. 2001. "The Marriages of Equally Dependent Spouses." *Journal of Family Issues* 22(6): 756–777.

Oláh, Livia Sz., and Eva M. Bernhardt. 2008. "Sweden: Combining Childbearing and Gender Equality." *Demographic Research* 19: 1105–1144.

Orbuch, Terri L., et al. 2002. "Who Will Divorce: A 14-Year Longitudinal Study of Black Couples and White Couples." *Journal of Social and Personal Relationships* 19(2): 179–202.

Pedersen, Frank A. 1991. "Secular Trends in Human Sex Ratios: Their Influence on Individual and Family Behavior." *Human Nature* 2(3): 271–291.

Peterson, Richard R. 1996. "A Re-evaluation of the Economic Consequences of Divorce." *American Sociological Review* 61: 528–536.

Phillips, Julie A., and Megan M. Sweeney. 2006. "Can Differential Exposure to Risk Factors Explain Recent Racial and Ethnic Variation in Marital Disruption?" *Social Science Research* 35(2): 409–434.

Phillips, Julie A., and Megan M. Sweeney. 2005. "Premarital Cohabitation and Marital Disruption among White, Black, and Mexican American Women." *Journal of Marriage and Family* 67: 296–314.

Pienta, Amy Mehraban, Mark D. Hayward, and Kristi Rahrig Jenkins. 2000. "Health Consequences of Marriage for the Retirement Years." *Journal of Family Issues* 21(5): 559–586.

Pinderhughes, Elaine B. 2002. "African American Marriage in the 20th Century." *Family Process* 41(2): 269–282.

Porter, Margaret M., and Arline L. Bronzaft. 1995. "Do the Future Plans of Educated Black Women Include Black Mates?" *The Journal of Negro Education* 64(2): 162–170.

Previti, Denise, and Paul R. Amato. 2003. "Why Stay Married? Rewards, Barriers, and Marital Stability." *Journal of Marriage and Family* 65: 561–573.

Qian, Zhenchao. 1999. "Who Intermarries? Education, Nativity, Region, and Interracial Marriage, 1980 and 1990." *Journal of Comparative Family Studies* 30(4): 579–597.

Qian, Zhenchao, and Daniel T. Lichter. 2007. "Social Boundaries and Marital Assimilation: Interpreting Trends in Racial and Ethnic Intermarriage." *American Sociological Review* 72: 68–94.

Raley, R. Kelly, and Larry Bumpass. 2003. "The Topography of the Divorce Plateau: Levels and Trends in Union Stability in the United States after 1980." *Demographic Research* 8(8): 245–260.

Raley, R. Kelly, and Megan M. Sweeney. 2009. "Explaining Race and Ethnic Variation in Marriage: Directions for Future Research." *Race and Social Problems* 1(3): 132–142.

Roberts, D. E. 2004. "The Social and Moral Cost of Mass Incarceration in African American Communities." *Stanford Law Review* 56: 1271–1306.

Roberts, Dorothy. 2000. "Black Women and the Pill." Guttmacher Institute, *Family Planning Perspectives* 32(2).

Ross, Louie E. 1997. "Mate Selection Preferences among African American College Students." *Journal of Black Studies* 27(4): 554–569.

Smock, Pamela J., Wendy D. Manning, and Sanjiv Gupta. 1999. "The Effect of Marriage and Divorce on Women's Economic Well-Being." *American Sociological Review* 64(6): 794–812.

Sobotka, Tomáš, and Laurent Toulemon. 2008. "Overview Chapter 4: Changing Family and Partnership Behaviour: Common Trends and Persistent Diversity across Europe." *Demographic Research* 19: 85–138.

South, Scott J. 1995. "Do You Need to Shop Around? Age at Marriage, Spousal Alternatives, and Marital Dissolution." *Journal of Family Issues* 16(4): 432–449.

South, Scott J. 1993. "Racial and Ethnic Differences in the Desire to Marry." *Journal of Marriage and the Family* 55(2): 357–370.

South, Scott J., and Kim L. Lloyd. 1992. "Marriage Opportunities and Family Formation: Further Implications of Imbalanced Sex Ratios." *Journal of Marriage and the Family* 54(2): 440–451.

South, Scott J., and Katherine Trent. 1988. "Sex Ratios and Women's Roles: A Cross-National Analysis." *The American Journal of Sociology* 93(5): 1096–1115.

Stephen, Elizabeth Hervey, and Anjani Chandra. 2006. "Declining Estimates of Infertility in the United States: 1982–2002." *Fertility & Sterility* 86(3): 516–523.

Stevenson, Betsy, and Justin Wolfers. 2007. "Marriage and Divorce: Changes and Their Driving Forces." *Journal of Economic Perspectives* 21(2): 27–52.

Stevenson, Betsy, and Justin Wolfers. 2009. "The Paradox of Declining Female Happiness." *American Economic Journal* 1(2): 190–225.

St. Lawrence, Janet S., et al. 1998. "Factors Influencing Condom Use among African American Women: Implications for Risk Reduction Interventions." *American Journal of Community Psychology* 26(1): 7–28.

Sweeney, Megan M., and Julie A. Phillips. 2004. "Understanding Racial Differences in Marital Disruption: Recent Trends and Explanations." *Journal of Marriage and Family* 66: 639–650.

Sweeney, Megan M. 2002. "Two Decades of Family Change: The Shifting Economic Foundations of Marriage." *American Sociological Review* 67: 132–147.

Toulemon, Laurent, Ariane Pailhé, and Clémentine Rossier. 2008. "France: High and Stable Fertility." *Demographic Research* 19: 503–556.

Treas, Judith, and Deirdre Giesen. 2000. "Sexual Infidelity among Married and Cohabiting Americans." *Journal of Marriage and the Family* 62(1): 48–60.

Tucker, M. Belinda, and Claudia Mitchell-Kernan. 1998. "Psychological Well-Being and Perceived Marital Opportunity among Single African American, Latina, and White Women." *Journal of Comparative Family Studies* 29: 57–72.

Wade, Joel T., and Sara Bielitz. 2005. "The Differential Effect of Skin Color on Attractiveness, Personality Evaluations, and Perceived Life Success of African Americans." *Journal of Black Psychology* 31(3): 215–236.

Washington, Thomas Alex, Yan Wang, and Dorothy Browne. 2008. "Difference in Condom Use among Sexually Active Males at Historically Black Colleges and Universities." *Journal of American College Health* 57(4): 411–416.

Weisberg, Robert, and Joan Petersilia. 2010. "The Dangers of Pyrrhic Victories against Mass Incarceration." *Daedalus* 139(3): 124–133.

Wellons, Melissa F., et al. "Racial Differences in Self-Reported Infertility and Risk Factors for Infertility in a Cohort of Black and White Women: The CARDIA Women's Study." *Fertility and Sterility* 90 (2008): 1640–1648.

Western, Bruce, and Christopher Wildeman. 2009. "The Black Family and Mass Incarceration." *The Annals of the American Academy of Political and Social Science* 621: 221–242.

Whyte, James, Maria D. Whyte, and Eileen Cormier. 2008. "Down Low Sex, Older African American Women, and HIV Infection." *Journal of the Association of Nurses in AIDS Care* 19(6): 423–431.

Wildeman, Christopher. 2009. "Parental Imprisonment, the Prison Boom, and the Concentration of Childhood Disadvantage." *Demography* 46(2): 265–280.

Wingwood, Gina M., and Ralph J. DiClemente. 1998. "The Influence of Psychosocial Factors, Alcohol, Drug Use on African-American Women's High-Risk Sexual Behavior." *American Journal of Preventive Medicine* 15(1): 54–59.

Wolfinger, Nicholas H. 2003. "Parental Divorce and Offspring Marriage: Early or Late." *Social Forces* 82(1): 337–353.

Wood, Robert G. 1995. "Marriage Rates and Marriageable Men: A Test of the Wilson Hypothesis." *The Journal of Human Resources* 30: 163–193.

Yancey, George. 2009. "Crossracial Differences in Racial Preferences of Potential Dating Partners: A Test of the Alienation of African Americans and Social Dominance Orientation." *Sociological Quarterly* 50(1): 121–143.

Yancey, George. 2007. "Homogamy over the Net: Using Internet Advertisements to Discover Who Interracially Dates." *Journal of Social and Personal Relationships* 24: 913–930.

Zhang, Yuanting, and Jennifer Van Hook. 2009. "Marital Dissolution among Interracial Couples." *Journal of Marriage and Family* 71: 95–107.

Reports and Papers

Acemoglu, Daron, and David Autor. 2010. "Skills, Tasks, and Technologies: Implications for Employment and Earnings." National Bureau of Economic Research, *NBER Working Paper* No. 16082 (June 2010).

Angrist, Josh. 2000. "Consequences of Imbalanced Sex Ratios: Evidence from America's Second Generation." National Bureau of Economic Research, *NBER Working Paper* No. 8042. http://www.nber.org/papers/w8042.

Autor, David. 2010. "The Polarization of Job Opportunities in the U.S. Labor Market: Implications for Employment and Earnings." Center for American Progress and The Hamilton Project. Available at http://www.brookings.edu/papers/2010/04_jobs_autor.aspx.

Autor, David H., and David Dorn. 2009. "The Growth of Low-Skill Service Jobs and the Polarization of the U.S. Labor Market." National Bureau of Economic Research, *NBER Working Paper* No. 15150 (July 2009).

Bell, Nathan E. 2009. "Graduate Enrollment and Degrees: 1998–2008." Council of Graduate Schools. Available at http://www.cgsnet.org/Default.aspx?tabid=168.

Bernhardt, Eva. 2004. "Cohabitation or Marriage? Preferred Living Arrangements in Sweden." Accessed May 20, 2009. http://www.oif.ac.at/sdf/sdf04-04-bernhardt.pdf.

Bramlett, Matthew D., and William D. Mosher. 2002. "Cohabitation, Marriage, Divorce, and Remarriage in the United States." National Center for Health Statistics, *Vital Health Statistics* 23(22).

Bramlett, Matthew D., and William D. Mosher. 2001. "First Marriage Dissolution, Divorce, and Remarriage: United States." Centers for Disease Control and Prevention, Advance Data, No. 323.

Carroll, Joseph. 2007. "Most Americans Approve of Interracial Marriages" Gallup Poll, Aug. 16, 2007, Gallup News Service. Accessed June 9, 2009. http://www.gallup.com/poll/28417/Most-Americans-Approve-Interracial-Marriages.aspx

Centers for Disease Control and Prevention. 2010. "Seroprevalence of Herpes Simplex Virus Type 2 among Persons Aged 14–49 Years—United States, 2005–2008." *Morbidity and Mortality Weekly Report (MMWR)* 59(15).

Centers for Disease Control and Prevention. 2008. "HIV/AIDS among African Americans." CDC HIV/AIDS Fact Sheet. Available at http://www.aidsatwork.org/education/HIVAIDS%20Among%20African%20Americans.pdf.

Centers for Disease Control and Prevention, Division of STD Prevention. 2007. "Consultation to Address STD Disparities in African American Communities." Atlanta, Georgia, June 5–6, Meeting Report.

Cohen, Susan A. 2008. "Abortion and Women of Color: The Bigger Picture." *Guttmacher Policy Review* (GPR) 11(3).

CONSAD Research Corporation. 2009. "An Analysis of the Reasons for the Disparity in Wages between Men and Women." Final Report, Prepared for U.S. Department of Labor, Employment Standards Administration. Available at http://consad.com/index.php?page=

an-analysis-of-reasons-for-the-disparity-in-wages-between-men-and-women.

Davis, Jessica W., and Kurt J. Bauman. 2008. "School Enrollment in the United States: 2006." U.S. Census Bureau, *Current Population Reports* P20-559.

Digest of Education Statistics. 2009. "Table 204. Enrollment rates of 18- to 24-year-olds in degree-granting institutions, by type of institution and sex and race/ethnicity of student: 1967 through 2008." U.S. Department of Education, Institute of Education Science (IES). Accessed August 10, 2010. http://NCES.ed.gov/programs/digest/d09/tables/dt09_204.asp.

Digest of Education Statistics. 2009. "Table 295. First-professional degrees conferred by degree-granting institutions, by sex, race/ethnicity, and field of study: 2007–2008." U.S. Department of Education, Institute of Education Science (IES). Accessed August 10, 2010. http://nces.ed.gov/programs/digest/d09/tables/dt09_295.asp.

Dye, Jane Lawler. 2010. "Fertility of American Women: 2008." U.S. Census Bureau, *Current Population Reports* P20-563.

Dye, Jane Lawler. 2008. "Fertility of American Women: 2006." U.S. Census Bureau, *Current Population Reports* P20-558.

Ellwood, David T., and Christopher Jencks. 2004. "The Spread of Single-Parent Families in the United States since 1960." John F. Kennedy School of Government, Working Paper Series No. rwp04-008. http://web.hks.harvard.edu/publications/workingpapers/Index.aspx.

Fein, David J. 2004. "Married and Poor: Basic Characteristics of Economically Disadvantaged Couples in the U.S." *MRDC Working Paper.* http://www.mdrc.org/publications/393/workpaper.html.

Fullilove, Robert E. 2006. "African Americans, Health Disparities, and HIV/AIDS: Recommendations for Confronting the Epidemic in Black America." National Minority AIDS Council.

Fry, Richard. 2010. "The Reversal of the College Marriage Gap." Pew Research Center. A *Social & Demographic Trends Report.*

Fry, Richard, and D'Vera Cohn. 2010. "Women, Men and the New Economics of Marriage." Pew Research Center, *Social & Demographic Trends Report.* http://pewsocialtrends.org/pubs/750/new-economics-of-marriage.

Goldin, Claudia, and Lawrence F. Katz. 2009. "The Future of Inequality: The Other Reason Education Matters So Much." *Aspen Institute Congressional Program* 24(4): 7–14. Education Reform: Sixteenth Conference, August 17–22, 2009. Washington, D.C. http://dash.harvard.edu/handle/1/4341691.

Gruber, Jonathan. 2000. "Is Making Divorce Easier Bad for Children? The Long-Run Implications of Unilateral Divorce." National Bureau of Economic Research, *NBER Working Paper* 7968. http://www.nber.org/papers/w7968.

Guttmacher Institute. 2010. "Facts on Induced Abortion in the United States." http://www.guttmacher.org/pubs/fb_induced_abortion.html.

Haines, Michael R. 2002. "Ethnic Differences in Demographic Behavior in the United States: Has There Been Convergence?" National Bureau of Economic Research, *NBER Working Paper* 9042. www.nber.org/papers.w9042.

Hamilton, Brady E., and Stephanie J. Ventura. 2006. "Fertility and Abortion Rates in the United States, 1960–2002." *International Journal of Andrology* 29: 34–45.

Hitsch, Guenter J., Ali Hortaçsu, and Dan Ariely. 2006. "What Makes You Click? Mate Preferences and Matching Outcomes in Online Dating." MIT Sloan Research Paper No. 4603-06. Available at Social Science Research Network, www.ssrn.com.

Isaacs, Julia B., Isabel V. Sawhill, and Ron Haskins. 2008. "Getting Ahead or Losing Ground: Economic Mobility in America." The Brookings Institutions, Economic Mobility Project.

Jones, Rachel K., Lawrence B. Finer, and Susheela Singh. 2010. "Characteristics of U.S. Abortion Patients, 2008." Guttmacher Institute, www.guttmacherinstitute.org.

Kreider, Rose M. 2005. "Number, Timing, and Duration of Marriages and Divorces: 2001." U.S. Census Bureau, *Current Population Reports* P70-97.

Kreider, Rose M., and Jason M. Fields. 2002. "Number, Timing, and Duration of Marriages and Divorces: 1996." U.S. Census Bureau, Population Profiles: Dynamic Version. www.census.gov/population/www/pop-profile/files/dynamic/FamiliesLA.pdf.

Lewis, Sharon, et al. 2010. "A Call for Change: The Social and Educational Factors Contributing to the Outcomes of Black Males in Urban Schools." The Council of Great City Schools.

Livingston, Gretchen and D'Vera Cohn. 2010. "Childlessness Up among All Women; Down among Women with Advanced Degrees." Pew Research Center. A *Social & Demographic Trends Report.* http://pewsocialtrends.org/2010/06/25/childlessness-up-among-all-women-down-among-women-with-advanced-degrees/.

Livingston, Gretchen, and D'Vera Cohn. 2010. "The New Demography of American Motherhood." Pew Research Center. A *Social & Demographic Trends Report.* http://pewresearch.org/pubs/1586/changing-demographic-characteristics-american-mothers.

Martin, Steven P. 2004. "Growing Evidence for a 'Divorce Divide'? Education and Marital Dissolution Rates in the U.S. since the 1970s." Russell Sage Foundation Working Papers: Series on Social Dimensions of Inequality.

Martinez, Chandra A., et al. 2005. "Fertility, Family Planning, and Reproductive Health of U.S. Women: Data from the 2002 National Survey of Family Growth." National Center for Health Statistics, Vital and Health Statistics Series 23(25).

Mather, Mark, and Dia Adams. 2007. "The Crossover in Female-Male College Enrollment Rates." Population Reference Bureau. http://www.prb.org/Articles/2007/CrossoverinFemaleMaleCollegeEnrollmentRates.aspx.

McKinnon, Jesse. 2003. "The Black Population in the United States: March 2002." U.S. Census Bureau, *Current Population Reports* P20-541.

Morbidity and Mortality Weekly Report (MMWR). 2010. "Seroprevalence of Herpes Simplex Virus Type 2 among Persons Aged 14–49 Years—United States, 2005–2008." 59(15).

MMWR. 2005. "HIV Transmission among Black Women—North Carolina, 2004." 54(04): 89–94.

Mosher, William D., et al. 2005. "Sexual Behavior and Selected Health Measures: Men and Women 15–44 Years of Age, United States, 2002." National Center for Health Statistics, Advance Data from Vital and Health Statistics No. 362.

Moynihan, Daniel Patrick. 1965. "The Negro Family: The Case for National Action." Office of Policy Planning and Research, U.S. Department of Labor. http://www.dol.gov/oasam/programs/history/webid-meynihan.htm.

Nitsche, Natalie, and Hannah Brueckner. 2009. "Opting Out of the Family? Social Change in Racial Inequality in Family Formation Patterns and Marriage Outcomes among Highly Educated Women." Unpublished paper, presented at the annual meeting of the American Sociological Association (ASA), San Francisco, Calif., August.

Passel, Jeffrey S., Wendy Wang, and Paul Taylor. 2010. "Marrying Out: One-in-Seven New U.S. Marriages is Interracial or Interethnic." Pew

Research Center Publications. http://pewresearch.org/pubs/1616/american-marriage-interracial-interethnic.

Pazol, Karen, et al. 2009. "Abortion Surveillance—United States, 2006." CDC, *Morbidity and Mortality Weekly Report (MMWR),* Surveillance Summaries 58(SS08): 1–35.

Pettersson, Thorleiff. 2003. "Basic Values and Civic Education: A Comparative Analysis of Adolescent Orientations towards Gender Equality and Good Citizenship." World Values Survey. http://www.worldvaluessurvey.com/library/latestpub.asp.

Pettifor, Audrey E., et al. 2004. "Sexual Power and HIV Risk, South Africa." International Conference on Women and Infectious Diseases, *Emerging Infectious Diseases* 10(11).

The Pew Forum on Religion and Public Life. 2009. "A Religious Portrait of African Americans." Pew Research Center. Accessed August 13, 2010. http://pewforum.org/A-Religious-Portrait-of-African-Americans.aspx.

Pew Research Center Report. 2010. "A Year after Obama's Election, Blacks Upbeat about Black Progress." *Social & Demographic Trends Report.* http://pewsocialtrends.org/pubs/749/blacks-upbeat-about-black-progress-obama-election.

Pew Research Center Report. 2006. "Guess Who's Coming to Dinner." *Social & Demographic Trends Report.* Accessed on July 23, 2009. http://pewsocialtrends.org/pubs/304/guess-whos-coming-to-dinner.

Pollak, Robert A. 2005. "Bargaining Power in Marriage: Earnings, Wage Rates and Household Production." http://apps.olin.wustl.edu/faculty/pollak/barg%20power%20mar%2005.pdf.

Provasnik, Stephen, and Linda L. Shafer. 2004. "Historically Black Colleges and Universities, 1976 to 2001." National Center for Education Statistics (NCES) 2004-062.

Rawlings, Steve W., and Arlene F. Saluter. 1995. "Household and Family Characteristics: March 1994." U.S. Census Bureau, *Current Population Reports* P20-483.

Rector, Robert E., Melissa G. Pardue, and Lauren R. Noyes. 2003. "'Marriage Plus': Sabotaging the President's Efforts to Promote Healthy Marriage." The Heritage Foundation, Backgrounder #1677. http://www.heritage.org/Research/Reports/2003/08/Marriage-Plus-Sabotaging-the-Presidents-Efforts-to-Promote-Healthy-Marriage.

Rodgers, William M., III, and Leslie S. Stratton. 2005. "The Male Marital Wage Differential: Race, Training, and Fixed Effects." Institute for the Study of Labor (IZA), Discussion Paper No. 1745.

Ruggles, Steven, et al. 2004. "Integrated Public Use Microdata Series: Version 3.0." Available at http://usa.ipums.org/usa/.

Sitgraves, Claudia. 2008. "The Benefits of Marriage for African American Men." Institute for American Values, Center for Marriage and Families, Research Brief No. 10.

Spraggins, Renee E. 2005. "We the People: Women and Men in the United States." U.S. Census Bureau, Census 2000 Special Reports.

Taylor, Paul, Cary Funk, and April Clark. 2007. "As Marriage and Parenthood Drift Apart, Public Is Concerned about Social Impact." Pew Research Center, *Social & Demographic Trends Report.* http://pewresearch.org/pubs/526/marriage-parenthood.

U.S. Census Bureau. 2010. "The Black Alone Population in the United States: 2008." Current Population Survey Reports. http://www.census.gov/population/www/socdemo/race/black.html.

U.S. Census Bureau. 2005. "America's Families and Living Arrangements: 2004." Current Population Survey. http://www.census.gov/population/www/socdemo/hh-fam/cps2004.html.

U.S. Census Bureau, Population Division, Fertility & Family Statistics Branch. 2004. "America's Families and Living Arrangements: 2004." Current Population Survey. http://www.census.gov/population/www/socdemo/hh-fam/cps2004.html.

U.S. Census Bureau. 2006. "School Enrollment—Social and Economic Characteristics of Students: October 2006." Current Population Survey. http://www.census.gov/population/www/socdemo/school/cps2006.html.

U.S. Census Bureau. 2009. "Births, Deaths, Marriages, and Divorces: Births." The 2009 Statistical Abstract: The National Data Book. Available at http://www.census.gov/compendia/statab/2009/cats/births_deaths_marriages_divorces.html.

U.S. Department of Health and Human Services. 2007. "Table 8. Temporary Assistance of Needy Families—Active Cases. Percent Distribution of TANF Families by Ethnicity/Race October 2005–September 2006." Office of Family Assistance. Accessed July 22, 2009. http://www.acf.hhs.gov/programs/ofa/character/FY2006/tab08.htm.

U.S. Department of Justice Bureau of Justice Statistics, Criminal Offender Statistics. Accessed June 23, 2009. http://www.bjs.ojp.usdoj.gov.

U.S. Department of Labor. 2010. "Labor Force Characteristics by Race and Ethnicity, 2009." U.S. Bureau of Labor Statistics, Report 1026.

U.S. Department of Labor. 2010. "Highlights of Women's Earnings in 2009." U.S. Bureau of Labor Statistics, Report 1025.

U.S. Department of Labor, Office of Policy Planning and Research. 1965. "The Negro Family: The Case for National Action." Available at http://www.dol.gov/oasam/programs/history/webid-meynihan.htm.

U.S. Department of Justice, Bureau of Justice Statistics, Prison Statistics (June 30, 2008), Accessed June 23, 2009. http://www.bjs.ojp.usdoj.gov.

Ventura, Stephanie J., et al. 2009. "Estimated Pregnancy Rates by Outcome for the United States, 1990–2004." National Center for Health Statistics, *National Vital Statistics Reports* 58(4).

Ventura, Stephanie J., et al. 2008. "Estimated Pregnancy Rates by Outcome for the United States, 1990–2004." National Center for Health Statistics, *National Vital Statistics Reports* 56(15).

Ventura, Stephanie J., et al. 2009. "Estimated Pregnancy Rates for the United States, 1990–2005: An Update." National Center for Health Statistics, *National Vital Statistics Reports* 58(4).

Wei, Shang-Jin, and Xiaobo Zhang. 2009. "The Competitive Saving Motive: Evidence from Rising Sex Ratios and Savings Rates in China." National Bureau of Economic Research, *NBER Working Paper* 15093. http://www.nber.org/papers/w15093.

West, Heather C., and William J. Sabol. 2008. U.S. Department of Justice, Bureau of Justice Statistics, "Prison Inmates at Midyear 2008—Statistical Tables," Table 19 (June 20, 2000–2008).

Winslow, Sarah. 2004. "She Earns, He Earns: Exploring Race and Class Variation in Wives' Contributions to Couples' Income." Population Association of America Annual Meeting, Philadelphia, PA, March-April 2005.

Wood, Robert G., Brian Goesling, and Sarah Avellar. 2007. "The Effects of Marriage on Health: A Synthesis of Recent Research Evidence." Prepared for the Department of Health and Human Services by Mathematica Policy Research, Inc. Available at http://aspe.hhs.gov/hsp/07/marriageonhealth/index.htm.

Xu, Jiaquan, et al. 2010. "Death: Final Data for 2007." National Center for Health Statistics, *National Vital Statistics Reports* 58(19).

Newspaper and Magazine Articles

Alexander, Brian. 2009. "Why Marriage Seems to Skip High-Achieving Black Women: Many Go through Life Single and Childless." *Black Christian News,* Blackchristiannews.com, August 17.

Alexander, Brian. 2009. "Marriage Eludes High-Achieving Black Women." MSNBC.com, August 13.

Allen, John L., Jr. 2008. "Slavery Comparisons on the Rise in Pro-Life Rhetoric." *National Catholic Reporter,* December 26.

Amber, Jeannine. 2003. "A Player 'Fesses Up." *Essence,* August.

Amber, Jeannine. 1998. "Somebody Else's Guy." *Essence,* February.

Bair, Deirdre. 2010. "The 40-Year Itch." *New York Times,* June 3.

Bambara, Toni Cade. 1973. "Black Woman/Black Man: Closer Together or Further Apart . . . Compared to What?" *Essence,* October.

Banks, Ralph Richard. 2010. "The Soulmate Factor." *New York Times,* Room for Debate Blog: "Divorce: It's Not Always about You," June 4.

Benen, Steve. 2010. "GOP Rep: Blacks Better Off under Slavery." *Washington Monthly,* Political Animal, February 27.

Blake, John. 2009. "Single Black Women Choosing to Adopt." CNN.com, July 1. http://www.cnn.com/2009/LIVING/07/01/bia.single.black.women.adopt/index.html.

Blow, Charles M. 2010. "Abortion's New Battle Lines." *New York Times,* May 1.

Blow, Charles M. 2008. "The Demise of Dating." *New York Times,* December 13.

Boo, Katherine. 2003. "The Marriage Cure: Is Wedlock Really a Way Out of Poverty?" *New Yorker,* August 18 and 25.

Bowman, Bobbi. 2010. "The (Poor) State of Black Families." Theroot.com, March 2.

Campbell, Bebe Moore. 1992. "Brothers and Sisters." *New York Times Magazine,* August 23.

Chambers, Veronica. 2010. "I'm Her Mother, Not Her Nanny." *Essence,* June.

Cherlin, Andrew J. 2010. "The Risks Men Take." *New York Times,* Room for Debate Blog: "Divorce: It's Not Always about You," June 4.

Cheshire, Godfrey. 1995. "Waiting to Exhale." *Variety,* Reviews, December 18.

Childs, Dan, and Carla Williams. 2007. "One in 10 Men Has Multiple Sex Partners." ABC News Medical Unit, ABCNews.go.com, October 30.

Clark-Flory, Tracy. 2010. "Banning Race-Based Abortions Is Wrong." Salon.com, March 11.

Coates, Ta-Nehisi. 2008. "This Is How We Lost to the White Man." *Atlantic,* May.

Cody, Edward. 2009. "Straight Couples in France Are Choosing Civil Unions Meant for Gays." *Washington Post,* February 14.

Cole, Harriette. 2009. "Real Love: What We All Crave . . . What Barack and Michelle Obama Have." *Ebony,* February.

Connolly, Katie. 2009. "That's One Classy Mom." *Newsweek,* May 11/18.

Cooper, Helene. 2009. "President Delivers Exhortation to Fathers." *New York Times,* June 20.

Cose, Ellis. 2003. "The Black Gender Gap." *Newsweek,* March 3.

Depass, Dee. 2006. "Looking for Mr. White." *Essence,* May 15.

Dewan, Shaila. 2010. "To Court Blacks, Foes of Abortion Make Racial Case." *New York Times,* February 26.

Dewan, Shaila. 2010. "Anti-Abortion Ads Split Atlanta." *New York Times,* February 6.

Dickerson, Debra J. 2003. "Post-Ghetto Fabulous: Coming to Grips with Black Women's Success." *Washington Monthly,* April.

DuBois, W. E. B. 1897. "Strivings of the Negro People." *Atlantic Monthly,* August.

Duke, Lynne, and Teresa Wiltz. 2005. "Katrina Blew In, and Tossed Up Reminders of a Tattered Racial Legacy." *Washington Post,* September 4.

Dvorak, Petula. 2010. "Bringing Home More Bacon, Still Cleaning the Pan." *Washington Post,* January 19.

Ebert, Roger. 1995. "Waiting to Exhale." *Sun Times,* Reviews, December 22. http://rogerebert/suntimes.com.

Eckholm, Erik. 2006. "Plight Deepens for Black Men, Studies Warn." *New York Times,* March 20.

The Economist. 2010. "The Worldwide War on Baby Girls." March 6.

The Economist. 2010. "Haryana's Lonely Bachelors." March 6.

The Economist. 2010. "Sex and the Single Black Woman: How the Mass Incarceration of Black Men Hurts Black Women." Lexington, April 8.

The Economist. 2010. "The Family in Figures: Men and Marriage." January 30.

The Economist. 2007. "Marriage in America: The Frayed Knot." May 24.

Edwards, Audrey. 2003. "Catch Him If You Can." *Essence,* September.

Ertelt, Steven. 2010. "Congressman Says Abortion More Devastating Than Slavery for Black Americans." Lifenews.com, February 26.

Ertelt, Steven. 2008. "New Report Finds Black, Older, Poor Women More Likely to Have Abortions." Lifenews.com, September 23.

Fields, C. Virginia. 2008. "Ending AIDS in Black America: 'Yes, We Can.'" *New York Amsterdam News,* November 27–December 3.

Fischer, Shell. 2010. "The Hush on Abortion." *In These Times,* April 9.

Fullilove, Robert, Adaora Adimora, and Peter Leone. 2008. "An Epidemic No One Wants to Talk About." *Washington Post,* March 21.

Gerson, Kathleen. 2010. "Uncharted Territory." *New York Times,* Room for Debate Blog: "Divorce: It's Not Always about You," June 4.

Gibbs, Nancy, and Michael Scherer. 2009. "The Meaning of Michelle Obama." *Time,* May 21.

Gilliam, Melissa. 2008. "Health-Care Inequality Is Key in Abortion Rates." Philly.com, August 10.

Grigoriadis, Vanessa. 2008. "Black & Blacker: The Racial Politics of the Obama Marriage." *New York Magazine,* August 10.

Guthmann, Edward. 1996. "'Waiting to Exhale' Mostly Sputters." SFGate.com, April 26.

Harris, Hamil R. 2004. "Some Blacks Find Nuggets of Truth in Cosby's Speech." *Washington Post,* May 26.

Harris-Lacewell, Melissa. 2010. "A Right to Life for the Living." *Nation,* April 15.

Hill, Dionne. 2008. "Black and Single: Is Marriage Really for White People?" CNN.com, July 22.

Hilton, Shani O. 2010. "Black Women Don't Need Billboards." *The American Prospect,* February 24.

Hoffman, Jan. 2009. "If They Can Find Time for Date Night . . ." *New York Times,* June 7.

Holden, Stephen. 1995. "Film Review: Divas Have Lots of Fun Telling Off Mr. Wrong." *New York Times,* December 22.

Hughes, Zondra. 2003. "Why Some Brothers Only Date Whites and 'Others.'" *Ebony,* January.

Hulse, Carl. 2009. "Obama Is Sworn In as the 44th President." *New York Times,* January 21.

Hurley, Dan. 2005. "Divorce Rate: It's Not as High as You Think." *New York Times,* April 19.

In Touch. 2009. "We Work at It Every Day." April 27.

Jackson, Susan. 2009. "Michelle Obama: A Charismatic Leader?" Washingtonpost.com, April 7.

Jaschik, Scott. 2005. "The Missing Black Men." *Inside Higher Ed,* December 5. http://www.insidehighered.com/news/2005/12/05/blackmale.

Jayson, Sharon. 2010. "In Economics of Marriage, Men Hit Jackpot." *USA Today,* January 19.

Johnson, Pamela K. 2004. "Men, Women, and the New Power Gap." *Essence,* June.

Jones, Charisse. 2003. "Somebody Else's Guy." *Essence,* November.

Jones, Joy. 2006. "Marriage Is for White People." *Washington Post,* March 26.

Jones, Vanessa E. 2006. "Younger Blacks Absorb a Wariness of Marriage." *Boston Globe,* August 9.

July, William. 2004. "The Confessions of an Ex-Bachelor." *Essence,* October.

Kalb, Claudia. 2009. "No Rest for an AIDS Veteran." *Newsweek,* April 6.

Kane, Eugene. 2004. "Cosby Didn't Let Down City; Let's Not Disappoint Him." *Milwaukee Journal Sentinel,* October 21.

Kantor, Jodi. 2009. "The First Marriage." *New York Times Magazine,* November 1.

Kantor, Jodi. 2009. "Nation's Many Faces in Extended First Family." *New York Times,* January 1.

Kinnon, Joy Bennett. 2003. "The Shocking State of Black Marriage: Experts Say Many Will Never Get Married." *Ebony,* November.

Krattenmaker, Tom. 2010. "Abortion's Middle Ground? Reducing Them." *USA Today,* updated May 2.

LaFraniere, Sharon. 2009. "Chinese Bias for Baby Boys Creates a Gap for 32 Million." *New York Times,* April 10.

Lamb, Yanick Rice, and Brenda Wade. 1996. "Single and Satisfied." *Essence.*

Lewin, Tamar. 2006. "At Colleges, Women Are Leaving Men in the Dust." *New York Times,* July 9.

Lyons, Douglas C. 1993. "Where the Men Are: The 10 Best Cities." *Ebony,* July.

Malveaux, Julianne. 1970. "Blacklove Is . . . A Bitter/Sweetness." *Essence,* College Essay Contest Winner, August.

McGreal, Chris. 2010. "Marriage in America: Who's the Big Earner Now?" *The Guardian* (London), January 20.

Montini, E. J. 2010. "Franks Equates Abortion with Slavery—Really." *Arizona Republic,* March 7.

Ms. magazine. 2010. "Victory against Georgia Anti-Choice Bill." Feminist Wire Newsbriefs, May 3.

Ndibo, Judy Amunga. 2009. "The Look of Love." *New African Woman,* February.

Norton, Amy. 2007. "Concurrent Sex Partners Not Uncommon for U.S. Men." Reuters, October 30.

Noveck, Jocelyn. 2009. "Obama Marriage Inspires Fascination, Imitation." Associated Press, February 12.

Offner, Paul. 2002. "What's Love Got to Do with It? Why Oprah's Still Single—Society and Opportunities for African American People." *Washington Monthly,* March.

O'Neill, Joseph. 2009. "Democracy and Its Discontents: Why We Crave a Royal Michelle—and Why We Shouldn't." *New York Magazine,* March 23.

Osunsami, Steve. 2010. "Abortion Billboards: Strong Words Spark Debate in Atlanta's Black Neighborhoods." ABCNews.com, February 22.

Parker-Pope, Tara. 2009. "Divorce, It Seems, Can Make You Ill." *New York Times,* August 3.

Peck, Don. 2010. "How a New Jobless Era Will Transform America." *Atlantic,* March.

Pope, Justin. 2009. "Under a Third of Men at Black Colleges Earn Degree in 6 Years." *USA Today,* March 30.

Porter, Eduardo. 2009. "Tales of Republicans, Bonobos, and Adultery." *New York Times,* July 3.

Powell, Michael, and Jodi Kantor. 2008. "After Attacks, Michelle Obama Looks for a New Introduction." *New York Times,* June 18.

Raspberry, William. 2005. "Why Our Black Families Are Failing." Washingtonpost.com, July 25.

Regnerus, Mark. 2009. "The Problem with Idealizing Marriage." *New York Times,* Room for Debate Blog: "A New Trend in Motherhood," May 17.

Roberts, Sam. 2010. "Black Women See Fewer Black Men at the Altar." *New York Times,* June 3.

Roberts, Sam. 2010. "In Education and Income, U.S. Women Move Ahead Faster Than Their Mates." *International Herald Tribune,* January 21.

Roberts, Sam. 2010. "More Men Marrying Better Educated, Wealthier Wives." *New York Times,* January 19.

Roberts, Sam. 2008. "Two-Parent Black Families Showing Gains." *New York Times,* December 17.

Romano, Andrew. 2009. "Our Model Marriage." *Newsweek,* February 23.

Rosin, Hanna. 2010. "The End of Men." *Atlantic,* July/August.

Saletan, William. 2010. "Black Death: The Selective Crusade against Black Women's Abortions." Slate.com, March 8.

Samuels, Adrienne P. 2007. "Will I Ever Get Married? (Do I Really Want To?)" *Ebony,* April.

Samuels, Allison. 2008. "What Michelle Means to Us." *Newsweek,* December 1.

Samuels, Allison. 2006. "She's Gotta Have Him: A Woman Agonizes about Race in 'Something New.'" *Newsweek* (Movie Review), January 30.

Scott, A. O. 2005. "Shedding Racial Prejudices, but Not Old Ideas of Virtue." *New York Times,* March 25.

Scott, Jill. 2010. "Commentary: Jill Scott Talks Interracial Dating." *Essence,* April.

Scott, Megan K. 2009. "Women Seeking: A Man Like Barack Obama." *Associated Press,* June 17.

Senior, Jennifer. 2009. "Regarding Michelle Obama: The Many Meanings of a New American Icon." *New York Magazine,* March 23.

Singletary, Michelle. 2010. "Wealth and Marriage." *Boston Globe,* January 21.

Singletary, Michelle. 2010. "Higher Earners Tend to Have Diplomas and Rings." *Washington Post,* January 21.

Singletary, Michelle. 2005. "Debunking Cosby on Blacks." *Washington Post,* November 13.

Smith, Taigi. 2005. "The New Man Sharing." *Essence,* January.

Stevenson, Betsey. 2010. "Divorce in the Golden Years." *New York Times,* Room for Debate Blog: "Divorce: It's Not Always about You," June 4.

St. George, Donna. 2010. "More Wives Are the Higher-Income Spouse." *Washington Post,* January 19.

Stone, Robin D. 2005. "The State of Our Unions: A Snapshot of Marriage in Black America." *Essence,* August.

Suggs, Ernie. 2010. "Senate Abortion Bill Continues to Stir Emotions." *Atlanta Journal-Constitution,* April 6.

Taylor, Susan L. 2004. "Fearless Love." *Essence,* In the Spirit, November 20.

Taylor, Susan L. 2003. "A Love Worth Giving." *Essence,* In the Spirit, November 22.

Tucker, Cynthia. 2008. "The Obamas Can Be Model for Marriage." *Atlanta Journal-Constitution,* November 16.

UNC News. 2007. "UNC Study Redefines Black Middle Class as More Adults Stay Single and Live Alone." UNCNews.unc.edu., December 19.

Voss, Gretchen. 2010. "Happy Marriage: How Not to Be the Starter Wife." *Women's Health,* April.

Walker, Rebecca. 2009. "Making of a Man." *Newsweek,* January 21.

Walters, Barry. 1995. "One Scary Truckload of Drama: 'Waiting to Exhale.'" SFGate.com, December 22.

Washington, Booker T. 1896. "The Awakening of the Negro." *Atlantic Monthly,* September.

Weathers, Diane. 2003. "Black America's Dirty Little Secret." *Essence,* July.

Weathers, Diane. 2003. "Do You Know What Love Is?" *Essence,* February.

Wellington, Darryl Lorenzo. 2008. "Barack Obama in the Public Imagination." *Dissent,* Fall.

Wetzstein, Cheryl. 2008. " 'Change' of Role Models." *Washington Times,* November 26.

White, Diane E. 2003. "To Me with Love." *Essence,* February.

White, Linda. 1977. "Black Woman/White Man." *Essence,* Point of View, February.

Williams, Alex. 2010. "The New Math on Campus." *New York Times,* February 7.

"As Jobs Fade Away." 2010. *The Economist,* May 6.

Wind, Rebecca. 2010. "Abortion Has Become More Concentrated among Poor Women." Guttmacher Institute, New Release, May 4.

Wu, Audrey. 1996. "Women in *Exhale* Cut the Strings of Strained Love." *The Tech* 115(66), January 24.

Young, Yolanda. 2010. "What about Black Men and Marriage?" *USA Today,* January 29.

Zacharek, Stephanie. 2005. " 'Guess Who': Ashton Kutcher and Bernie Mac Try to Bridge Color Lines in This Reverse Take on 'Guess Who's Coming to Dinner?' " Salon.com, March 25.

"Sister Poll." 1998. Compiled by Pamela Johnson, *Essence,* April, p. 16.

"Where Are All the Men?" 2005. Letter to the Editor, *Essence,* October, p. 24.

Cases

Eisenstadt v. Baird, 405 U.S. 438 (1972).

Goodridge v. Department of Public Health, 440 Mass. 309 (Mass. 2003).

Griswold v. Connecticut, 381 U.S. 479 (1965).

Levy v. Levy, 900 So.2d 737 (Fla.App. 2 Dist. 2005).

Loving v. Virginia, 388 US 1 (1967).

Marvin v. Marvin, 134 Cal.Rptr. 815 (Cal. 1976).

Maynard v. Hill, 125 U.S. 190 (1888).

Rankin v. Rankin, 124 A. 2d 639 (1956)

Roe v. Wade, 410 U.S. 113 (1973).

Stanley v. Illinois, 405 U.S. 645 (1972).

Legislative Enactments

Personal Responsibility and Work Opportunity Reconciliation Act of 1996, Pub. L. 104-193 § 101 (1996).

Prenatal Nondiscrimination Act. Georgia General Assembly HB 1155. Withdrawn March 11, 2010.

Specify Certain Acts that Constitute Abortion. Georgia General Assembly SB 529.

Dissertations

Clarke, Averil Y. 2003. "The Sexless Lives of College-Educated Black Women: When Education Means No Man, Marriage, or Baby." Unpublished dissertation, University of Pennsylvania.

Eto, Sandra M. 2003. "Exploring Receptiveness to Interracial Marriage and Levels of Self-Perception among African American Women." Dissertation, California School of Professional Psychology.

Kitchen, Deborah Lynn. 2003. "Interracial Marriage in the United States, 1900–1980." Dissertation, University of Michigan.

Films

Daddy's Little Girls. 2007. DVD. Directed by Tyler Perry. Lions Gate Films.

Diary of a Mad Black Woman. 2005. DVD. Directed by Darren Grant. Diary of a Woman Productions, Inc.

Guess Who. 2005. DVD. Directed by Kevin Rodney Sullivan. Sony Pictures Entertainment.

Guess Who's Coming to Dinner. 1967. DVD. Directed by Stanley Kramer. Columbia Pictures Corp.

Jungle Fever. 1991. Directed by Spike Lee. 40 Acres & A Mule Filmworks.

Lakeview Terrace. 2008. DVD. Directed by Neil La Bute. Sony Pictures Entertainment.

Never Scared. 2004. DVD. Directed by Joel Gallen. HBO Home Video.

School Daze. 1988. DVD. Directed by Spike Lee. 40 Acres & A Mule Filmworks.

Something New. 2006. DVD. Directed by Sanaa Hamri. Focus Features.

Waiting to Exhale. 1995. DVD. Directed by Forest Whitaker. Twentieth Century Fox Film Corp.

Why Did I Get Married? 2007. DVD. Directed by Tyler Perry. Lions Gate Films.

Speeches

Cosby, Bill. 2004. "Address at the NAACP on the 50th Anniversary of *Brown v. Board of Education.*" May 17. Constitution Hall, Washington, D.C.

Obama, Barack. 2008. "Remarks of Senator Barack Obama: Apostolic Church of God." June 15. http://www.barackobama.com/2008/06/15/remarks_of_senator_barack_obam_78.php.

Websites

Alexandrovna, Larisa. 2010. "Racist Anti-Abortion Group Billboard: Black Children Are an 'Endangered Species.'" http://www.atlargely.com/atlargely/2010/02/racist-antiabortion-group-billboard-black-children-are-an-endangered-species.html.

Belle, Nicole. 2010. "Rep. Trent Franks Suggests That Blacks Had It Better during Slavery." Crooksandliars.com, February 27. http://

crooksandliars.com/nicole-belle/rep-trent-franks-suggests -blacks-had.

Berardinelli, James. 1995. "*Waiting to Exhale:* A Film Review by James Berardinelli." http://www.reelviews.net/movies/w/ waiting.html.

Black, Isaac. "College? Where Are the Black Males?" Accessed August 19, 2009. http://blackexcel.org/ratios.htm.

Blackmarriageday.com. "Celebrate the Joy." Accessed February 24, 2010. http://www.blackmarriageday.com/Black_Marriage_Day/ Welcome.html.

Chait, Jonathan. 2010. "Trent Franks Is Too Frank." *New Republic,* March 1. Available at www.trn.com/blog/jonathan -chait/trent-franks-too-frank/html.

Davis, Catherine. 2010. "Black Children Are an Endangered Species." GRTL's E-News, February 5. http://georgialife.wordpress.com/2010/ 02/05/black-children-are-an-endangered-species/.

Dixon, Carmen. 2010. "GOP Congressman Says Abortion Worse Than Slavery for Blacks." BlackVoices, March 1. http://www .bvblackspin.com/2010/03/01/gop-congressman-says-abortion-worse -than-slavery-for-blacks/.

Farai.com. "How Does It Feel to Be a Black, Female, Single Problem?" Farai Chideya. Accessed May 11, 2000. http://www.faraichideya .com/how-does-it-feel-to-be-a-black-female-single-problem/.

Feministing.com. "Georgia Right to Life Using Racialized Gender Narratives to Garner Support." Accessed May 25, 2010. http://www .feministing.com/archives/020050.html.

Holman, Adrian. 2010. "Controversy over Abortion Billboards." February 23. http://www.allvoices.com/contributed-news/5282902-controversy -over-abortion-billboards.

Holman. Curt. 2005. "The In-Laws: Time Isn't the Only Thing That Separates *Guess Who* from the Original *Guess Who's Coming to Dinner*." Creative Loafing Atlanta, March 23. http://clatl.com/2005-03-23/flicks_review.html.

Libby, Sara. 2010. "Congressman Calls Black Abortions 'More Devastating' Than Slavery." February 26. http://trueslant.com/saralibby/2010/02/26/congressman-calls-black-abortions-more-devastating-than-slavery/.

National Healthy Marriage Resource Center. "NHMRC Media Campaign." Accessed May 24, 2009. http://www.healthymarriageinfo.org/nhmrc-media-campaign.

Politico. "Breaking the Last Racial Taboo." Accessed October 22, 2009. http://www.politico.com/news/stories/1009/28175.html.

Theradiancefoundation.org. "Our Bios." Accessed May 6, 2010. http://www.theradiancefoundation.org/ourbios.html.

RHrealitycheck.org. 2010. "The Real Danger in Black Communities: Maternal and Infant Mortality." March 23. http://www.rhrealitycheck.org/blog/2010/03/23/real-danger-black-communities-maternal-infant-mortality.

Scheidler, Joe. 2010. "'Too Many Aborted' Billboard Gets Great Press." March 4. Available at http://prolifeaction.org/hotline/2010/billboard/.

The Sentencing Project. "Racial Disparity." Accessed June 23, 2009. http://www.sentencingproject.org/IssueAreaHome.aspx?IssueID=3.

"The State of Our Unions 2005: The Social Health of Marriage in America." The National Marriage Project (2005). http://stateofourunions.org/past_issues.php.

Toomanyaborted.com. "The Truth (in Black & White). Accessed October 28, 2010. http://www.toomanyaborted.com/?page_id=2.

U.S. Department of Health and Human Services, Administration for Children and Families. "President Bush's Healthy Marriage Initiative," February 2002. http://www.acf.hhs.gov/healthymarriage/about/president_announces.htm.

Zafar, Walid. 2010. "Rep Trent Franks: Blacks Better Off under Slavery." *Media Matters Acton Network*, blog, February 26.

NOTES

CHAPTER I

1. Some of the sources that were most useful in the researching and writing of this chapter include: Angela J. Hattery and Earl Smith. 2007. *African American Families.* Los Angeles: Sage Publications; M. Belinda Tucker and Claudia Mirchell-Kernan, eds. 1995. *The Decline in Marriage among African Americans.* New York: Russell Sage Foundation.
2. According to a Pew Research Center analysis of recent data from the United States Census Bureau, "only 33 percent of black women were married in 2007." Richard Fry and D'Vera Cohn. 2010. "Women, Men, and the New Economics of Marriage." Pew Research Center, *Social & Demographic Trends Report,* p. 6; p. 22, ages 30–44.
3. Richard Fry and D'Vera Cohn. 2010. "Women, Men, and the New Economics of Marriage." Pew Research Center, *Social & Demographic Trends Report,* p. 6; ages 30–44. Black women in 1970, at the early stages of marriage decline, were nearly twice as likely to be married as are black women now.
4. Richard Fry and D'Vera Cohn. 2010. "Women, Men, and the New Economics of Marriage." Pew Research Center, *Social & Demographic Trends Report,* p. 6; p. 22, ages 30–44.

5. Only 44 percent of black men were married in 2007. Richard Fry and D'Vera Cohn. 2010. "Women, Men, and the New Economics of Marriage." Pew Research Center, *Social & Demographic Trends Report,* p. 6; p. 22, ages 30–44.
6. Vanessa E. Jones. 2006. "Younger Blacks Absorb a Wariness of Marriage." *Boston Globe,* August 9.
7. According to an analysis of United States Census data by the Pew Research Center, the percentage of adults between ages thirty and forty-four who are married declined from 84 percent in 1970 to 60 percent in 2007. What this means is that adults are more than twice as likely to be unmarried now as in 1970. Pew Report, *New Economics of Marriage.* The percentage of white men who are married dropped from 88 percent in 1970 to 63 percent in 2007. Pew Report, *New Economics of Marriage,* p. 6.
8. Richard Fry and D'Vera Cohn. 2010. "Women, Men, and the New Economics of Marriage." Pew Research Center, *Social & Demographic Trends Report.* http://pewsocialtrends.org/pubs/750/new-economics-of-marriage.
9. Daniel Patrick Moynihan. 1965. "The Negro Family: The Case for National Action." Office of Policy Planning and Research, U.S. Department of Labor. Available at http://www.dol.gov/oasam/programs/history/webid-meynihan.htm. The best contemporaneous account of the Moynihan Report and the firestorm it generated is Lee Rainwater and William L. Yancy. 1967. *The Moynihan Report and the Politics of Controversy* Cambridge: MIT Press.
10. See, e.g., Douglas S. Massey and Robert J. Sampson, eds. 2009. "The Moynihan Report Revisited: Lesson and Reflections after Four Decades." *The Annals of the American Academy of Political and Social Science* 621, January.
11. Richard Fry and D'Vera Cohn. 2010. "Women, Men, and the New Economics of Marriage." Pew Research Center, *Social & Demographic Trends Report,* p. 6; ages 30–44. Black men, too, are substantially less likely than white men to be married. Fewer than half of black men are married, compared to nearly three out of four white men. Only 44 percent of black men were married in 2007. Richard Fry and D'Vera Cohn. 2010. "Women, Men, and the New Economics of Marriage." Pew Research Center, *Social & Demographic Trends Report,* p. 6; p. 22, ages 30–44. The percentage of white men who are married dropped from 88 percent in 1970 to 74 percent in 2007. Richard Fry and D'Vera Cohn. 2010. "Women, Men, and the New Economics of Marriage." Pew Research Center, *Social & Demographic Trends Report,* p. 6.

12. According to recent census data, 10 percent of white women between the ages of forty and forty-four have never married. In contrast, more than two out of ten black women in the same age range have not married. Steven Ruggles, et al., Integrated Public Use Microdata Series: Version 3.0 (2004), available at http://www.ipums.umn.edu/usa/cite.html; Current Population Survey, America's Families and Living Arrangements: 2004, available at http://www.census.gov/population/www/socdemo/hh-fam/cps2004.html. Further, the Census Bureau estimates that women who reach age forty without ever marrying have a smaller chance of marriage. Rose M. Kreider and Jason M. Fields. 2002. "Number, Timing, and Duration of Marriages and Divorces: 1996." U.S. Census Bureau, February, http://www.census.gov/population/www/pop-profile/files/dynamic/FamiliesLA.pdf

13. Forty-three percent of black adults have never been married at all, compared to only 25 percent of white adults. Jesse McKinnon. 2003. "The Black Population in the United States: March 2002," U.S. Census Bureau, *Current Population Reports* P20-541, April, p. 2. At times in the past, as many as 95 percent of women would marry at some point in their lives. According to recent projections, approximately 90 percent of women are expected to marry at some point. Andrew J. Cherlin. 2009. *The Marriage-Go-Round.* New York: Random House, p. 136.

14. Now, the average age at marriage for black women is twenty-eight, which is later in life than for any other group of women. U.S. Department of Health and Human Services. 2002. "Cohabitation, Marriage, Divorce, and Remarriage in the United States." *Vital Health Statistics* 23(22), July, p. 26.

15. M. Belinda Tucker and Claudia Mitchell Kernan, "Trends in African American Family Formation: A Theoretical and Statistical Overview." In M. Belinda Tucker and Claudia Mitchell-Kernan, eds. 1995. *The Decline in Marriage among African Americans.* New York: Russell Sage Foundation, pp. 3–26, 12. They note that "black women divorce at a rate that is more than double that of either white or Hispanic women." Matthew D. Bramlett and William D. Mosher. 2001. "First Marriage Dissolution, Divorce, and Remarriage: United States" Advance Data, Centers for Disease Control and Prevention, No. 323, May 31, p. 13.

16. "A Religious Portrait of African Americans." The Pew Forum on Religion and Public Life (January 30, 2009). Accessed August 13, 2010. http://pewforum.org/A-Religious-Portrait-of-African-Americans.aspx.

17. Nearly eight in ten African Americans, for example, describe religion as "very important" in their lives, a sentiment expressed by fewer than six in ten adults in the United States. "A Religious Portrait of African Americans." The Pew

Forum on Religion and Public Life (January 30, 2009). Accessed August 13, 2010. http://pewforum.org/A-Religious-Portrait-of-African-Americans.aspx.

18. Among the general population, fewer than six in ten people report that they pray daily and fewer than four in ten attend church weekly. More than three out of four blacks, in contrast, state that they pray every day, and more than half say they attend church at least once a week. "A Religious Portrait of African Americans," The Pew Forum on Religion and Public Life (January 30, 2009). Accessed August 13, 2010. http://pewforum.org/A-Religious-Portrait-of-African-Americans.aspx.
19. M. Belinda Tucker and Claudia Mitchell-Kernan. 1995. "Trends in African American Family Formation: A Theoretical and Statistical Overview." In *The Decline in Marriage Among African Americans,* edited by M. Belinda Tucker and Claudia Mitchell-Kernan, pp. 3–26. New York: Russell Sage Foundation, 1995.
20. Some discussions of the black middle class include: Karyn R. Lacy. 2007. *Blue-Chip Black: Race, Class, and Status in the New Black Middle Class.* Berkeley: University of California Press; Mary Patillo-McCoy. 2000. *Black Picket Fences: Privilege and Peril among the Black Middle Class.* Chicago: University of Chicago Press; Bruce D. Haynes. 2001. *Red Lines, Black Spaces: The Politics of Race and Space in a Black Middle-Class Suburb.* New Haven: Yale University Press.
21. Paul Attewell, David Lavin, Thurston Domina, and Tania Levey. 2004. "The Black Middle Class: Progress, Prospects, and Puzzles." *Journal of African American Studies* 8(1), Summer–Fall: 7, 6–19.
22. Paul Attewell, David Lavin, Thurston Domina, and Tania Levey. 2004. "The Black Middle Class: Progress, Prospects, and Puzzles." *Journal of African American Studies* 8(1), Summer–Fall: 6–19.
23. According to data from the National Center of Education Statistics, nearly a third of nonincarcerated African Americans between the ages of eighteen and twenty-four are enrolled in a degree-granting postsecondary educational institution. Digest of Education Statistics, Table 204. Accessed August 10, 2010. http://NCES.ed.gov/programs/digest/d09/tables/dt09_204.asp.
24. Thomas M. Shapiro and Melvin L. Oliver. 1996. *Black Wealth/White Wealth: A New Perspective on Racial Inequality.* New York: Routledge.
25. U.S. Department of Labor. 2010. "Labor Force Characteristics by Race and Ethnicity, 2009." U.S. Bureau of Labor Statistics, Report 1026; U.S. Department of Labor. 2010. "Highlights of Women's Earnings in 2009." U.S. Bureau of Labor Statistics, Report 1025.

26. Paul Attewell. 2004. "The Black Middle Class: Progress, Prospects, and Puzzles." *Journal of African American Studies* 8(1), Summer–Fall: 6–19. Racial gaps in individual income are not nearly so large as racial gaps in household income.
27. Averil Y. Clarke. 2003. "The Sexless Lives of College-Educated Black Women: When Education Means No Man, Marriage, or Baby." Unpublished dissertation, University of Pennsylvania.
28. Paul Attewell, David Lavin, Thurston Domina, and Tania Levey. 2004. "The Black Middle Class: Progress, Prospects, and Puzzles." *Journal of African American Studies* 8(1), Summer–Fall: 6–19.
29. Orlando Patterson. 1998. *Rituals of Blood: The Consequences of Slavery in Two American Centuries.* New York: Basic Civitas Books; Orlando Patterson. 1997. *The Ordeal of Integration: Progress and Resentment in America's "Racial" Crisis.* Washington, D.C.: Civitas/Counterpoint.
30. W. E. B. DuBois. 1908. *The Negro American Family.* Georgia: Atlanta University Press, p. 21.
31. W. E. B. DuBois. 1908. *The Negro American Family,* Georgia: Atlanta University Press, p. 37.
32. Some scholars have argued that historical evidence indicates that African Americans emerged from slavery with their families more or less intact. Herbert G. Gutman. 1976. *The Black Family in Slavery and Freedom, 1750–1925.* New York: Pantheon Books.
33. William J. Wilson. 1996. *When Work Disappears.* New York: Alfred A. Knopf; William J. Wilson. 1987. *The Truly Disadvantaged: The Inner City, the Underclass, and Public Policy.* Chicago: University of Chicago Press.
34. Wilson has spent four decades, practically his entire career, studying the employment and family formation patterns of the poor inner-city residents of Chicago, a group he termed the "truly disadvantaged." William Julius Wilson. 1996. *When Work Disappears.* New York: Alfred A. Knopf, pp. 87–89. In recent years, a younger generation of sociologists has extended Wilson's research by examining so-called fragile families in urban areas and by exploring why poor women so often have children without being married.
35. Murray marched through an array of correlations between the growth of the welfare rolls and the increase in out-of-wedlock childbearing among African Americans. He noted, for example, that in 1950, before the development of the welfare program, about 17 percent of all black births were to single women. Charles

Murray. 1984. *Losing Ground: American Social Policy 1950–1980.* New York: Basic Books, p. 126. By 1980, after a generation of women had come of age aware of the availability of welfare, 48 percent of black births were to single mothers. According to Murray, not only did welfare diminish the likelihood that a couple would marry, but it made it less likely that the couple would stay together. The dissolution of marriages was 42 percent higher for blacks receiving welfare payments than for those who did not, and 36 percent higher for whites. Charles Murray. 1984. *Losing Ground: American Social Policy 1950–1980.* New York: Basic Books, p. 152.

36. According to Robert Rector at the Heritage Foundation, welfare encourages births to unwed parents and in fact discourages marriage, since a mother will receive greater benefits if single. Rector notes, "Welfare not only serves as a substitute for a husband, but actually penalizes marriage because a low-income couple will experience a significant drop in combined income if they marry." Robert E. Rector, Melissa G. Pardue, Lauren R. Noyes. 2003. "'Marriage Plus': Sabotaging the President's Efforts to Promote Healthy Marriage." The Heritage Foundation, Backgrounder #1677. August 22.
37. Debra J. Dickerson. 2003. "Post-Ghetto Fabulous: Coming to Grips with Black Women's Success." *Washington Monthly,* April.

CHAPTER 2

38. Some of the sources that were most useful in the researching and writing of this chapter include: Stephanie Coontz. 2005. *Marriage, a History: How Love Conquered Marriage.* New York: Penguin Books; Andrew J. Cherlin. 2009. *The Marriage-Go-Round.* New York: Alfred A. Knopf; E. J. Graff. 1999. *What Is Marriage For?* Boston: Beacon Press.
39. *Rankin v. Rankin,* 181 Pa.Super. 414, 124 A.2d 639 (1956).
40. *Stanley v. Illinois,* 405 U.S. 645 (1972); *Levy v. Levy,* 900 So.2d 737 (Fla.App. 2 Dist. 2005).
41. This trend was initiated by the California case *Marvin v. Marvin,* 134 Cal.Rptr. 815 (Cal. 1976).
42. *Griswold v. Connecticut,* 381 U.S. 479 (1965); *Eisenstadt v. Baird,* 405 U.S. 438 (1972).
43. Elaine Tyler May. 2010. *America and the Pill: A History of Promise, Peril, and Liberation.* New York: Basic Books; Johanna Schoen. 2005. *Choice & Coercion:*

Birth Control, Sterilization, and Abortion in Public Health and Welfare. Chapel Hill: University of North Carolina Press.

44. *Roe v. Wade,* 410 U.S. 113 (1973).
45. The social security system, for example, grants benefits to surviving spouses, and immigration law grants preference to the spouses of legal immigrants. There are other privileges accorded adults who occupy the status of spouse.
46. Spouses are liable, for example, for each other's medical expenses or credit card debts.
47. Personal Responsibility and Work Opportunity Reconciliation Act of 1996, Pub. L. 104-193 § 101 (1996).
48. It did so by reducing the so-called marriage penalty in the federal tax code, which requires married people filing jointly to pay slightly higher taxes than two people who file separate tax returns.
49. "President Announces Welfare Reform Agenda." February 26, 2002. http://www.acf.hhs.gov/healthymarriage/about/president_announces.htm.
50. The Healthy Marriage Project eventually passed as part of the Deficit Reduction Omnibus Reconciliation Bill of 2005 (S. 1932), which amended 42 U.S.C. 603(a)(2).
51. Healthy Marriage Initiative media campaign. Accessed May 24, 2009. http://www.healthymarriageinfo.org/nhmrc-media-campaign.
52. This billboard and many others are the products of a commission established by the Supreme Court of Georgia. The Chief Justice who established the commission hoped not only to promote the well-being of children and families, but also to lessen the burden on the judicial system resulting from so many time-consuming divorce, custody, and child support cases.
53. Andrew J. Cherlin. 2009. *The Marriage-Go-Round.* New York: Alfred A. Knopf, p. 137.
54. In *Goodridge v. Department of Public Health,* the Massachusetts Supreme Judicial Court asserted that "marriage is a vital social institution. The exclusive commitment of two individuals to each other nurtures love and mutual support; it brings stability to our society." *Goodridge v. Department of Public Health,* 440 Mass. 309 (Mass. 2003).
55. Betsey Stevenson and Justin Wolfers. 2007. "Marriage and Divorce: Changes and Their Driving Forces." *Journal of Economic Perspectives* 21(2), Spring:

p. 40, Table 2, showing that in Sweden only 45.2 percent of the adult population is "currently married."

56. Tomáš Sobotka and Laurent Toulemon. 2008. "Changing Family and Partnership Behaviour: Common Trends and Persistent Diversity across Europe." *Demographic Research* 19, July–December: 85–138. Rostock, Germany: Max Planck Institute for Demographic Research.

57. Tomáš Sobotka and Laurent Toulemon. 2008. "Changing Family and Partnership Behaviour: Common Trends and Persistent Diversity across Europe." *Demographic Research* 19, July–December: 85–138, at 99–102. Rostock, Germany: Max Planck Institute for Demographic Research.

58. Livia Sz. Oláh and Eva M. Bernhardt. 2008. "Sweden: Combining Childbearing and Gender Equality." *Demographic Research* 19, July–December: 1105–1144, at 1114. Rostock, Germany: Max Planck Institute for Demographic Research; noting that "nearly 60 percent of all children" in Sweden are born into nonmarital cohabitating relationships. See also David Popenoe. 2005. *The State of Our Unions.* New York: Institute for American Values, p. 9, noting that 90 percent of nonmarital births in Sweden are to cohabitating couples.

59. Tomáš Sobotka and Laurent Toulemon. 2008. "Changing Family and Partnership Behaviour: Common Trends and Persistent Diversity across Europe." *Demographic Research* 19, July–December: 85–138, at 123. Rostock, Germany: Max Planck Institute for Demographic Research; reporting that 52 percent of children in the United States will live with a single parent before reaching the age of fifteen, which rate is higher than for any of the western or southern European countries.

60. Edward Cody. 2009. "Straight Couples in France Are Choosing Civil Unions Meant for Gays." *Washington Post,* February 14.

61. See Andrew J. Cherlin. 2009. *The Marriage-Go-Round.* New York: Alfred A. Knopf, p. 28, citing Thorleif Pettersson. 2003. "Basic Values and Civic Education: A Comparative Analysis of Adolescent Orientations towards Gender Equality and Good Citizenship." World Values Survey.

62. Eva Bernhardt. 2004. "Cohabitation or Marriage? Preferred Living Arrangements in Sweden." Accessed May 20, 2009. http://www.oif.ac.at/sdf/sdf04-04-bernhardt.pdf; Matthew D. Bramlett and William D. Mosher. 2002. "Cohabitation, Marriage, Divorce, and Remarriage in the United States." National Center for Health Statistics, *Vital Health Statistics* 23(22); Julie A. Phillips and Megan M. Sweeney. 2005. "Premarital Cohabitation and Marital Disruption

among White, Black, and Mexican American Women." *Journal of Marriage and Family* 67: 296–314; Linda J. Waite, ed. 2000. *The Ties That Bind: Perspectives on Marriage and Cohabitation.* New York: Aldine de Gruyter.

63. Tomáš Sobotka and Laurent Toulemon. 2008. "Changing Family and Partnership Behaviour: Common Trends and Persistent Diversity across Europe." *Demographic Research* 19, July–December: 85–138, at 102. Rostock, Germany: Max Planck Institute for Demographic Research; reporting that 91 percent of cohabitating couples in the United States either marry or separate within five years.

64. Andrew J. Cherlin. 2004. "The Deinstitutionalization of American Marriage." *Journal of Marriage and Family* 66(4): 848–861.

65. Andrew J. Cherlin. 2009. *The Marriage-Go-Round.* New York: Alfred A. Knopf; Andrew J. Cherlin. 2004. "The Deinstitutionalization of American Marriage." *Journal of Marriage and Family* 66(4): 848–861.

66. The National Marriage Project. 2001. "The State of Unions 2001: The Social Health of Marriage in America." http://www.virginia.edu/marriageproject/annualreports.html, p. 11.

67. Paul Taylor, Cary Funk, and April Clark. 2007. *"As Marriage and Parenthood Drift Apart, Public Is Concerned about Social Impact."* Pew Research Center, July 1, p. 2.

68. Paul Taylor, Cary Funk, and April Clark. 2007. *"As Marriage and Parenthood Drift Apart, Public Is Concerned about Social Impact."* Pew Research Center, July 1, p. 29.

69. Barbara Dafoe Whitehead and David Popenoe. 2001. "Who Wants to Marry a Soul Mate?" In *The State of Our Unions, 2001,* by the National Marriage Project. http://www.virginia.edu/marriageproject/specialreports.html.

70. Steven P. Martin. 2004. "Growing Evidence for a 'Divorce Divide'? Education and Marital Dissolution Rates in the U.S. since the 1970s." Russell Sage Foundation Working Papers: Series on Social Dimensions of Inequality.

71. Naomi Cahn and June Carbone. 2010. *Red Families v. Blue Families: Legal Polarization and the Creation of Culture.* New York: Oxford University Press, pp. 39–40.

CHAPTER 3

72. Todd R. Clear. 2007. *Imprisoning Communities: How Mass Incarceration Makes Disadvantaged Neighborhoods Worse.* New York: Oxford University

Press; Mary Patillo, David F. Weiman, and Bruce Western, eds. 2004. *Imprisoning America: The Social Effects of Mass Incarceration.* New York: Russell Sage Foundation; Jeremy Travis and Michelle Waul, eds. 2003. *Prisoners Once Removed: The Impact of Incarceration and Reentry of Children, Families, and Communities.* Washington, D.C.: The Urban Institute Press; D. E. Roberts. 2004. "The Social and Moral Cost of Mass Incarceration in African American Communities." *Stanford Law Review* 56: 1271–1306; Robert Weisberg and Joan Petersilia. 2010. "The Dangers of Pyrrhic Victories against Mass Incarceration." *Daedalus* 139(3): 124–133; Bruce Western and Christopher Wildeman. 2009. "The Black Family and Mass Incarceration." *The ANNALS of the American Academy of Political and Social Science* 621: 221–242.

73. Bruce Western and Christopher Wildeman. 2009. "The Black Family and Mass Incarceration." *The ANNALS of the American Academy of Political and Social Science* 621: 221–242.

74. Mary Patillo, David F. Weiman, and Bruce Western, eds. 2004. *Imprisoning America: The Social Effects of Mass Incarceration.* New York: Russell Sage Foundation.

75. Through the 1970s, the incarceration rate of black men was not that much higher than for white men. But the war on drugs changed that. Since the inception of the drug war in the mid-1980s, the number of people incarcerated in the United States has increased many times over. Our nation now has nearly two million people in state or federal prison. We incarcerate a higher percentage of our population than any other democracy in the world.

76. Heather C. West. 2010. "Prison Inmates at Midyear 2009—Statistical Tables." Bureau of Justice Statistics, NCJ 230113. Table 15. On June 30, 2009, there were 2,297,400 total inmates in custody in federal prison, state prison, or local jails.

77. Heather C. West. 2010. "Prison Inmates at Midyear 2009—Statistical Tables." Bureau of Justice Statistics, NCJ 230113, Table 16.

78. Heather C. West and William J. Sabol. 2009. "Prison Inmates at Midyear 2008—Statistical Tables." Table 19 (June 20, 2000–2008). U.S. Department of Justice, Bureau of Justice Statistics. More than a tenth of all black men in the United States between ages thirty and thirty-four are incarcerated. In 2008, for every 100,000 black men aged thirty to thirty-four, 11,137 were in prison.

79. The Sentencing Project. "Racial Disparity." Accessed June 23, 2009. http://www.sentencingproject.org/IssueAreaHome.aspx?IssueID=3.

80. Allen J. Beck and Thomas P. Bonczar. 1997. "Lifetime Likelihood of Going to State or Federal Prison." Bureau of Justice Statistics. http://bjs.ojp.usdoj.gov/index.cfm?ty=pbdetail&iid=1042. As of 2008, there were 846,000 black men in state or federal prisons and local jails in the United States. Heather C. West and William J. Sabol. 2009. "Prison Inmates at Midyear 2008—Statistical Tables." Bureau of Justice Statistics. http://bjs.ojp.usdoj.gov/index.cfm?ty=pbdetail&iid=839, Table 17.

    In 2008, there were 4,777 black male prison or local jail inmates per 100,000 black males in the U.S. population. Heather C. West and William J. Sabol. 2009. "Prison Inmates at Midyear 2008—Statistical Tables." Bureau of Justice Statistics. http://bjs.ojp.usdoj.gov/index.cfm?ty=pbdetail&iid=839, Table 18.

    To compare, there were 727 white male prison/jail inmates per 100,000 white males, and 1,760 Hispanic males.

81. Bruce Western and Christopher Wildeman. 2009. "The Black Family and Mass Incarceration." *The ANNALS of the American Academy of Political and Social Science* 621: 228.

82. Bruce Western and Christopher Wildeman. 2009. "The Black Family and Mass Incarceration." *The ANNALS of the American Academy of Political and Social Science* 621: 231.

83. Bruce Western and Christopher Wildeman. 2009. "The Black Family and Mass Incarceration." *The ANNALS of the American Academy of Political and Social Science* 621: 221–242.

84. According to Bruce Western, just over one out of every ten black men in prison is married, compared to one out of every four outside of prison. Bruce Western and Christopher Wildeman. 2009. "The Black Family and Mass Incarceration." *The ANNALS of the American Academy of Political and Social Science* 621: 235.

85. Ronald B. Mincy, ed. 2006. *Black Males Left Behind.* Washington, D.C.: Urban Institute Press.

86. Donald Braman. 2002. "Families and Incarceration." In Marc Mauer and Meda Chesney-Lind, eds. 2002. *Invisible Punishment: The Collateral Consequences of Mass Imprisonment,* pp. 117–135. New York: The New Press; Christopher Wildeman. 2009. "Parental Imprisonment, the Prison Boom, and the Concentration of Childhood Disadvantage." *Demography* 46(2): 265–280.

87. Kathryn Edin and Maria Kefalas. 2005. *Promises I Can Keep: Why Poor Women Put Motherhood before Marriage.* Berkeley: University of California Press; Kathryn Edin and Joanna M. Reed. 2005. "Why Don't They Just Get Married? Barriers to Marriage among the Disadvantaged." *The Future of Children* 15(2): 117–137.

88. Kerwin Kofi Charles and Ming Ching Luoh. 2010. "Male Incarceration, the Marriage Market, and Female Outcomes." *The Review of Economics and Statistics* 92(3): 614–627.

89. According to the most recent available data, 5.5 percent of black wives are married to someone of another race, which makes them the least likely of all minority groups to be interracially married. An alternative measure of interracial marriage would consider only recent marriages, which would yield a better sense of the likelihood that someone today would marry someone of a different race. Nearly 9 percent of black women who married in 2008 married across racial lines. Still, this rate is less than half of the 22 percent of black men who married interracially during the same time period, and approximately a third less than the 26 percent of Latinos and 31 percent of Asians who married someone of a different race during 2008. Jeffrey S. Passel, Wendy Wang, and Paul Taylor. 2010. "Marrying Out: One-in-Seven New U.S. Marriages Is Interracial or Interethnic." Pew Research Center Publications. http://pewresearch.org/pubs/1616/american-marriage-interracial-interethnic.

90. Jeffrey S. Passel, Wendy Wang, and Paul Taylor. 2010. "Marrying Out: One-in-Seven New U.S. Marriages Is Interracial or Interethnic." Pew Research Center Publications. http://pewresearch.org/pubs/1616/american-marriage-interracial-interethnic. Rates of interracial marriage also increase as education level increases. In 2000, 9 percent of African Americans with a bachelor's degree or higher married someone of another race, whereas only six percent of African American high school graduates married someone of another race. Sharon M. Lee and Barry Edmonston. 2005. "New Marriages, New Families: U.S. Racial and Hispanic Intermarriage." *Population Bulletin* 60(2): 16. Additionally, the rate of interracial marriage varies geographically. A higher percentage of new marriages are interracial in the Western states (21 percent) than elsewhere in the U.S. This means that "blacks who live in the West are three times as likely to outmarry as are blacks who live in the South and twice as likely as blacks in the Northeast or Midwest." Jeffrey S. Passel, Wendy Wang, and Paul Taylor. 2010. "Marrying Out: One-in-Seven New U.S. Marriages Is Interracial or

Interethnic." Pew Research Center Publications. http://pewresearch.org/pubs/1616/american-marriage-interracial-interethnic.

91. Black men are a scarce resource, many black women would say, and should stay with black women. As *Ebony* noted in 1993, "Finding an eligible Black man, as almost any single 'sister' will tell you, has become an increasingly difficult task. . . . Black men dating White women, for example, cause most single Black women to see red in almost any community." Douglas C. Lyons. 1993. "Where the Men Are: The 10 Best Cities." *Ebony*, July.

92. Patricia Johnson. 1998. "Sister Poll." *Essence*, April.

93. Zondra Hughes. 2003. "Why Some Brothers Only Date Whites and 'Others.'" *Ebony*, January.

94. "Where Are All the Men?" 2005. Letter to the Editor. *Essence*, October, p. 24.

95. Christie D. Batson, et al. 2006. "Interracial and Intraracial Patterns of Mate Selection among America's Diverse Black Populations." *Journal of Marriage and Family* 68: 658–672.

96. Kingsley Davis. 1941. "Intermarriage in Caste Societies." *American Anthropologist* 43(3): 376–395; Robert K. Merton. "Intermarriage and the Social Structure: Fact and Theory." *Psychiatry* 4: 361–374.

97. Michael J. Rosenfeld. "A Critique of Exchange Theory in Mate Selection." *American Journal of Sociology* 110(5): 1284–1325.

98. Bebe Moore Campbell. 1993. "White Women: A Sister Relinquishes Her Anger." In Marita Golden, ed. 1993. *Wild Women Don't Wear No Blues*. New York: Doubleday, p. 117.

99. Bebe Moore Campbell. 1993. "White Women: A Sister Relinquishes Her Anger." In Marita Golden, ed. 1993. *Wild Women Don't Wear No Blues*. New York: Doubleday, p. 117.

100. Jeffrey S. Passel, Wendy Wang, and Paul Taylor. 2010. "Marrying Out: One-in-Seven New U.S. Marriages Is Interracial or Interethnic." Pew Research Center Publications. http://pewresearch.org/pubs/1616/american-marriage-interracial-interethnic, p. ii.

101. Sharon Lewis, et al. 2010. "A Call for Change: The Social and Educational Factors Contributing to the Outcomes of Black Males in Urban Schools." Washington, D.C.: The Council of Great City Schools.

102. In 2007–2008, the national high school graduation rate for black male students was 47 percent. Schott Foundation for Public Education. 2010. "Yes We

Can: The Schott 50 State Report on Public Education and Black Males." http://blackboysreport.org/.

103. In 2007–2008, New York's high school graduation rate for black male students was 25 percent—the lowest of any state. Schott Foundation for Public Education. 2010. "Yes We Can: The Schott 50 State Report on Public Education and Black Males." http://blackboysreport.org/.

104. U.S. Census Bureau. 2006. "School Enrollment—Social and Economic Characteristics of Students: October 2006." *Current Population Survey.* http://www.census.gov/population/www/socdemo/school/cps2006.html, Table 5. In 2003, there were more than 1,300,000 black women enrolled in college to fewer than 800,000 black men. U.S. Census Bureau. 2005. "School Enrollment—Social and Economic Characteristics of Students: October 2003." *Current Population Survey.* http://www.census.gov/population/www/socdemo/school/cps2003.html.

    Counting only full-time enrollment at four-year universities, there are 600,000 black female students and fewer than 400,000 black male students. U.S. Census Bureau. 2006. "School Enrollment—Social and Economic Characteristics of Students: October 2006." *Current Population Survey.* http://www.census.gov/population/www/socdemo/school/cps2006.html, Table 5.

105. Anonymous. 2007. "African Americans Making Solid Gains in Bachelor's and Advanced Degrees: Black Women Far Out Ahead." *Journal of Blacks in Higher Education* 57, Autumn.

106. Justin Pope. 2009. "Under a Third of Men at Black Colleges Earn Degree in 6 Years." *USA Today.* March 30.

107. Nathan E. Bell. 2009. "Graduate Enrollment and Degrees: 1998–2008." Council of Graduate Schools. http://www.cgsnet.org/Default.aspx?tabid=168, p. 14.

108. *Digest of Education Statistics.* 2009. "Table 295. First-professional degrees conferred by degree-granting institutions, by sex, race/ethnicity, and field of study: 2007–2008." U.S. Department of Education, Institute of Education Science (IES). Accessed August 10, 2010. http://nces.ed.gov/programs/digest/d09/tables/dt09_295.asp.

109. David Autor. 2010. "The Polarization of Job Opportunities in the U.S. Labor Market: Implications for Employment and Earnings." Center for American Progress and the Hamilton Project. http://www.brookings.edu/papers/2010/04_jobs_autor.aspx, Figure 12.

110. David Autor. 2010. "The Polarization of Job Opportunities in the U.S. Labor Market: Implications for Employment and Earnings." Center for American Progress and the Hamilton Project. http://www.brookings.edu/papers/2010/04_jobs_autor.aspx, Figure 12.

111. David Autor. 2010. "The Polarization of Job Opportunities in the U.S. Labor Market: Implications for Employment and Earnings." Center for American Progress and the Hamilton Project. http://www.brookings.edu/papers/2010/04_jobs_autor.aspx, Figure 12.

112. "As Jobs Fade Away," *The Economist* 33, May 8, 2010.

113. Daron Acemoglu and David Autor. 2010. "Skills, Tasks, and Technologies: Implications for Employment and Earnings." National Bureau of Economic Research, *NBER Working Paper* No. 16082, June; David H. Autor and David Dorn. 2009. "The Growth of Low-Skill Service Jobs and the Polarization of the U.S. Labor Market." National Bureau of Economic Research, *NBER Working Paper* No. 15150, July; David Autor. 2010. "The Polarization of Job Opportunities in the U.S. Labor Market: Implications for Employment and Earnings." Center for American Progress and the Hamilton Project. http://www.brookings.edu/papers/2010/04_jobs_autor.aspx.

114. Daron Acemoglu and David Autor. 2010. "Skills, Tasks, and Technologies: Implications for Employment and Earnings." National Bureau of Economic Research, *NBER Working Paper* No. 16082, June.

115. Daron Acemoglu and David Autor. 2010. "Skills, Tasks, and Technologies: Implications for Employment and Earnings." National Bureau of Economic Research, *NBER Working Paper* No. 16082, June.

116. David Autor. 2010. "The Polarization of Job Opportunities in the U.S. Labor Market: Implications for Employment and Earnings." Center for American Progress and the Hamilton Project. http://www.brookings.edu/papers/2010/04_jobs_autor.aspx.

117. David Autor. 2010. "The Polarization of Job Opportunities in the U.S. Labor Market: Implications for Employment and Earnings." Center for American Progress and the Hamilton Project. http://www.brookings.edu/papers/2010/04_jobs_autor.aspx.

118. There is a large body of literature concerning the relation between education and income. See, for example, Claudia Goldin and Lawrence F. Katz. 2009. "The Future of Inequality: The Other Reason Education Matters So Much." Aspen

Institute Congressional Program 24(4): 7–14. Education Reform: Sixteenth Conference, August 17–22, 2009. Washington, D.C. http://dash.harvard.edu/handle/1/4341691; Donald R. Deere and Jelena Vesovic. 2006. "Educational Wage Premiums and the U.S. Income Distribution: A Survey. In Eric A. Hanushek and Finis Welch, eds. 2006. *Handbook of the Economics of Education.* Amsterdam: North-Holland.

119. Daron Acemoglu and David Autor. 2010. "Skills, Tasks, and Technologies: Implications for Employment and Earnings." National Bureau of Economic Research, *NBER Working Paper* No. 16082, June, p. 7. The authors' analysis of national data suggests that the "earnings of the average college graduate in 2008 were 1.97 times those of the average high school graduate."

120. U.S. Department of Labor. 2010. "Labor Force Characteristics by Race and Ethnicity, 2009." U.S. Bureau of Labor Statistics, Report 1026. In contrast, white women are paid only 80 percent of what white men are paid.

121. Jesse McKinnon. 2003. "The Black Populations in the United States: March 2002," U.S. Census Bureau, *Current Population Reports* P20-541, April, p. 5.

122. Paul Offner. 2002. "What's Love Got to Do with It? Why Oprah's Still Single—Society and Opportunities for African American People." *Washington Monthly,* March.

123. David Autor. 2010. "The Polarization of Job Opportunities in the U.S. Labor Market: Implications for Employment and Earnings." Center for American Progress and the Hamilton Project, April, p. 31. Appendix Figures 1A and 1B.

124. Paul Offner. 2002. "What's Love Got to Do with It? Why Oprah's Still Single—Society and Opportunities for African American People." *Washington Monthly,* March.

125. Pew Research Center Report. 2007. "Optimism about Black Progress Declines; Blacks See Growing Values Gap between Poor and Middle Class." *Social & Demographic Trends.*

126. The emerging gender gap among men and women has recently been the subject of media attention. See, for example, Hanna Rosin. 2010. "The End of Men." *Atlantic,* July/August.

127. Paul Taylor, Richard Fry, D'Vera Cohn, Wendy Wang, Gabriel Velasco, Daniel Dockterman. 2010. "Women, Men, and the New Economics of Marriage," Pew Research Center 21, January 19. Data for both groups taken from U.S.-born citizens between the ages of thirty and forty-four.

128. Paul Taylor, Richard Fry, D'Vera Cohn, Wendy Wang, Gabriel Velasco, Daniel Dockterman. 2010. "Women, Men, and the New Economics of Marriage." Pew Research Center 21, January 19. Observing that women "accounted for 57 percent of those who gained their undergraduate degrees in the 2006–2007 school year" the report also noted that "in 2007 66 percent of U.S.-born women ages 30–44 had attended or graduated from college, compared with 59 percent of men in that age group."

129. Jessica W. Davis and Kurt J. Bauman. 2008. "School Enrollment in the United States: 2006." U.S. Census Bureau, *Current Population Reports* P20-559, p. 6.

130. Richard Fry and D'Vera Cohn. 2010. "Women, Men, and the New Economics of Marriage." Pew Research Center, January 19, p. 2. Data for both groups taken from U.S.-born citizens between the ages of thirty and forty-four.

131. Richard Fry and D'Vera Cohn. 2010. "Women, Men, and the New Economics of Marriage." Pew Research Center, January 19, p. 2.

132. Richard Fry and D'Vera Cohn. 2010. "Women, Men, and the New Economics of Marriage." Pew Research Center, *Social & Demographic Trends Report.* http://pewsocialtrends.org/pubs/750/new-economics-of-marriage, p. 2.

133. David Autor. 2010. "The Polarization of Job Opportunities in the U.S. Labor Market: Implications for Employment and Earnings." Center for American Progress and the Hamilton Project, April, p. 27, Figure 13.

134. David Autor. 2010. "The Polarization of Job Opportunities in the U.S. Labor Market: Implications for Employment and Earnings." Center for American Progress and The Hamilton Project, April, p. 20, Figure A.

135. Richard Fry and D'Vera Cohn. 2010. "Women, Men, and the New Economics of Marriage," Pew Research Center, January 19, p. 2. Data for both groups taken from U.S.-born citizens between the ages of thirty and forty-four.

136. Richard Fry and D'Vera Cohn. 2010. "Women, Men, and the New Economics of Marriage," Pew Research Center, January 19, p. 9. Data for both groups taken from U.S.-born citizens between the ages of thirty and forty-four. "Median earnings of full-year female workers in 2007 were 71% of earnings of comparable men, compared with 52% in 1970."

137. Kathryn Edin and Maria Kefalas. 2005. *Promises I Can Keep: Why Poor Women Put Motherhood before Marriage.* Berkeley: University of California Press; Paula England and Kathryn Edin, eds. 2007. *Unmarried Couples with Children.* New York: Russell Sage Foundation.

138. Richard Fry and D'Vera Cohn. 2010. "Women, Men, and the New Economics of Marriage." Pew Research Center, *Social & Demographic Trends Report.*

139. Richard Fry and D'Vera Cohn. 2010. "Women, Men, and the New Economics of Marriage." Pew Research Center, *Social & Demographic Trends Report.*

CHAPTER 4

140. Adaora A. Adimora, Victor J. Schoenbach, and Irene A. Doherty. 2007. "Concurrent Sexual Partnerships among Men in the United States." *American Journal of Public Health* 97(12): 2230–2237; Amy Norton. 2007. "Concurrent Sex Partners Not Uncommon for U.S. Men." Reuters, October 30.

141. Audrey B. Chapman. 1986. *Man Sharing: Dilemma or Choice.* New York: William Morrow & Co.

142. Jeannine Amber, "Somebody Else's Guy." 1998. *Essence,* February, pp. 103, 104.

143. Edward O. Laumann, et al. 1994. *The Social Organization of Sexuality: Sexual Practices in the United States.* Chicago: University of Chicago Press; Edward O. Laumann and Robert T. Michael, eds. 1994. *Sex, Love, and Health in America: Private Choices, Public Policies.* Chicago: University of Chicago Press. Edward O. Laumann, et al., eds. 2004. *The Sexual Organization of the City.* Chicago: University of Chicago Press.

144. Yossik Youm and Anthony Paik. 2004. "The Sex Market and Its Implications for Family Formation." In Edward O. Laumann, et al., eds. 2004. *The Sexual Organization of the City.* Chicago: University of Chicago Press.

145. Of course, one should be cautious in interpreting this sort of data. The sample size that it relies on is in the thousands, but as one looks at narrower and narrower categories (e.g., black women who are college-educated and divorced, for example), the sample sizes shrink. One therefore hesitates to draw strong conclusions from these small sample sizes. The evidence drawn is suggestive more than definitive. It is for this reason that to the best extent possible, I consider multiple sources of data, and different types of information that might bear on the same phenomenon.

146. Jenna Mahay and Edward O. Laumann. 2004. "Neighborhoods as Sex Markets," in Edward O. Laumann, et al., eds. 2004. *The Sexual Organization of the City.* Chicago: University of Chicago Press, p. 89.

147. Yoosik Youm and Anthony Paik. "The Sex Market and Its Implications for Family Formation," in Edward O. Laumann, et al., eds. 2004. *The Sexual Organization of the City.* Chicago: University of Chicago Press, pp. 177–179.

148. Yoosik Youm and Anthony Paik. "The Sex Market and Its Implications for Family Formation," in Edward O. Laumann, et al., eds. 2004. *The Sexual Organization of the City.* Chicago: University of Chicago Press, pp. 177–179.

149. A 2007 study published in the *American Journal of Public Health* found man sharing to be much more prevalent than previously thought. While 11 percent of American men were found to have had concurrent sexual relationships in the preceding year, concurrent relationships were much more common among African American men. Adaora A. Adimora, et al. 2007. "Concurrent Sexual Partnerships among Men in the United States." *American Journal of Public Health* 97(12).

150. Judith Treas and Deirdre Giesen. 2000. "Sexual Infidelity among Married and Cohabiting Americans." *Journal of Marriage and the Family* 62(1): 48–60.

151. Judith Treas and Deirdre Giesen. 2000. "Sexual Infidelity among Married and Cohabiting Americans." *Journal of Marriage and the Family* 62(1): 48–60.

152. Yossik Youm and Anthony Paik. "The Sex Market and Its Implications for Family Formation," in Edward O. Laumann, et al., eds. 2004. *The Sexual Organization of the City.* Chicago: University of Chicago Press.

153. In the discussion that follows, I use the term "multiple-partner relationships." In quotes from published research that refers to "polygamy" I have substituted the term "multiple-partner relationships."

154. Michael P. Carey, et al. 2010. "Urban African-American Men Speak Out on Sexual Partner Concurrency: Findings from a Qualitative Study." *AIDS and Behavior* 14: 38–47.

155. Paula England and Kathryn Edin, eds. 2007. *Unmarried Couples with Children.* New York: Russell Sage Foundation, p. 116.

156. Scott J. South. 1993. "Racial and Ethnic Differences in the Desire to Marry." *Journal of Marriage and the Family* 55(2): 357–370.

157. Alex Williams. 2010. "The New Math on Campus." *New York Times,* February 7.

158. Other factors contribute to hookups as well. Part of the explanation no doubt has to do with the fact that college students no longer feel the need to establish a serious relationship in college because people are marrying later now than

their parents or grandparents did. The ritual of dating—one man and one woman alone together—has given way among young people to group outings that don't promote the intimacy that characterizes an exclusive relationship. Add to that the general loosening of strictures surrounding sexual activity. As a result, women in particular may feel freer to have sex outside of a relationship; the "friends with benefits" construct appeals to both sexes now more than ever. The loosening of the strictures or constraints on sexual expression in the aftermath of the sixties, the delayed age in marriage, with the result that people may not be thinking about marriage while they're in college—these are certainly factors that affect the spread of hookups.

159. Kathleen A. Bogle. 2008. *Hooking Up: Sex, Dating, and Relationships on Campus.* New York: New York University Press, p. 23.

160. Shang-Jin Wei and Xiaobo Zhang. 2009. "The Competitive Saving Motive: Evidence from Rising Sex Ratios and Savings Rates in China." National Bureau of Economic Research, *NBER Working Paper* 15093. http://www.nber.org/papers/w15093; *The Economist*. 2010. "The Worldwide War on Baby Girls." March 6.

161. Yossik Youm and Anthony Paik. "The Sex Market and Its Implications for Family Formation." In Edward O. Laumann, et al., eds. 2004. *The Sexual Organization of the City.* Chicago: University of Chicago Press.

162. Adaora A. Adimora, Victor J. Schoenbach, and Irene A. Doherty. 2007. "Concurrent Sexual Partnerships among Men in the United States." *American Journal of Public Health* 97(12), December.

163. Yoosik Youm and Anthony Paik. "The Sex Market and its Implications for Family Formation," in Laumann, et al., eds. 2004. *The Sexual Organization of the City.* Chicago: University of Chicago Press, p. 179.

164. Adaora A. Adimora, Victor J. Schoenbach, and Irene A. Doherty. 2007. "Concurrent Sexual Partnerships among Men in the United States." *American Journal of Public Health* 97(12): 2230–2237; Adaora A. Adimora, Victor J. Schoenbach, and Irene Doherty. 2006. "HIV and African Americans in the Southern United States: Sexual Networks and Social Context." *Sexually Transmitted Diseases* 33(7): S39–S45; Adaora A. Adimora and Victor J. Schoenbach. 2005. "Social Context, Sexual Networks, and Racial Disparities in Rates of Sexually Transmitted Infections." *Journal of Infectious Diseases* 191: S115–S122; Adaora A. Adimora, et al. 2002. "Concurrent Sexual Partnerships among Women in the United States" *Epidemiology* 13(3): 320–327.

165. Centers for Disease Control and Prevention. 2010. "Seroprevalence of Herpes Simplex Virus Type 2 among Persons Aged 14–49 Years—United States, 2005–2008." *Morbidity and Mortality Weekly Report (MMWR)* 59(15): 456.

166. Centers for Disease Control and Prevention. 2010. "Seroprevalence of Herpes Simplex Virus Type 2 among Persons Aged 14–49 Years—United States, 2005–2008." *Morbidity and Mortality Weekly Report (MMWR)* 59(15): 457.

167. Irene A. Doherty, Victor J. Schoenbach, and Adaora A. Adimora. 2009. "Condom Use and Duration of Concurrent Partnerships among Men in the United States." *Sexually Transmitted Diseases* 36(5): 265–272; Thomas Alex Washington, Yan Wang, and Dorothy Browne. 2008. "Difference in Condom Use among Sexually Active Males at Historically Black Colleges and Universities." *Journal of American College Health* 57(4): 411–416; Janet S. St. Lawrence, et al. 1998. "Factors Influencing Condom Use among African American Women: Implications for Risk Reduction Interventions." *American Journal of Community Psychology* 26(1): 7–28.

168. Centers for Disease Control and Prevention. 2010. "Seroprevalence of Herpes Simplex Virus Type 2 among Persons Aged 14–49 Years—United States, 2005–2008." *Morbidity and Mortality Weekly Report (MMWR)* 59(15): 456.

169. Adaora A. Adimora, Victor J. Schoenbach, and Irene A. Doherty. 2007. "Concurrent Sexual Partnerships among Men in the United States." *American Journal of Public Health* 97(12): 2230–2237; Adaora A. Adimora and Victor J. Schoenbach. 2005. "Social Context, Sexual Networks, and Racial Disparities in Rates of Sexually Transmitted Infections." *Journal of Infectious Diseases* 191: S115–S122; Adaora A. Adimora, et al. 2002. "Concurrent Sexual Partnerships among Women in the United States." *Epidemiology* 13(3): 320–327.

170. William D. Mosher, et al. 2005. "Sexual Behavior and Selected Health Measures: Men and Women 15–44 Years of Age, United States, 2002." National Center for Health Statistics, Advance Data from *Vital and Health Statistics* 362.

171. For comparison: 8 percent of non-Hispanic whites and 14 percent of Hispanics reported having three or more sexual partners in the past twelve months. William D. Mosher, et al. 2005. "Sexual Behavior and Selected Health Measures: Men and Women 15–44 Years of Age, United States, 2002," Advance Data from *Vital and Health Statistics* 362, September 15, at Table 1 and Table 10. U.S. Centers for Disease Control and Prevention.

172. William D. Mosher, et al. 2005. "Sexual Behavior and Selected Health Measures: Men and Women 15–44 Years of Age, United States, 2002." National Center for Health Statistics, Advance Data from *Vital and Health Statistics* 362, Table 10.

173. Centers for Disease Control and Prevention. 2010. "HIV among African Americans." Last modified September 9. http://www.cdc.gov/hiv/topics/aa/index.htm.

174. Centers for Disease Control and Prevention. 2010. "Diagnoses of HIV Infection and AIDS in the United States and Dependent Areas, 2008." *HIV Surveillance Report* 20, http://www.cdc.gov/hiv/surveillance/resources/reports/2008report/index.htm, Table 3a.

175. Centers for Disease Control and Prevention. 2010. "Diagnoses of HIV Infection and AIDS in the United States and Dependent Areas, 2008." *HIV Surveillance Report* 20, http://www.cdc.gov/hiv/surveillance/resources/reports/2008report/index.htm, Table 3a.

176. Centers for Disease Control and Prevention. 2010. "Diagnoses of HIV infection and AIDS in the United States and Dependent Areas, 2008." *HIV Surveillance Report* 20, http://www.cdc.gov/hiv/surveillance/resources/reports/2008report/index.htm, Table 5a.

CHAPTER 5

177. U.S. Census Bureau, Population Division, Fertility & Family Statistics Branch. 2004. "America's Families and Living Arrangements: 2004. Table C3: Living Arrangements of Children under 18 Years and Marital Status of Parents, by Age, Gender, Race, and Hispanic Origin of the Child for All Children: March 2004." Current Population Survey. http:// www.census.gov/population/www/socdemo/hh-fam/cps2004.html.

178. Larry Bumpass. 1984. "Children and Marital Disruption, a Replication and Update." *Demography* 21(1): 75.

179. Jesse McKinnon. 2003. "The Black Populations in the United States: March 2002." U.S. Census, *Current Population Reports* P20-541, April.

180. Daniel Patrick Moynihan. 1965. "The Negro Family: The Case for National Action." Office of Policy Planning and Research, U.S. Department of Labor. http://www.dol.gov/oasam/programs/history/webid-meynihan.htm; Douglas S. Massey and Robert J. Sampson, eds. 2009. "The Moynihan Report Revisited: Lessons and Reflections after Four Decades." *The Annals of the American*

Academy of Political and Social Science 621(1); Kathryn Edin and Maria Kefalas. 2005. *Promises I Can Keep: Why Poor Women Put Motherhood before Marriage.* Berkeley: University of California Press; Paula England and Kathryn Edin, eds. 2007. *Unmarried Couples with Children.* New York: Russell Sage Foundation.

181. Paula England and Kathryn Edin, eds. 2007. *Unmarried Couples with Children.* New York: Russell Sage Foundation.

182. Stephanie J. Ventura, et al. 2008. "Estimated Pregnancy Rates by Outcome for the United States, 1990–2004." National Center for Health Statistics, *National Vital Statistics Reports* 56(15).

183. Bill Cosby. 2004. "Address at the NAACP on the 50th Anniversary of *Brown v. Board of Education.*" May 17, Constitution Hall, Washington, D.C.

184. Bill Cosby and Alvin F. Poussaint. 2007. *Come On, People: On the Path from Victims to Victors.* Nashville: Thomas Nelson.

185. Paula England and Kathryn Edin, eds. 2007. *Unmarried Couples with Children.* New York: Russell Sage Foundation; Kathryn Edin and Maria Kefalas. 2005. *Promises I Can Keep: Why Poor Women Put Motherhood before Marriage.* Berkeley: University of California Press.

186. Matthew D. Bramlett and William D. Mosher. 2002. "Cohabitation, Marriage, Divorce, and Remarriage in the United States." National Center for Health Statistics, *Vital Health Statistics* 23(22).

187. Kris Marsh, et al. 2007. "The Emerging Black Middle Class: Single and Living Alone." *Social Forces* 86(2), December; Averil Y. Clark. 2003. "The Sexless Lives of College-Educated Black Women: When Education Means No Man, Marriage, or Baby." Unpublished dissertation, University of Pennsylvania, pp. 406–408.

188. Bill Cosby. 2004. "Address at the NAACP on the 50th Anniversary of *Brown v. Board of Education.*" May 17, Constitution Hall, Washington, D.C.

189. Barack Obama. 2008. "Remarks of Senator Barack Obama: Apostolic Church of God." June 15, http://www.barackobama.com/2008/06/15/remarks_of_senator_barack_obam_78.php.

190. Gary S. Becker. 1981. *A Treatise on the Family.* Cambridge: Harvard University Press.

191. Lindsay M. Monte. 2007. "Blended but Not the Bradys: Navigating Unmarried Multiple Partner Fertility." In Paula England and Kathryn Edin, eds. *Unmarried Couples with Children.* New York: Russell Sage Foundation, pp. 183–203.

192. Katherine Magnuson and Christina M. Gibson-Davis. 2007. "Child Support among Low-Income Noncustodial Fathers." In Paula England and Kathryn Edin, eds. *Unmarried Couples with Children.* New York: Russell Sage Foundation, pp. 228–251.

193. Paul R. Amato and Juliana M. Sobolewski. 2004. "The Effects of Divorce and Marital Discord on Adult Children's Psychological Well-Being." *American Sociological Review* 66(6): 900–921; Paul R. Amato. 2000. "The Consequences of Divorce for Adults and Children." *Journal of Marriage and the Family* 62: 1269–1287; Larry Bumpass. 1984. "Children and Marital Disruption, a Replication and Update." *Demography* 21(1): 71–82.

194. Melissa F. Wellons, et al. 2008. "Racial Differences in Self-Reported Infertility and Risk Factors for Infertility in a Cohort of Black and White Women: The CARDIA Women's Study." *Fertility and Sterility* 90: 1640–1648.

195. Melissa F. Wellons, et al. 2008. "Racial Differences in Self-Reported Infertility and Risk Factors for Infertility in a Cohort of Black and White Women: The CARDIA Women's Study." *Fertility and Sterility* 90: 1640–1648.

196. John Blake. 2009. "Single Black Women Choosing to Adopt." CNN, July 1, available at http://www.cnn.com/2009/LIVING/07/01/bia.single.black.women.adopt/index.html.

197. Personal communication from Census Bureau analyst.

198. Susan A. Cohen. 2008. "Abortion and Women of Color: The Bigger Picture." *Guttmacher Policy Review (GPR)* 11(3); Guttmacher Institute. 2010. "Facts on Induced Abortion in the United States." http://www.guttm acher.org/pubs/fb_induced_abortion.html; Rachel K. Jones, Lawrence B. Finer, and Susheela Singh. 2010. "Characteristics of U.S. Abortion Patients, 2008." Guttmacher Institute, Guttmacherinstitute.org; Karen Pazol, et al. 2009. "Abortion Surveillance—United States, 2006." CDC, *Morbidity and Mortality Weekly Report (MMWR), Surveillance Summaries* 58(SS08): 1–35; Brady E. Hamilton and Stephanie J. Ventura. 2006. "Fertility and Abortion Rates in the United States, 1960–2002." *International Journal of Andrology* 29: 34–45.

199. Susan A. Cohen. 2008. "Abortion and Women of Color: The Bigger Picture." *Guttmacher Policy Review (GPR)* 11(3).

200. Karen Pazol, et al. 2009. "Abortion Surveillance—United States, 2006." CDC, *Morbidity and Mortality Weekly Report (MMWR), Surveillance Summaries* 58(SS08): 1–35.

201. Averil Y. Clarke, 2003. "The Sexless Lives of College-Educated Black Women: When Education Means No Man, Marriage, or Baby." Unpublished dissertation, University of Pennsylvania, p. 353.

202. Stephanie J. Ventura, et al. 2009. "Estimated Pregnancy Rates for the United States, 1990–2005: An Update." National Center for Health Statistics, *National Vital Statistics Reports* 58(4): 5–10, Table 2.

203. Data assembled by the National Center for Health Statistics indicates that the proportion of black women's pregnancies that are unwanted is 26 percent, compared to only 11 percent among whites and 17 among Latinos. Stephanie J. Ventura, et al. "Estimated Pregnancy Rates by Outcome for the United States, 1990–2004." National Center for Health Statistics, *National Vital Statistics Reports* 56(15): 9, Table B.

204. The pivotal significance of access to reliable contraception is reflected in the fact that poor women have a disproportionate number of abortions across racial groups. If all women were given sufficient information about and access to the most effective forms of contraception, then fewer unplanned pregnancies would result and the need for abortion would diminish.

205. Lawrence B. Finer and Stanley K. Henshaw. 2006. "Disparities in Rates of Unintended Pregnancy in the United States, 1994–2001." *Perspectives on Sexual and Reproductive Health* 38(2): 92.

206. Lawrence B. Finer and Stanley K. Henshaw. 2006. "Disparities in Rates of Unintended Pregnancy in the United States, 1994–2001." *Perspectives on Sexual and Reproductive Health* 38(2): 93.

207. Averil Y. Clarke. 2003. "The Sexless Lives of College-Educated Black Women: When Education Means No Man, Marriage, or Baby." Unpublished dissertation, University of Pennsylvania.

208. Averil Y. Clarke, 2003. "The Sexless Lives of College-Educated Black Women: When Education Means No Man, Marriage, or Baby." Unpublished dissertation, University of Pennsylvania, p. 33.

CHAPTER 6

209. Richard Fry and D'Vera Cohn. 2010. "Women, Men, and the New Economics of Marriage." Pew Research Center. January 19, p. 1. Data taken from U.S.-born

blacks between the ages of thirty and forty-four. A third of black wives are more educated than their husbands.

210. Richard Fry and D'Vera Cohn. 2010. "Women, Men, and the New Economics of Marriage." Pew Research Center, January 19, p. 23. Data taken from U.S.-born blacks between the ages of thirty and forty-four.
211. Richard Fry and D'Vera Cohn. 2010. "Women, Men, and the New Economics of Marriage." Pew Research Center, January 19, p. 31.
212. Paul Offner. 2002. "What's Love Got to Do with It? Why Oprah's Still Single—Society and Opportunities for African American People." *Washington Monthly,* March. Among college-educated white women nearly two-thirds have a husband who is at least as well educated as they are. Richard Fry and D'Vera Cohn. 2010. "Women, Men, and the New Economics of Marriage." Pew Research Center. January 19, pp. 13, 31. Researchers found that 64 percent of married college-educated women had a spouse with equal or greater education, while only 46 percent of black college-educated women did. Data for both groups taken from U.S.-born citizens between the ages of thirty and forty-four.
213. Donna Franklin. 2000. *What's Love Got to Do With It?* New York: Simon & Schuster, p. 191.
214. Richard Fry and D'Vera Cohn. 2010. "Women, Men, and the New Economics of Marriage." Pew Research Center, January 19, p. 33. Data taken from U.S.-born blacks between the ages of thirty and forty-four.
215. Richard Fry and D'Vera Cohn. 2010. "Women, Men, and the New Economics of Marriage." Pew Research Center, January 19, p. 1. Researchers found that 64 percent of married college-educated women had a spouse with equal or greater education, while only 46 percent of black college-educated women did. Data for both groups taken from U.S.-born citizens between the ages of thirty and forty-four.
216. Richard Fry and D'Vera Cohn. 2010. "Women, Men, and the New Economics of Marriage." Pew Research Center, *Social & Demographic Trends Report.* http://pewsocialtrends.org/pubs/750/new-economics-of-marriage.
217. Hanna Rosin. 2010. "The End of Men." *Atlantic,* July/August; Don Peck. 2010. "How a New Jobless Era Will Transform America." *Atlantic,* March.
218. Richard Fry and D'Vera Cohn. 2010. "Women, Men, and the New Economics of Marriage." Pew Research Center, January 19, p. 1. Researchers found that in

1970, 28 percent of couples involved a more educated husband, while 20 percent included a more educated wife. In 2007, 19 percent featured a more educated husband and 29 percent a more educated wife.

219. Now, the better-educated spouse is the wife in nearly three out of ten couples, and the husband in only two out of ten couples. Researchers found that in 1970, 28 percent of U.S.-born married women ages thirty to forty-four had husbands with more education than they did, and 20 percent had husbands with less. In 2007, 19 percent of wives had husbands with more education than they, and 28 percent had husbands with less education. Richard Fry and D'Vera Cohn. 2010. "Women, Men, and the New Economics of Marriage." Pew Research Center, January 19, p. 12.

220. Richard Fry and D'Vera Cohn. 2010. "Women, Men, and the New Economics of Marriage." Pew Research Center, January 19, p. 4—noting that 64 percent of college-educated wives had a college-educated husband in 2007, compared to 70 percent of college-educated wives who had a college-educated husband in 1970.

221. "As Jobs Fade Away." *The Economist* 33 (May 8, 2010).

222. Patricia K. Johnson. 2004. "Men, Women, and the New Power Gap." *Essence,* June, p. 178.

223. Richard Fry and D'Vera Cohn. 2010. "Women, Men, and the New Economics of Marriage." Pew Research Center, January 19, p. 18.

224. Bart Landry. 2002. *Black Working Wives: Pioneers of the American Family Revolution.* Berkeley: University of California Press.

CHAPTER 7

225. I borrow this term from Andrew Hacker. Hacker. 2003. *Mismatch: The Growing Gulf between Men and Women.* New York: Scribner.

226. Patrick O'Donnell and Tonya Sams. 2010. "Wife, Now Slain, Ignored Judge on Leaving Husband; Pastor, Friends Have Theories on Why Counselor Stayed in Troubled Marriage." *The Plain Dealer* (Cleveland, Ohio), July 31; Patrick O'Donnell. 2010. "Husband of Marriage Counselor Charged with Her Stabbing Death." *The Plain Dealer* (Cleveland, Ohio), July 27; "Lost Warrant, Lost Life: Slaying Reveals Police and Court Deficiencies that Heighten Risks of Domestic Violence in Cleveland"; *The Plain Dealer* (Cleveland, Ohio), August 8, 2010. Leila Atassi and Rachel

Dissell. 2010. "Slain Women Underscore Risks When Fleeing Abuse; Victims Often Aren't Aware of Protections." *The Plain Dealer* (Cleveland, Ohio), August 15.

227. Ephphatha. 2010. "Shana Gardner." Posted on August 9. http://ephphatha3.blogspot.com/2010/08/shana-gardner.html.

228. Judith Treas and Deirdre Giesen. 2000. "Sexual Infidelity among Married and Cohabiting Americans." *Journal of Marriage and the Family* 62(1): 48–60.

229. Rachel Dunifon and Linda Kowaleski-Jones. 2002. "Who's in the House? Race Differences in Cohabitation, Single Parenthood, and Child Development." *Child Development* 73(4): 1249–1264.

230. An important qualification is that the magnitude of the benefits that marriage offers children depends very much on the level of public investment in children in a given society. While marriage may yield some benefits for children in all societies, the relative advantage of two-married-parent families compared to single-parent or cohabiting-couple families, for example, depends in part on the extent to which the responsibilities of child rearing are borne solely by private parties rather than the state. In other words, in countries where the state assumes more of the economic obligations associated with child rearing, the outcome disparities between children from married-couple families and children from other family settings are narrower than in the United States where, by and large, the responsibilities for children have been privatized.

CHAPTER 8

231. Jeffrey S. Passel, Wendy Wang, and Paul Taylor. 2010. "Marrying Out: One-in-Seven New U.S. Marriages Is Interracial or Interethnic." Pew Research Center Publications. http://pewresearch.org/pubs/1616/american-marriage-interracial-interethnic, p. 2.

232. The actual percentage of black wives with a husband of a different race is 5.5 percent. Jeffrey S. Passel, Wendy Wang, and Paul Taylor. 2010. "Marrying Out: One-in-Seven New U.S. Marriages is Interracial or Interethnic." Pew Research Center Publications. http://pewresearch.org/pubs/1616/american-marriage-interracial-interethnic, p. 11.

233. Jeffrey S. Passel, Wendy Wang, and Paul Taylor. 2010. "Marrying Out: One-in-Seven New U.S. Marriages Is Interracial or Interethnic." Pew Research Center Publications. http://pewresearch.org/pubs/1616/american-marriage-interracial-interethnic, p. 11.

234. Specifically, 26 percent of Latinos and 31 percent of Asians who married during 2008 wed someone of a different race. Jeffrey S. Passel, Wendy Wang, and Paul Taylor. 2010. "Marrying Out: One-in-Seven New U.S. Marriages is Interracial or Interethnic." Pew Research Center Publications. http://pewresearch.org/pubs/1616/american-marriage-interracial-interethnic, p. ii.

235. Jeffrey S. Passel, Wendy Wang, and Paul Taylor. 2010. "Marrying Out: One-in-Seven New U.S. Marriages Is Interracial or Interethnic." Pew Research Center Publications. http://pewresearch.org/pubs/1616/american-marriage-interracial-interethnic, p. 17.

236. Jeffrey S. Passel, Wendy Wang, and Paul Taylor. 2010. "Marrying Out: One-in-Seven New U.S. Marriages is Interracial or Interethnic." Pew Research Center Publications. http://pewresearch.org/pubs/1616/american-marriage-interracial-interethnic, p. 35.

237. I rely on the best available estimates of intermarriage rates, derived from United States Census data. It is important, though, not to overstate the accuracy of statistics regarding African American intermarriage. Because black-white intermarriage during the periods I discuss is such a rare event, the statistics that I present should not be taken as exact measures of intermarriage.

238. Aaron Gullickson. 2006. "Black/White Interracial Marriage Trends, 1850–2000." *Journal of Family History* 31(3): 14–16.; Ronald G. Fryer Jr. 2007. "Guess Who's Been Coming to Dinner? Trends in Interracial Marriage over the 20th Century." *The Journal of Economic Perspectives* 21(2): 71–90.

239. According to data published by the Census Bureau, in 1960 there were twenty-six thousand black women married to white men, and twenty-five thousand black men married to white women. U.S. Census Bureau. 1998. "Table 1. Race of Wife by Race of Husband: 1960, 1970, 1980, 1991, and 1992." Interracial Tables. http://www.census.gov/population/www/socdemo/interrace.html.

240. *Loving v. Virginia,* 388 US 1 (1967); R. Richard Banks. 2007. "The Aftermath of *Loving v. Virginia:* Sex Asymmetry in African American Intermarriage." 2007 *Wisconsin Law Review:* 533–542.

241. *See* Kingsley Davis. 1941. "Intermarriage in Caste Societies." *American Anthropologist* 43(3): 376–395; Robert K. Merton. "Intermarriage and the Social Structure: Fact and Theory." *Psychiatry* 4: 361–374.

242. *See* Matthijs Kalmijn. 1998. "Intermarriage and Homogamy: Causes, Patterns, Trends." *Annual Review of Sociology* 24: 395–421.

243. Rachel F. Moran. 2001. "Interracial Intimacy: The Regulation of Race and Romance." Chicago: University of Chicago Press, p. 104.
244. Rachel F. Moran, 2001. "Interracial Intimacy: the Regulation of Race and Romance." Chicago: University of Chicago Press, pp. 103–105.
245. George Yancey. 2009. "Crossracial Differences in Racial Preferences of Potential Dating Partners: A Test of the Alienation of African Americans and Social Dominance Orientation." *Sociological Quarterly* 50(1): 121; Paul Spickard. 1989. *Mixed Blood: Intermarriage and Ethnic Identity in Twentieth Century America*. Madison: University of Wisconsin Press; Claudia Mitchell-Kernan and Belinda M. Tucker. 1990. "New Trends in Black American Interracial Marriage: The Social Structural Context." *Journal of Marriage and the Family* 52: 209–18; Richard Wilson and George Yancey. 1995. "Bi-Racial Marriages in the United States: An Analysis of Variation in Family Member Support of the Decision to Marry." *Sociological Spectrum* 15: 443–462.
246. George Yancey. 2009. "Crossracial Differences in Racial Preferences of Potential Dating Partners: A Test of the Alienation of African Americans and Social Dominance Orientation." *Sociological Quarterly* 50(1): 121–143.
247. Cynthia Feliciano, Belinda Robnett, and Golnaz Komaie. 2009. "Gendered Racial Exclusion among White Internet Daters." *Social Science Research* 38: 39–54. Seventy-two percent of white women and 59 percent of white men expressed a racial preference, while only 42 percent of women and 23 percent of men expressed a religious preference.
248. Cynthia Feliciano, Belinda Robnett, and Golnaz Komaie. 2009. "Gendered Racial Exclusion among White Internet Daters." *Social Science Research* 38: 39–54.
249. Cynthia Feliciano, Belinda Robnett, and Golnaz Komaie. 2009. "Gendered Racial Exclusion among White Internet Daters." *Social Science Research* 38: 39–54, at 46. Black women were the least preferred racial group for white men, but black men were only the fourth least-preferred racial group for white women.
250. Christina Rudder. 2009. "How Race Affects the Messages You Get." OkTrends. http://blog.okcupid.com/index.php/your-race-affects-whether-people-write-you-back/.
251. Cynthia Feliciano, Belinda Robnett, and Golnaz Komaie. 2009. "Gendered Racial Exclusion among White Internet Daters." *Social Science Research* 38: 39–54, at 50. The authors note that this preference is consistent with the idea that stereotypes of black women conflict with many idealized conceptions of femininity.

252. One study using a major online dating site found that women were more than twice as likely as men to express a preference for a partner of their own race. Thirty-eight percent of women had such a preference, but only 18 percent of men did. Guenter J. Hitsch, Ali Hortaçsu, and Dan Ariely. 2006. "What Makes You Click? Mate Preferences and Matching Outcomes in Online Dating." MIT Sloan Research Paper N. 4603-06, February. Available on SSRN.

253. This gender difference is likely due to the fact that men are less concerned than women with the acceptance of family and friends, as men invest less in such relationships than do women.

254. Cynthia Feliciano, Belinda Robnett, and Golnaz Komaie. 2009. "Gendered Racial Exclusion among White Internet Daters." *Social Science Research* 38: 23.

255. Gunter J. Hitsch, Ali Hortaçsu, and Dan Ariely. 2006. "What Makes You Click? Mate Preferences and Matching Outcomes in Online Dating." MIT Sloan Research Paper N. 4603-06, February, p. 22. Available on SSRN.

256. Raymond Fisman, Sheena Iyengar, Emir Kamenica, and Itamar Simonson. 2007. "Racial Preferences in Dating." *Review of Economic Studies* 75(1): 117–132, at 124. Cynthia Feliciano, Belinda Robnett, and Golnaz Komaie. 2009. "Gendered Racial Exclusion among White Internet Daters." *Social Science Research* 38: 39–54. More than 90 percent of the 72 percent of white women who name a racial preference stated that they would not date a black man. Among men, 58 percent stated a racial preference, and 93 percent would exclude black women; Gunter J. Hitsch, Ali Hortaçsu, and Dan Ariely. 2006. "What Makes You Click? Mate Preferences and Matching Outcomes in Online Dating." MIT Sloan Research Paper N. 4603-06, February. Available on SSRN. This study found that 38 percent of all women say that they prefer to meet someone of the same ethnic background as themselves, while only 18 percent of men do so; Robert Kurzban and Jason Weeden 2007. "Do Advertised Preferences Predict the Behavior of Speed Daters?" *Personal Relationships* 14: 623–632. This study examined data from speed-dating participants and found that women were more likely to state racial preferences than men.

CHAPTER 9

257. Gunter J. Hitsch, Ali Hortaçsu, and Dan Ariely. 2006. "What Makes You Click? Mate Preferences and Matching Outcomes in Online Dating." MIT Sloan Research Paper N. 4603-06, February, p. 22. Available on SSRN.

258. Renee C. Romano. 2003. *Race Mixing: Black-White Marriage in Postwar America.* Cambridge: Harvard University Press, p. 238.

259. Renee C. Romano. 2003. *Race Mixing: Black-White Marriage in Postwar America.* Cambridge: Harvard University Press, p. 238.

260. Raymond Fisman, et al. 2008. "Racial Preferences in Dating," *Review of Economic Studies* 75: 117–132.

261. George Yancey. 2007. "Homogamy over the Net: Using Internet Advertisements to Discover Who Interracially Dates." *Journal of Social and Personal Relationships* 24: 913–930, at 926.

262. Guenter J. Hitsch, Ali Hortaçsu, and Dan Ariely. 2006. "What Makes You Click? Mate Preferences and Matching Outcomes in Online Dating." MIT Sloan Research Paper N. 4603-06, February. Available on SSRN.

263. *See,* e.g., George Yancey. 2007. "Homogamy over the Net: Using Internet Advertisements to Discover Who Interracially Dates." *Journal of Social and Personal Relationships* 24: 913–930; Guenter J. Hitsch, Ali Hortaçsu, and Dan Ariely. 2006. "What Makes You Click? Mate Preferences and Matching Outcomes in Online Dating." MIT Sloan Research Paper N. 4603-06, February. Available on SSRN; Raymond Fisman, et al. 2007. "Racial preferences in Dating." *Review of Economic Studies* 75(1): 117–132; Robert Kurzban and Jason Weeden. 2007. "Do Advertised Preferences Predict the Behavior of Speed Daters?" *Personal Relationships* 14: 623–632.

264. Patricia Hill Collins. 2000. *Black Feminist Thought,* 2nd edition. New York: Routledge, p. 162.

265. Renee C. Romano. 2003. *Race Mixing: Black-White Marriage in Postwar America.* Cambridge: Harvard University Press, p. 217.

266. Candace Jenkins. 2007. *Private Lives, Proper Relations: Regulating Black Intimacy.* Minneapolis: University of Minnesota Press, p. 44.

267. *See,* e.g., Douglas S. Massey and Robert J. Sampson, eds. 2009. *The Moynihan Report Revisited: Lesson and Reflections after Four Decades. The Annals of the American Academy of Political and Social Science,* January: 621.

268. Susan L. Taylor. 2003. "A Love Worth Giving." *Essence,* November, p. 7.

269. Susan L. Taylor, 2008. "Black Love under Siege." *The State of Black America 2008.* (The official publication of the National Urban League.)

CHAPTER 10

270. *Something New*. 2006. DVD. Directed by Sanaa Hamri. Focus Features.

271. Veronica Chambers. 2010. "I'm Her Mother, Not Her Nanny." *Essence*, June.

272. Karyn R. Lacy. 2007. *Blue-Chip Black: Race, Class, and Status in the New Black Middle Class*. Berkeley: University of California Press, p. 161.

273. Pew Research Center Report. 2010. "A Year after Obama's Election, Blacks Upbeat about Black Progress." *Social & Demographic Trends Report*. http://pewsocialtrends.org/pubs/749/blacks-upbeat-about-black-progress-obama-election. Of the four groups asked about, openness to a family member's marriage to an African American ranks lowest. About two-thirds of nonblacks (66 percent) say they would be fine with it; by contrast, about three-quarters of non-Hispanics (73 percent) say they would be fine with a marriage to a Hispanic American. A similar percentage of non-Asians (75 percent) say the same about marriage to an Asian American and more than eight-in-ten nonwhites (81 percent) say they would be fine with a family member's marriage to a white American.

274. Pew Research Center, "Guess Who's Coming to Dinner." March 14, 2006. Accessed July 23, 2009. http://pewsocialtrends.org/pubs/304/guess-whos-coming-to-dinner.

275. Joseph Carroll. 2007. "Most Americans Approve of Interracial Marriages." Gallup Poll, August 16, 2007, Gallup News Service. Accessed June 9, 2009. http://www.gallup.com/poll/28417/Most-Americans-Approve-Interracial-Marriages.aspx.

276. Joseph Carroll. 2007. "Most Americans Approve of Interracial Marriages." Gallup Poll, August 16, 2007, Gallup News Service. Accessed June 9, 2009. http://www.gallup.com/poll/28417/Most-Americans-Approve-Interracial-Marriages.aspx.

277. Pew Research Center Report. 2006. "Guess Who's Coming to Dinner." *Social & Demographic Trends Report*. Accessed on July 23, 2009. http://pewsocialtrends.org/pubs/304/guess-whos-coming-to-dinner.

CHAPTER 11

278. Darrick Hamilton, Arthur H. Goldsmith, William Darity Jr. 2009. "Shedding 'Light' on Marriage: The Influence of Skin Shade on Marriage for Black Females." *Journal of Economic Behavior & Organization* 72: 30–50.

INDEX